POLITICS TO THE EXTREME

POLITICS TO THE EXTREME

AMERICAN POLITICAL INSTITUTIONS IN THE TWENTY-FIRST CENTURY

Edited by
Scott A. Frisch and Sean Q Kelly

Foreword by
*Thomas E. Mann and
Norman J. Ornstein*

palgrave
macmillan

POLITICS TO THE EXTREME
Copyright © Scott A. Frisch and Sean Q Kelly, 2013.

First published in 2013 by
PALGRAVE MACMILLAN®
in the United States—a division of St. Martin's Press LLC,
175 Fifth Avenue, New York, NY 10010.

Where this book is distributed in the UK, Europe and the rest of the world,
this is by Palgrave Macmillan, a division of Macmillan Publishers Limited,
registered in England, company number 785998, of Houndmills,
Basingstoke, Hampshire RG21 6XS.

Palgrave Macmillan is the global academic imprint of the above companies
and has companies and representatives throughout the world.

Palgrave® and Macmillan® are registered trademarks in the United States,
the United Kingdom, Europe and other countries.

ISBN: 978–1–137–36142–4 (paperback)
ISBN: 978–1–137–32492–4 (hardcover)

Library of Congress Cataloging-in-Publication Data is available from the
Library of Congress.

A catalogue record of the book is available from the British Library.

Design by Newgen Knowledge Works (P) Ltd., Chennai, India.

First edition: December 2013

10 9 8 7 6 5 4 3 2 1

CONTENTS

List of Illustrations   vii

Acknowledgments   ix

Foreword   xi
Thomas E. Mann and Norman J. Ornstein

Introduction: Politics to the Extreme   xv
Scott A. Frisch and Sean Q Kelly

Part I   Causes and Consequences of Partisan Polarization

1 Appropriations to the Extreme: Partisanship and the
  Power of the Purse   3
  Geoffrey W. Buhl, Scott A. Frisch, and Sean Q Kelly

2 The Gingrich Senators, the Tea Party Senators, and
  Their Effect on the US Senate   23
  Sean M. Theriault

3 The Weaponization of Congressional Oversight:
  The Politics of the Watchful Eye, 1947–2010   47
  David C. W. Parker and Matthew Dull

4 Taking Incivility Seriously: Analyzing Breaches of
  Decorum in the US Congress (1891–2012)   71
  Lawrence C. Dodd and Scot Schraufnagel

5 Let's Play Hardball: Congressional Partisanship in
  the Television Era   93
  Douglas B. Harris

6 Profile Politics: Examining Polarization through
  Congressional Member Facebook Pages   117
  José Marichal

7 Necessary and Damaging: Presidential Base Electoral
  Strategies and Partisan Polarization   135
  Lara M. Brown

8 A Polarizing Court? Analyzing Judicial Decisions
   in a Red/Blue America   161
   Kevin J. McMahon

Part II   Bridging the Partisan Divide

9 Growing Apart: "Civilista" Attempts to Bridge the Partisan Rift   187
   Frank H. Mackaman

10 Can Polarization Be "Fixed"? California's Experiment with
   the Top-two Primary   205
   Seth E. Masket

11 How to Turn Democrats and Republicans into Americans   219
   Mickey Edwards

About the Authors   227

Index   233

ILLUSTRATIONS

FIGURES

0.1	The "Disappearing Center" in the House of Representatives	xviii
0.2	The "Disappearing Center" in the Senate	xix
0.3	Party Unity Votes in the House (Solid Line) and Senate (Dashed Line)	xx
0.4	Theoretical Distributions of Voters in an American-style Two-stage Election	xxi
1.1	Intra- and Interparty Distances on Appropriations Votes in the House	14
1.2	Intra- and Interparty Distances on Appropriations Votes in the Senate	16
1.3	Interparty difference in the House and Senate and the Passage of Appropriations Bills	18
2.1	Polarization Scores for the Democrats, Gingrich Senators, and the Other Republicans	32
2.2	Polarization Scores Based on Roll-Call Votes in 2011	33
2.3	Presidential Support Scores of Democrats, Other Republicans, Gingrich Senators, and Tea Party Senators	35
2.4	Amendments offered by Democrats, Other Republicans, Gingrich Senators, and Tea Party Senators	38
3.1	Congressional Investigations by Chamber, 1947–2010	55
3.2	Congressional Committee Investigations, Days, and Pages by Chamber, 1947–2010	56
3.3	*The New York Times* Coverage of High-publicity Congressional Committee Probes, 1947–2010	60
4.1	Party Polarization and the Differentiation between the Depolarized and Polarized Spectrums of Conflict	78
4.2	Incivility and Party Polarization over Time: $r = 0.58$, $p < 0.001$	82
4.3	Percent of Articles on Incivilities by Partisan Context: Different Polarization Scenarios	84

4.4	Percent of Articles on Incivilities by Topic: Different Polarization Scenarios	89
5.1	House "Democratic Message Board" Membership by Ideological Decile, One Hundred and First Congress.	100
5.2	House Republican "Theme Team" Membership by Ideological Decile	101
5.3	House Democrats' Appearances on Hardball by Ideological Decile	102
5.4	House Republicans' Appearances on Hardball by Ideological Decile	102
7.1	Percent of Polarized States, 1872–1892	147
7.2	Percent of Polarized States, 1992–2012	147
7.3	Difference of Means (DW-NOMINATE) in Congress, 1878–1892 and 1996–2010	149
7.4	Turnout Levels (VAP) in Presidential Elections, 1872–1892 and 1992–2012	150
10.1	Polarization in California	206
10.2	Percentage of Incumbents Challenged from Within their Party in Primaries, by Office	212
10.3	Percentages of Incumbents Challenged from Within their Party in Primaries, by Party	213
10.4	Same-party Runoffs in Assembly, Senate, and US House Elections	215

TABLES

2.1	DeMint Campaign Contributions to Senate Candidates, 2010	29
2.2	Polarization Scores for Republicans, 2011	31
3.1	The Mean Number and Intensity of Congressional Investigations in Divided and Unified Government, 1947–2010	57
3.2	Divided Government, Watergate, and the Effect of Increasing Committee Staff on Congressional Investigations, 1947–2010	58
3.3	High-publicity Congressional Probes in Divided and Unified Government, Pre- and Post-1974	61
4.1	Bivariate Correlations between Three Forms of Incivility and Landmark Productivity in Polarized versus Depolarized Congresses, 1891–1994	86
7.1	National Electoral Comparison of 1872–1894 and 1992–2012	143
7.2	Party Means by Chamber (DW-NOMINATE), 1878–1892 and 1996–2010	149
9.1	Obstacles and Solutions to Civility	190

Acknowledgments

The chapters for this book were first written for a conference titled *Politics to the Extreme: American Political Institutions in the Twenty-First Century* held on the campus of California State University Channel Islands October 17–18, 2012. In the course of our research on a book about the congressional appropriations process, it was becoming increasingly clear that ideological and partisan extremism was infiltrating a traditional bastion of bipartisanship. With the encouragement of our campus president, Dr. Richard Rush, we resolved to invite some of the nation's leading political scientists and political commentators to our campus to gauge the extent to which extremity was affecting American politics generally.

Shortly thereafter, Tom Mann and Norm Ornstein released their book *It's Even Worse Than It Looks: How the American Constitutional System Collided With the New Politics of Extremism*. Mann and Ornstein eagerly accepted our invitation to participate in the discussion, as did Mickey Edwards who was preparing to publish his own book *The Parties Versus the People: How to Turn Republicans and Democrats into Americans*. The core of academics who presented the papers reflected in this volume enthusiastically agreed to participate and contribute their essays, which reflect novel and creative attempts to understand the causes and consequences of extremity in American politics, and offer potential solutions for the hyperconflictual state of our contemporary national politics.

It was not our purpose, however, to allow political scientists to simply "talk among themselves." We included both political scientists and political practitioners and pundits in our sessions. The "practitioners and pundits" ensured that the political scientists did not bathe themselves in excessive and lofty theoretical debate; academic commentators ensured that the papers were properly vetted for academic quality. By combining academic and practical perspectives in the conference, these chapters reflect both points of view. We thank Brian Newman, Jennifer Merolla, Michael Willis, Christian Grose, Howard Marlowe, Lawrence Becker, Thomas Brunell, Les Francis, Darry Sragow, Sarah Anderson, Chris den Hartog, Lou Cannon, Rick Hasen, Amanda Hollis-Brusky, Timm Herdt, and Joe Mathews for their willingness to play an integral part in the conference and provide valuable feedback for the authors.

An undertaking of this size and breadth is not possible without contributions of time and effort from our entire campus community, especially the Communication and Marketing team Michael Berman, Nancy Gill, and Joanna Murphy. JB provided for our sound and computer needs. Multimedia Coordinator Tom Emmens designed the *Politics to the Extreme* image that inspired the cover of the book. Extra special recognition is due to Chanda Cunningham-Spence who handled the logistics for the conference. Merissa Stith was in charge of space and event planning. CI President Richard Rush provided moral and material support.

As a student-centered and interdisciplinary institution, we were pleased (but not surprised) by the support of our faculty colleagues across the disciplines and our students. In particular, we want to acknowledge the support of Jim Meriwether (History), Don Rodriguez (Environmental Science), Simone Aloisio (Chemistry), Tiina Itkonen (Education), and Matt Cook (Library) from the faculty; and two standout student leaders, David Ashley and Steven Jordan.

Financial support for the conference was generously provided by the students of CSU Channel Islands through the Instructionally Related Activities fund, the Office of the President, the Channel Islands Political Science Department, the Dirksen Congressional Center, and Palgrave-Macmillan. The *Ventura County Star* and KADY-TV were our media sponsors.

Finally, but most important, we acknowledge the support of our families: Dr. Elizabeth Rothrock and Colin Frisch, and Dr. Sheen Rajmaira and Shriya Kelly. In all the extreme madness of our professional lives, they represent the vital center.

FOREWORD

Thomas E. Mann and Norman J. Ornstein

The two of us had the good fortune of participating in the conference from which this volume was produced. The setting—the campus of California State University Channel Islands—was lovely. The presentations and conversations were stimulating and informative. The subject matter—political polarization—was depressing, but is the defining feature of contemporary American politics and policymaking.

The conference convened near the end of the highly contentious and unproductive one hundred and twelfth Congress, weeks before the 2012 elections that many hoped might alter the political dynamic that has contributed to an increasingly dysfunctional government. Polarized politics is widely seen as the major source of our governing problems, yet many questions about it remained unanswered, among scholars, reporters, and citizens. We used our time at the plenary session to weigh in on a number of them.

The first is that polarization is defined by its linkage to partisanship. Politics in America today is extreme because the two major parties have become more ideologically homogeneous and distant from one another. This is true not just for Washington, but for elected officials and party activists in most states, and also increasingly for Democrats and Republicans in the electorate. Voters have sorted themselves, by residential choice or psychological attachment, into one party or the other based on their values and beliefs. This sorting into two camps has important political consequences beyond any overall increase in extreme views in the public as a whole.

Moreover, the rough parity between the parties in recent decades—with either party capable of winning the White House or the majority in the House and Senate—means the partisan polarization is as much strategic and tribal as it is ideological. The prevailing strategy is not, "Our philosophy is different," but "If they are for it, then we must be against it—even if we were for it yesterday." Lawmaking is less about solving problems than defining differences. The permanent campaign, in which the boundaries between campaigning and governing became evermore blurred, has morphed into an ongoing political war between two tribes.

The parties now operate through their own distinctive networks, extending beyond party caucuses in government and national and state organizations to loyal partisans in the electorate, sympathetic interest groups, media outlets, advocacy organizations, megadonors, and super-PACs. No aspect of the rules of our democracy—from campaign finance and redistricting to minority voting rights and the casting and counting of ballots—is free of partisan contestation.

Perhaps most importantly, today's partisan polarization is not symmetric. Democrats went through a difficult period of policy extremism and electoral defeat, but after 1988, thanks in large part to the Democratic Leadership Council and Bill Clinton, repositioned itself as a center-left party, less ideological and more pragmatic. Now the Republicans have abandoned the center-right and veered far off course, dominated by a hard-right, radical insurgency that has driven most GOP moderates and pragmatists into retirement, defeat or marginalization within their party. The resolute and unyielding Republican opposition to President Obama in the first two years of his presidency, followed by a destructive brinkmanship on the budget and debt ceiling after they won control of the House in 2010, illustrated just how badly extreme parliamentary-style opposition parties operate in a separation-of-powers governing system.

This asymmetric partisan polarization is deeply rooted, not likely displaced by a single election. Indeed, it was not altered fundamentally by the decisive results of 2012. Despite the comfortable reelection victory of Barack Obama, the unexpected gain of two seats by Democrats in the Senate, and the Republican loss of seats in the House of Representatives, many fundamentals of dysfunction continued in place after the election.

The foreshadowing of this roadblock came right after the election with the remarkably ungenerous words of Senate Republican leader Mitch McConnell:

The American people did two things: they gave President Obama a second chance to fix the problems that even he admits he failed to solve during his first four years in office, and they preserved Republican control of the House of Representatives.

The voters have not endorsed the failures or excesses of the President's first term, they have simply given him more time to finish the job they asked him to do together with a Congress that restored balance to Washington after two years of one-party control. Now it's time for the President to propose solutions that actually have a chance of passing the Republican-controlled House of Representatives and a closely-divided Senate, step up to the plate on the challenges of the moment, and deliver in a way that he did not in his first four years in office."[1]

To be sure, McConnell stepped in at the end of 2012, at the eleventh hour before the "fiscal cliff" resulted in sharp and massive tax increases, to cut a deal with Vice President Joe Biden. That deal, which enabled taxes on those making over $400,000 to return to pre-Bush levels, also postponed for three months the sequestration, the across-the-board cuts in discretionary spending put into the 2011 deal to avert a debt ceiling crisis that were designed never to actually be implemented. It was adopted overwhelmingly by the Senate, 89–88, including support from conservative icons such as Jim Inhofe and Tom Coburn, both of Oklahoma—but when it was brought up for a vote in the House, Speaker John Boehner could corral barely a third of his members, the rest either cowed by the Grover Norquist no-new-tax pledge and the opposition of the Club for Growth, or determined not to vote for anything supported by Barack Obama. The deal passed only with support from the vast majority of House Democrats.

The state of House Republicans was well described by Ryan Lizza in his March 2013 New Yorker profile of House Majority Leader Eric Cantor: "House Republicans as a group are farther to the right than they have ever been. The overwhelming majority still fear a primary challenge from a more conservative rival more than a general-election campaign against a Democrat. They may hope that the Party's national brand improves enough to help win the White House in 2016, but there is little incentive for the average member of the House to moderate his image."[2]

If there were promising signs in the Senate's "Gang of Eight" negotiations to craft a bipartisan comprehensive immigration bill, and in the president's cordial dinners with two dozen Senate Republicans where there was discussion of a fiscal bargain to include both revenues and changes in Social Security and Medicare, those signs were at best modestly encouraging. The immigration progress was driven not by a newfound desire to craft bipartisan compromises but far more by the Republican desire to find a way to expand its narrowing electoral base. When the president responded to the insistence of Senate Republicans that he go first on a fiscal compromise, openly endorsing a change in cost-of-living adjustments for Social Security and other programs, he was met not with a corresponding gesture by the GOP, but criticism for his willingness to hit seniors.

Another discouraging sign came with the Senate vote on background checks for gun purchases in the aftermath of the Newtown massacre. The bill, a bipartisan effort by conservative Republican Pat Toomey (PA) and moderate Democrat Joe Manchin (WV), got support from a clear majority of the Senate—but, in a reflection of the current dysfunctional reality of the Senate, needed 60 votes to prevail. Much of the media focus was on four recalcitrant Democrats who voted against the bill—but even with their votes, it would have fallen short, because 41 of 45 Republican senators voted no. Pat Toomey himself underscored the tribal phenomenon, in a conversation with reporters: "In the end it didn't pass because we're so politicized. There were some on my side who did not want to be seen helping the president do something he wanted to get done, just because the president wanted to do it."[3]

The Senate, nevertheless, does have its share of members who want to solve major national problems—but bills that pass the Senate with 70 or more votes have no guarantee of making it through the even more polarized and tribal House. Such is the state of American politics—politics, as the title of the conference, and this book, describe it, to the extreme.

Introduction

Politics to the Extreme

Scott A. Frisch and Sean Q Kelly

Unfortunately, we have an increasing number of legislators in both parties
who have adopted an unrelenting partisan viewpoint. This shows up in countless vote studies that find diminishing intersections between Democrat and
Republican positions. Partisans at both ends of the political spectrum are
dominating the political debate in our country. And partisan groups, including outside groups...are determined to see that this continues. They have
worked to make it as difficult as possible for a legislator of either party to hold
independent views or engage in constructive compromise. If that attitude pre-
vails in American politics, our government will remain mired in the dysfunction we have witnessed during the last several years.

Too often bipartisanship is equated with centrism or deal cutting. Bipartisanship
is not the opposite of principle. One can be very conservative or very liberal
and still have a bipartisan mindset. Such a mindset acknowledges that the
other party is also patriotic and may have some good ideas. It acknowledges
that national unity is important, and that aggressive partisanship deepens cynicism, sharpens political vendettas, and depletes the national reserve of good
will that is critical to our survival in hard times.

Senator Richard Lugar (R-IN)

May 8, 2012

Richard Lugar is one of several of Republican incumbents who were defeated
in primary elections by more conservative Republicans who criticized incumbents for staking out moderate positions, compromising, and occasionally
working in a bipartisan manner with Democrats. In his concession speech,
Lugar referred to studies that describe the trend toward more partisan and
ideological congressional contingents on the left and the right in American
politics. The departure of ideologically moderate and instinctively bipartisan
senators such as Lugar and Olympia Snowe (R-ME) in the Senate exacerbate

an already dire situation. Lugar warned his victorious opponent of the dangers of excessive partisanship for his potential constituents and for the country:

> [Partisanship] is not conducive to problem solving and governance. And he will find that unless he modifies his approach, he will achieve little as a legislator. Worse, he will help delay solutions that are totally beyond the capacity of partisan majorities to achieve. The most consequential of these is stabilizing and reversing the Federal debt in an era when millions of baby boomers are retiring. There is little likelihood that either party will be able to impose their favored budget solutions on the other without some degree of compromise.

The United States currently faces challenges of historic proportions: The deepest recession since the Great Depression, an international economy teetering toward a partial collapse, two wars, and structural deficits to name just a few. Simultaneously, every indication is that the political center in American politics has collapsed. American politics has come to be dominated by ideological and partisan extremists. Political analysts—both academic political scientists and political practitioners—are left to wonder whether an American political system dominated by the extreme views of the political left and right is capable of responding to these historic challenges.

American Constitutional design is premised on the ability of political actors—legislators, executives, and judges—to achieve compromise to arrive at solutions to national problems. The American system of "separate institutions sharing power" requires agreement between House and Senate, between Congress and the president, and the balanced judgments of the Courts to respond successfully to policy challenges. The designers of the Constitution rejected the fusion of legislative and executive power represented by parliamentary institutions; they preferred to encourage government inaction of as a means limiting power and built a governing system biased toward gridlock. On those occasions when government action was necessary, the founders preferred a high degree of consensus within the governing class.

In recent years, political elites have become polarized along ideological lines to a degree not seen in the United States since the Civil War. American political parties have come to resemble the "responsible party" organizations often found in parliamentary systems, where partisan legislators vote in lockstep with the party leadership. In the absence of parliamentary institutions equipped to respond to rigid partisanship, American political institutions seize up. With political parties often uninterested in the compromise necessary to navigate the natural institutional fissures in the American system, American political institutions are crippled by the forces of ideological and partisan extremism.

In October 2012, we invited some of the most innovative and sophisticated political scientists in the country to our campus to consider the causes and consequences of ideological extremism in contemporary politics. We asked some of them to focus on potential solutions to political extremity in contemporary American politics. The chapters in this volume represent two days of lively discussion. This book is primarily aimed at political science undergraduate students and readers with a general interest in the current state of our polarized politics. For the purposes of this book, we sought to have these scholars present their research in a manner that is understandable to students.

The book is divided into two parts. In the first part of the book, chapters focus on the causes and consequences of ideological extremity, partisanship, and the decline of comity. While there is a heavy focus on Congress, we chose authors who would focus on the media, presidency, and the courts. The second part of the book is dedicated to discussion of possible "solutions" to extremity. Chapters in this section should make clear that there is no "silver bullet," no single reform or even set of reforms that will reduce extreme behavior. The provocative nature of these essays should provide for lively discussion in a classroom and deep contemplation by general readers and political practitioners.

We hope that this two-pronged approach makes this book both a contribution to the political science literature, and suitable for courses ranging from introductory American politics, to those that focus on American political institutions.

What Is Extremity?

Extremity is not a one-dimensional concept. It can be reflected in a variety of behavioral indicators. Throughout the chapters in this volume, extremity is expressed in several different behaviors: ideological extremity, partisanship, and a lack of civility.

Ideology

One way to capture extremity in American politics is by examining the ideological sentiments of institutional actors. NOMINATE is a computer algorithm developed by Keith Poole and Howard Rosenthal (2000) that uses the votes that members of Congress (MCs) cast in the House or Senate to estimate the ideological position of politicians on a scale from very liberal to very conservative. Nominate scores are expressed on a scale from negative-one (-1 = very liberal) to one (1 = very conservative); a value of zero indicates that an MC is in the middle of the ideological spectrum (moderate). Generally speaking, political scientists find that when parties are polarized—that is when MCs are grouped tightly at the extreme ends of the political spectrum, with little overlap between partisans—it will be more difficult for members of Congress to find the common ground necessary to achieve a compromise.

Figures 0.1 and 0.2 illustrate the evolution of ideological positions in the House and Senate by party between the ninety-first Congress (1969) and the one hundred and eleventh Congress (2011). In the earlier Congresses, there is considerable overlap between Democrats and Republican MCs

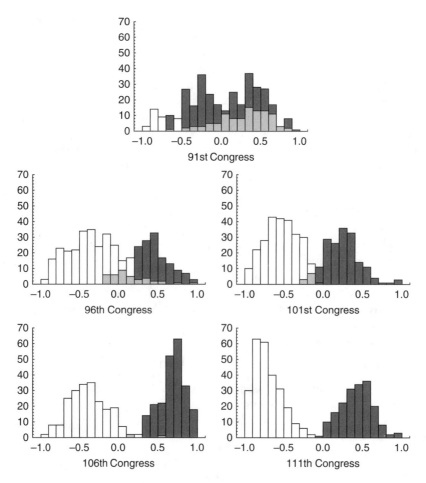

Figure 0.1 The "Disappearing Center" in the House of Representatives. Selected Congresses, 1969–2010.

near the center of the political spectrum. In fact, it was common to find Republicans with voting records that identified them as more liberal than some Democrats; some Democratic MCs are identified as more conservative than some Republicans. But observe the space between the two distributions of members. With the passage of each 10-year period, the overlap between partisans at the center of the distribution grows smaller until, in the one hundred and eleventh Congress, there is virtually no overlap at all. Note also that as time passes the two parties become more tightly bunched toward the liberal and conservative extremes of the ideological spectrum. This indicates that members of the two political parties have become more ideologically homogeneous (alike), and more polarized than at any time since just prior to the Civil War.

Buhl, Frisch, and Kelly use the NOMINATE algorithm to describe how and why ideological extremity has infiltrated one of the last bastions of moderation

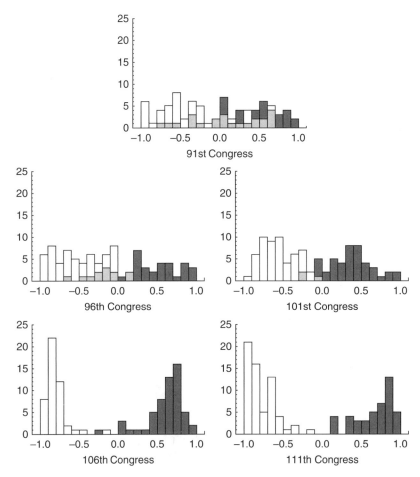

Figure 0.2 The "Disappearing Center" in the Senate. Selected Congresses, 1969–2010.

and bipartisanship in the Congress: the House and Senate Appropriations Committees. They contend that increased partisanship in the appropriations process has undermined the ability of Congress to exercise its "power of the purse." As a result, Congress has lost much of its ability to exert control over vital public policies and ceded considerable power to the executive branch.

Theriault examines the impact of the "Gingrich Senators" in the early 1990s (also employing NOMINATE scores), and the influx of TEA Party Republicans since 2010. He demonstrates that they shifted the gravitational center of the Republican Party in the Senate, exacerbating ideological and partisan tensions in the Senate and within the Republican Party.

Dodd and Shraufnagel weave a more nuanced interpretation of the role of ideological divisions within Congress. They explore the linkage between ideology, civility, and legislative productivity. They suggest that some level of ideological homogeneity improves civility and legislative productivity,

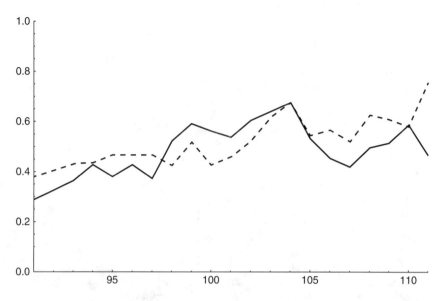

Figure 0.3 Party Unity Votes in the House (Solid Line) and Senate (Dashed Line), ninety-first to one hundred and eleventh Congress.

but that when polarization achieves a "tipping point," civility suffers, and Congress is less able to fulfill its legislative responsibilities.

Partisanship

Another indicator of extremity is the degree to which members of Congress adhere to partisan patterns of voting on the House and Senate floor. Political scientists turn, once again, to roll-call votes to capture this behavior. A common indicator of partisanship is the percentage of votes on which a majority of one party votes against a majority of the other party. These are commonly known as "party unity votes."

As figure 0.3 indicates, party unity votes in the House began to surge in earnest in the 1980s, and the Senate followed suit beginning about 1990. By the mid-1990s, party unity votes composed about half of the votes taken in the House and Senate in each Congress.

SOME CAUSES OF EXTREMITY

Increased ideological and partisan extremity in contemporary politics has several sources. Some of these are external to those institutions, and some are internal.[4]

Electoral Causes

Actors in our democratic political institutions are, by definition, chosen by the people. Even members of the Supreme Court, while not directly elected, are nominated and confirmed by directly elected officials. At least part of the explanation for our extreme politics lies with the electorate. However, elections occur within a given context, and voters choose among the candidate options that are presented to them.

American elections proceed in two steps. First, the parties select their nominees using primary elections or, in some cases, party caucuses. Regardless of the method of nomination, it is usually a small slice of the electorate that engages in the nomination process. This nomination constituency, as illustrated in figure 0.4, is usually overrepresentative of voters on the ideological left and right. In the general election stage, ordinary voters, who are typically more moderate than the nominating constituencies, are constrained by the choices determined during the first stage of the election. In short, they have a choice between a liberal Democrat and a conservative Republican; there is no moderate candidate more in line with the ideological predispositions of the general electorate. It is a truism that in an election someone *will* win. Given the choices offered the general electorate as a result of the nomination process, in many elections, an ideologically extreme candidate of one party or the other will be elected and thus represent a given subset of voters in American democratic institutions (see chapter 11).

These electoral arrangements have been in place for some time. So the question arises why we are witnessing this pattern of ideological and partisan extremity now? Several trends explain the increased divergence of party nominees from the political center. One factor is that the House and Senate partisan campaign committees began aggressively recruiting candidates who reflected the ideological preferences of leaders, and providing material support for these candidates. More important, in recent years, is the emergence of liberal and conservative groups that seek to enforce a level of ideological

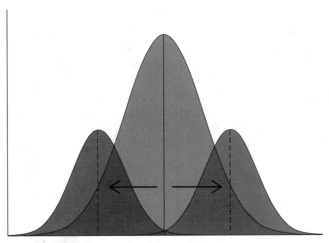

Democratic nominating constituency

Figure 0.4 Theoretical Distributions of Voters in an American-style Two-stage Election.

purity within the parties (Masket 2009; see also chapter 10). Groups like MoveOn.org (liberal) and the Club for Growth (conservative) bring pressure on sitting members of Congress to adhere to the groups' ideological agenda. One of their chief tactics is to threaten to recruit and support monetarily primary challengers against members of Congress who do not adhere to the groups' agendas. The *threat* of a primary challenge by a more "ideologically pure" partisan candidate is usually enough to cause politicians to heed the warning. It takes only a few successful cases, one like Richard Lugar's that began this chapter, to convince sitting politicians that the groups' threats are credible and potentially career ending. Actual primary challenges may be rare (Boatright 2013); it is the threat that changes politicians' behaviors.

Partisanship in Congress may also be exacerbated by how electoral districts are drawn. In the majority of states, congressional districts are drawn by elected officials. It is widely assumed that as partisans they seek to maximize the number of districts that can be captured by the dominant political party in the state through partisan gerrymandering. To achieve this, they concentrate partisan voters into districts that assure the election of a legislator from one party or the other. Politicians, unconcerned about the need to be reelected, stake out more extreme positions than they would if they feared electoral competition from a challenger of the other party. The explanatory value of this argument is limited, however, by the fact that there are similar patterns of ideological extremity in the Senate; Senate constituencies are determined by state lines and thus not dependent on the gerrymandering activities of state political actors.

The Role of the Media

Also contributing to ideological and partisan extremism is a fragmented media environment in which citizens, and especially politically active citizens, choose news outlets that are consistent with their existing views (what psychologists call selective perception). The rise of cable television, and then the advent of the internet, has led to a proliferation of news outlets. As news outlets battle for customers, many offer news and information that appeal to the ideological predilections of their audience. According to a survey conducted by the Pew Research Center (2011, 43), voters on the conservative side of the political spectrum are far more likely than the average American to watch FOX News regularly, and to regularly listen to conservative commentators Glenn Beck and Rush Limbaugh. Liberals are more likely than average Americans to watch reliably liberal MSNBC and The Daily Show, and read the *New York Times*. As Doug Harris suggests in his chapter, the partisan messages of members of Congress on television shows like MSNBC's "Hardball" (that appeals to more liberal viewers) tend to be delivered by members of Congress who represent the ideological extremes of the parties. Taken together, this suggests that liberal and conservative activists—the kind who tend to participate in nominating candidates for election—are exposed to more extreme partisan messages that further reinforce viewers' ideological predispositions.

Social media likely intensifies the dynamic. Political science research on social media and political attitudes is in its infancy. It is plausible that social media choices (who to follow on media sites such as Facebook, Twitter, Tumblr, and the like) are similar to the choices individuals make when choosing news sources; they choose to surround themselves with friends and political commentators who agree with their existing beliefs. In chapter 6, José Marichal argues that members of Congress use Facebook as a means of personally presenting themselves to their constituents—rather than as a place to promote their partisanship—it is likely the case that the choice to "friend" a member of Congress is often a partisan choice, and consumption of these relatively innocuous message support the assumption that an ideological and partisan extremist is "reasonable."

Internal Changes in Congress

Between 1933 and 1994, Democrats controlled a majority in the US House, except during the eightieth (1947–1949) and the eighty-third (1953–1955) congresses. Democrats were almost as successful at controlling the Senate over this period; only 10 years of that 60-year period were Democrats not the majority in the Senate. This seeming domination masks the fact that congressional Democrats were consistently split along regional lines. Conservative Southern Democrats and more liberal Northern and Western Democrats were held together through the "Boston-Austin" connection (Champagne et al. 2009), an arrangement in which liberal and conservative Democrats shared in the leadership of the party.

With the collapse of this coalition in the late 1980s, and the rise of a viable Republican Party in the former solid Democratic South, Republicans were poised to seize control of the House of Representatives. A coordinated campaign by a growing number of Republicans aimed at discrediting Democratic control of the House as corrupt and imperious. Led by a young firebrand named Newt Gingrich, the strategy led to the resignation of Democratic Speaker Jim Wright (D-TX) over allegations of corruption, resulted in the revelations of the House banking scandal, and ultimately in the Republican Party seizing a majority in the House for the first time in 40 years following the 1994 congressional elections.

The "Republican Revolution" was widely interpreted as a repudiation of Democratic control of Congress (and the sitting Democratic President Bill Clinton) and as a victory for Newt Gingrich's "Contract with America," an ambitious policy agenda that became the immediate focus of the new Republican majority. Gingrich believed that the Republican Party leadership in the House should exercise strong control over the legislative process. The Republican leadership seized control over committee assignments, threatening to remove members from plum committee assignments for bucking the party (Frisch and Kelly 2006). Party leaders developed the use of political "pork" (earmarks) as an incentive (and sometimes a punishment) for supporting party positions on the floor (Frisch and Kelly 2011). Achieving the policy agenda laid down by the party leadership became the sole focus of the Republican leadership. Where Democrats had tried, and mostly failed to impose "party discipline," Gingrich largely succeeded. Within 100 days House Republicans passed all of the components of the Contract, although most of the bills languished in the Senate.

Despite Gingrich's exit from the House in early 1999 under a cloud (and his miscalculation of Americans' appetite for impeaching and removing President Clinton), the party leadership machinery that he put into place—and his strong right arm Tom DeLay—managed to maintain an efficient partisan machine. In the 1994 election, and in subsequent elections, Republican Senators also moved considerably to the political right (see chapter 2). Levels of ideological and partisan extremity in the House and Senate reached new heights over the 20 years since Gingrich's ascendance to the speakership.

Democrats, for their part, resented how they were marginalized in the Republican House; they also learned a few lessons of their own. Democratic Minority leader Dick Gephardt (MO) and then his successor Nancy Pelosi (CA) sought to consolidate power in the Democratic leadership offices. When the Democrats regained the majority in 2006, Nancy Pelosi and Democrats used many of the same tactics to muffle House Republicans. With the election of Barak Obama and two years of united party government, Speaker Pelosi presided over one of the most prolific, and polarizing, congresses in history. House Republicans refused to cooperate with any major element of the Obama–Pelosi agenda, and where House Democrats ran into resistance they rolled over Republicans as Republicans had rolled over them in the past.

Summary

American politics over the last two decades is characterized by the intense ideological polarization and partisanship that are evident. The sources of this extremity are a dynamic and reinforcing combination of external and internal forces. As ideological extremity and partisanship has intensified in Congress, it has sharpened the lines of conflict among liberal Democratic and conservative Republican activists. This extremity is highlighted and encouraged by a fragmented news media that dramatizes the "battle lines," further sharpening divisions between political actors and between party activists on the left and right. Outside interest groups encourage the dynamic by recruiting (or threatening to recruit) ideologically pure candidates to challenge sitting politicians who are not toeing the line, and pour millions of dollars into demonizing those who oppose them. To some degree, the average American likely feels trapped between warring factions, but is routinely called on to adjudicate these differences during elections.

SOLUTIONS

It is not enough to describe the pathologies of contemporary politics and explain their sources; it is incumbent upon political scientists and political practitioners to offer potential solutions to these pathologies. In the second part of this book, we asked three observers of American politics to discuss possible solutions.

In the wake of the hyperpartisanship that followed the 1994 "Republican Revolution" in the House and the subsequent bitter budget fights, several Democrats and Republicans promoted the idea of bipartisan retreats. They argued that these retreats would allow members of the House to discuss the sources of partisan discord and search for solutions. Frank Mackaman discusses this failed attempt from the point of view of one of its leaders, Ray LaHood. Spearheaded by David Skaggs (D-CO) and Ray LaHood (R-IL), the effort leads to a series of retreats that, in part due to the partisanship they sought to address, collapsed.

Reforms of American electoral institutions are a favorite target of activists attempting to promote greater bipartisanship. Adopting the analysis of elections offered above, they maintain that certain reforms can promote electoral competition between more ideologically moderate candidates. Our home state of California is the site of recent attempts at several of these electoral reforms. In 2008, California voters approved Proposition 11, which created a citizen-led districting commission. The purpose of the commission was to take the job of drawing legislative districts away from the legislature. A newly formed bipartisan group of citizens would presumably draw district lines with an emphasis on "communities of interest" and the promotion of electoral competition, rather than drawing district lines that concentrated Democratic and Republican voters to create electorally safe districts for partisans.

Another experiment taking place in California arises as a result of Proposition 14. Approved in June 2010, this proposition created a "blanket primary" in which candidates of all parties run against one another in a first-round election, with the top two vote getters (regardless of party) face each other in the general election. Promoters of this new system argue that it will encourage moderate candidates to enter elections where before they would be unable to prevail in a closed-party primary. The first election under this new blanket primary system occurred in 2012. In chapter 10, Seth Masket evaluates whether this new system had the results anticipated by its proponents. He concludes that, at least in the short run, the political parties were reasonably successful at maintaining control over electoral outcomes.

Mickey Edwards concludes the volume by expertly summarizing some of the causes of extremity, and what he believes are some solutions. Edwards is an enthusiastic supporter of both of the measures examined by Masket, but he offers a number of additional reforms aimed at reducing the centrality of parties in Congress. A former Republican member of Congress, and a strong ally of President Ronald Reagan, Edwards believes that fealty to the congressional parties undermines the essential nature of representation in the American system. Among his more bold recommendations is reconceiving the position of speaker of the House as a nonpartisan position, perhaps held by someone who is not an elected member of Congress, which is a possibility given that the Constitution does not require the speaker to be a member of Congress.

NOTES

1. "McConnell Statement on the Re-election of President Obama," Office of U.S. Senate Republican Leader Mitch McConnell, November 7, 2012.
2. Lizza, "The House of Pain." *The New Yorker* March 14, 2013, 47.
3. Evan Brandt, 2013, "Toomey Doubts Second Senate Gun-control Vote Any Time Soon." *Main Line Media News* May 1. http://mainlinemedianews.com/articles/2013/05/01/main_line_times/news/doc5180f9ddb3dee859736381.txt?viewmode=fullstory.
4. The direct role of public opinion in producing extremity among members of Congress is a matter of considerable debate. Abramowitz (2011, 2012) contends that extremity is a result of a divided public. Fiorina (2011) challenges this formulation, arguing that ideological divisions in the population are mild to nonexistent; extremity in contemporary politics is an elite behavior and suggests that American political institutions are out of touch with ordinary Americans. In this volume we focus on the institutional causes and consequences of political extremity.

REFERENCES

Abramowitz, Alan I. 2011. *The Disappearing Center: Engaged Citizens, Polarization, and American Democracy.* New Haven, CT: Yale University Press.

———. 2012. *The Polarized Public: Why American Government is So Dysfunctional.* New York: Pearson.

Boatright, Robert G. 2013. *Getting Primaried: The Changing Politics of Congressional Primary Challenges.* Ann Arbor: University of Michigan.

Champagne, Anthony, Douglas B. Harris, James W. Riddlesperger Jr., and Garrison Nelson. 2009. *The Austin-Boston Connection: Five Decades of House Democratic Leadership, 1937–1989.* College Station, TX: Texas A&M Press.

Fiorina, Morris P. 2011. *Disconnect: The Breakdown of Representation in American Politics.* Norman: University of Oklahoma Press.

Frisch, Scott A., and Sean Q Kelly. 2011. *Cheese Factories on the Moon: Why Earmarks are Good for American Democracy.* Boulder, CO: Paradigm Publishers.

———. 2006. *Committee Assignment Politics in the US House of Representatives.* Norman: University of Oklahoma Press.

Masket, Seth. 2011. *No Middle Ground: How Informal Party Organizations Control Nominations and Polarize Legislatures.* Ann Arbor: University of Michigan.

Pew Research Center for the People and the Press. 2011. "Beyond Red vs. Blue." http://www.people-press.org/files/legacy-pdf/Beyond-Red-vs-Blue-The-Political-Typology.pdf (accessed April 2013).

Poole, Keith T., and Howard Rosenthal. 2000. *Congress: A Political-Economic History of Roll Call Voting.* New York: Oxford University Press.

Part I

Causes and Consequences of Partisan Polarization

1

APPROPRIATIONS TO THE EXTREME: PARTISANSHIP AND THE POWER OF THE PURSE

Geoffrey W. Buhl, Scott A. Frisch, and Sean Q Kelly

On July 15, 2010, senators filed into the Appropriations Committee meeting room. They were there to vote on 302(b) spending levels, which dictate the amount that each subcommittee has to spend on programs within their sub-committee's jurisdiction. Then chairman Daniel Inouye (D-HI) laid his pro-posal before the committee. Historically, votes on such allocations were not controversial, having been worked out by the chair and ranking member prior to the meeting. However, things were different this time. Senate Republican leader and Appropriations Committee member Mitch McConnell (KY) who typically does not attend such meetings responded with lower allocation spending numbers, claiming that in the absence of a Budget Resolution, it was up to the Appropriations Committee to show leadership on reduc-ing spending. Inouye suggested spending levels that fell between their two proposals. It appeared that the two sides were moving toward a compromise. Typically, 302(b) allocations are made on a bipartisan basis. What happened next shocked a senior Senate Appropriations Committee staffer: "[Ranking Republican member] Senator Cochran said 'well that seems like a good deal to me.' He said that, and he stared daggers at McConnell; and McConnell just threw him under the bus and said 'No.' [Republican] members all fell into line behind Senator McConnell... a lot of them didn't like it... but they felt they had to support the leadership."[1] Thirty-eight billion dollars sepa-rated the two sides: "In the broader scheme of things it's irrelevant... but those are ideological issues that are creeping into the debate," said a former

Senate Appropriations staffer. Inouye ended up passing the allocation on a straight party line vote. That year none of the 12 spending bills needed to fund the government's operations passed the Senate by the start of the fiscal year.

House Appropriations Committee chairman David Obey (D-WI) gaveled his committee to order on June 26, 2008. The order of the day was consideration of the Labor, Health, and Human Services (Labor-H) Appropriations bill. Republicans on the committee had a surprise up their sleeves. Obey was under pressure from the Democratic leadership to prevent the Interior Appropriations bill from coming up for consideration. Democrats felt vulnerable. With gas prices on the rise, support for an amendment aimed at increasing offshore drilling was gaining steam. Sensing a political advantage, Republicans had schemed to use initial consideration of the Labor-H bill to press the issue. According to Ranking Republican Jerry Lewis (R-CA), "We had one of our members present an amendment that was a substitute for his entire [Labor-H] bill...that would allow for drilling on the continental shelf." According to a staffer who attended the hearing, "Obey went through the flippin' roof" because he realized that there was bipartisan support for the drilling provisions and he would lose any vote in the subcommittee.[2] Obey "exploded," said Lewis. He "slammed the gavel down and turned to me and said, 'Well I'll see you at the end of the year.' That was the second committee hearing of the year...We never had another committee hearing."[3]

The House and Senate Appropriations Committees have typically been considered the most bipartisan committees in Congress. Their power and prestige emanate from the necessity of passing Appropriations bills, which fund much of the federal government, and the committees' ability to "move" their legislation in a bipartisan manner drawing broad bipartisan support for their bills. Today's Appropriations process can be described in a single word; "Dysfunctional" says an Appropriations Committee staffer. Members of the committee, he continued, have "lost the desire to work together."[4] In the words of another staffer, "This place has become incredibly partisan, dysfunctional and demoralizing...the institution has an inability to deal with the challenges facing the country; there is a breakdown in fundamentals...it feels like a revolutionary time."[5]

Using interviews and House and Senate roll call data, we explore the rise of partisanship in the Appropriations process between the ninety-first and the one hundred and eleventh Congress (1969–2011). We conclude that the textbook Appropriations process is, if not dead, on life support. Ideological extremity and partisanship are largely to blame for the inability of Congress to exercise its power of the purse. Congressional gridlock is causing Congress to cede power to the executive branch to make funding decisions in a manner inconsistent with constitutional design. Furthermore, reliance on Continuing Resolutions and omnibus spending bills as mechanisms to fund many federal programs means Congress is abdicating its responsibility to adapt spending to existing policy realities.

Textbook Appropriations

Richard Fenno's (1966) account of the Appropriations Committees remains the definitive work with regard to the operation of the committees.[6] He stresses the mission-driven organization of the committee toward what he calls their "single, paramount task—*to guard the Federal Treasury*" (1962, 311). As a result, members of Appropriations conceive of their legislative task as making decisions about money rather than policy: "They deal immediately with dollars and cents...theirs is a 'business' rather than a 'policy' committee" (Fenno 1962, 312). Members of Congress are drawn to Appropriations because of its power—the "power of the purse"—but are chosen for their skills and abilities as legislators, that is, their ability to adhere to the norms of the institution acting as "responsible legislators."

Fenno highlights the ability of the committee to maintain internal norms that promote unity within the subcommittees and across the Full Committee. The bulk of the legislative work in the committee occurs at the subcommittee level. A hallmark of the committee is the autonomy of the subcommittees: the degree to which subcommittees defer to one another's decisions, and subcommittee "unity"—the obligation of subcommittee members to support internal decisions. This unity norm is supported by selecting members who are responsible legislators. Unity at the subcommittee extends to the Full Committee. According to an appropriator, "I tell them (the Full Committee) we should have a united front. If there are any objections or changes, we ought to hear it now, and not wash our dirty laundry out on the floor" (Fenno 1962, 317).

The power and prestige of the Appropriations Committee, Fenno argues, depends upon indispensability of its work, and its ability to gain passage of their bills on the floor; the unity norm is critical to the legislative mission, and supporting the power and prestige of the committee:

> The committee's own conviction is that its floor success depends on its ability to present a united front in its confrontations with the House. And floor success...is important to the Committee members because it enhances Committee influence and individual prestige. Unity is the one key variable over which Committee members can exercise some control, and they bend every effort to do so. (Fenno 1966, 460)

Fenno depicts the Appropriations Committee as largely impervious to external influences: a closed club of sorts. The exclusive club is even off-limits to party leaders: "Party leaders do not normally exercise much influence during Committee decision-making ...Committee-based norms far more than party-based norms govern the behavior of members inside the committee" (Fenno 1966, 415).

Joseph White (1989) revisited the House Appropriations Committee in the 1980s and discovered a committee similar to that described by Fenno, if a bit worn by the political winds. The relative budgetary stability of the 1950s and 1960s gave way to the fiscal pressures of mounting deficits.

Concerns about deficits shifted the ethos of committee decision-making from "guardianship"—looking for places to cut expenditures—to stretching available resources in a manner that serves the interests of their colleagues. Likewise, the political stability of Fenno's committee gave way to a new political environment. Congressional reforms shifted power away from the "old bull" committee chairs, enhancing the power of rank-and-file members of Congress and party leaders. Despite the erosion of the budgetary and political environment that supported Fenno's Appropriations Committee, White argued that

> the [Appropriations] Committee remained one of the most non-partisan on the Hill. Chairmen still dominated subcommittees, though through command of staff more than norms of deference. New members were trained, though more through inducements than sanctions. The staff became more clearly the home of budgetary values, but those still shaped many of the committee's questions and answers. (White 1989, 15)

According to White the authority of the Appropriations Committee relies less on the norms described by Fenno than on two broad factors: maintaining a wall between appropriating and policy making, that is, steering clear of the work of the authorizing committees, and maintaining control over executive activities "while satisfying member demands for a rough fairness in the distribution of district benefits" (White 1989, 17).

Consistent with Fenno, White finds that the success of the Appropriations Committee depends on the bipartisan nature of their internal functioning. The power and prestige of the committee depends on their ability to "move" their bills and serve the interests of their colleagues:

> Appropriations [Committee] members...see the need for internal nonpartisanship. In other committees, one may become powerful by stopping action. For those purposes one needs only a majority within the committee. [The Appropriations Committee] is powerful only if it passes bills. To do that it must reach out to the House floor, and that is much easier if the committee coalition is as wide as possible. Their party colleagues' interest in a broad distribution of the available benefits further disposes members to cooperate within the committee...they share a disposition to cooperate, that is favored by outsiders, is powerfully in their self-interest, and is reinforced by shared experience (White 1989, 242; emphasis added).

Joshua Gordon (2002) offers a peek at a possible sea-change in the House Appropriations Committee. An increasing number of Republicans—dissatisfied with their role as a "permanent minority" and led by Newt Gingrich—engaged in a sustained attack on "those norms in the House that served to keep them in the minority. They severed bridging social ties with Democrats, preferring instead ideological and partisan ties bonding Republicans together" (Gordon 2002, 241). Gordon suggests that the success of the "Republican Revolution" ushered in a new period of partisan control over the Appropriations Committee that obliterated the internal norms of the committee. More junior and ideologically extreme members were appointed to the committee, members who were less likely to respect committee norms. The historic autonomy of the committee "was challenged by the [Republican] party leadership," resulting in a committee that is "more partisan and less integrated around consensual norms" (Gordon 2002, 243). Gordon provides evidence of changing dynamics in the committee; Aldrich and Rohde's (2000) findings support the conjecture that the Republican leadership exercised increasing influence over the Appropriations process. Consistent with Gordon, they demonstrate that votes on Appropriations legislation between the 1970s and the 1990s are marked by increasing levels of partisanship.

The literature over the last five decades suggests a changing "textbook" Appropriations Committee. Fenno's committee was possessed of a strong internal structure, committee unity, and a nonpartisan approach that generated widespread support within the institution. White's committee operated in a different budgetary and political context. Despite eroding norms, the bipartisan ethic of the committee, and a combined interest in maintaining the power and prestige of the committee led members into a common search for legislation that would attract bipartisan support throughout the institution. As White finished his dissertation, however, confrontational, conservative Republicans were fighting an increasingly open war to undermine institutional norms and achieve a partisan majority. Gordon found a committee substantially changed by ideological and partisan warfare. Internal norms in tatters and partisan control over the committee tightening; Gordon's committee was in danger of collapse.

THE NEW TEXTBOOK APPROPRIATIONS COMMITTEES

Gordon's work identifies the beginnings of an important change within the committee. We contend that the Appropriations process has—as the Appropriations staffers in the introduction contend—become dysfunctional. Growing ideological polarization is a root cause of the dysfunction. Ideological polarization surrounding Appropriations is at its highest level in more than 45 years (see below), and that polarization is evident among members of the Appropriations Committees. Ideological and partisan combat has left the internal norms of the committee in tatters. Leaders in both parties have successfully infiltrated the committee's decision-making process to promote their own interests, aggravating ideological and partisan rifts. Finally, a successful attack on the distributive role of the committee—and especially the committee's ability to use earmarks to build coalitions—has neutered the power and prestige of the committee.

Ideology and Partisanship

Ideological polarization is necessary but not sufficient to explain the near-total collapse of the Appropriations process. Ideologically opposed

members of Congress can cooperate. Legislative cooperation between liberal Ted Kennedy (D-MA) and conservatives such as Oren Hatch (R-UT)
and Dirk Kempthorne (R-ID) illustrates that opposites can cooperate. The
Appropriations Committees have not been devoid of ideological and partisan
differences; the relative autonomy of the committee from intrusion by party
leaders and the tendency to assign effective, proven legislators to the committees ensured a reasonable level of cooperation within the committees.

Our interviews suggest that the efforts of party leaders on both sides of
the aisle to gain control over the Appropriations process to promote broad
partisan interests has robbed it of the autonomy necessary to appropriate.

Elected in 1969, David Obey (D-WI) was appointed to House
Appropriations as a first-term member and served on the committee until
his retirement in 2011. In 1994, he was elected Chair of the committee,
and served in that role, or as the ranking democrat, until he left Congress.
Through the 1970s until the early 1990s, he observed, "It was still a fairly
bipartisan committee." That changed, he says, following the Republican
takeover of Congress in 1995. New Speaker Newt Gingrich (R-GA) departed
from the practice of assigning more senior and proven members to the committee: "When Newt [Gingrich] became Speaker he appointed a number of
fire-breathing conservatives to the committee and they had the attitude that
somehow, because we had been there before them, we were impure and not
worthy of respect." According to Obey, the impact of these new members
was not immediate; "the guys in charge of the subcommittees were still
largely the old school guys who wanted to get along with people."

Despite being Gingrich's hand-picked choice as Appropriations chair, Bob
Livingston (R-LA) was willing to push back against the party leadership.
"He was an institutionalist and he understood that the best legislation is
guided by party leadership, but leavened from the bottom up by people who
have enough expertise to understand the detailed impact of what the wiz-
ards in the leadership were trying to do." Throughout Livingston's tenure as
chairman, there was tension between him and the House leadership. Speaker
Gingrich required each Appropriations Subcommittee Chair to sign a pledge
to support Republican priorities, and there was considerable effort on the
part of leadership to influence the process. This tension reached a head on
November 6, 1998, when Livingston wrote a letter to then-Speaker Gingrich
making 16 separate demands for increased autonomy for the Committee and
power for himself as its chair.[7] The letter asserts:

> I believe that it is imperative that you acknowledge and agree to these sug-
> gested changes in House procedure, without exception. 1. I as Chairman of
> the Appropriations Committee, shall run the Committee as I see fit and in
> the best interest of the Republican majority, with full consultation with the
> leadership, but without being subject to the dictates of any other member of
> Congress. 2. That I be the final authority to determine content of legislation
> within the Appropriations Committee, and the schedule under which legis-
> lation is produced, without interference...(the letter continues in a similar
> manner).

Soon after this letter was written, Speaker Gingrich announced his intent to step down and Livingston was selected by his colleagues to become the next Republican House Leader. Unfortunately for Livingston, not long after he was chosen, he announced his stunning resignation from the House in the wake of allegations of marital infidelity.

When Livingston left Congress, the new Republican leadership seized the opportunity to further consolidate power within the Appropriations process. The Republican Steering Committee is empowered to choose committee chairs. The structure of the committee is such that the Speaker—along with the Majority Leader and Whip— effectively control the votes necessary to appoint a committee chair (or make any committee assignment [Frisch and Kelly 2006a]). This provides considerable leverage over the committee chair; it allows the leadership to command a level of influence over the committee chair who owes his chairmanship to party leaders.

Speaker Hastert took the reins from Newt Gingrich, and Tom DeLay (R-TX), a former appropriator, rose to become Majority Leader in place of retiring Dick Armey (R-TX). This was a pivotal turn of events according to Obey and others: "DeLay became the enforcer. DeLay was a member of the committee as well as on the Leadership, and it became very much a leadership-directed committee." Observing the process from the outside, and two years before Obey shared his perspective, Bob Livingston acknowledged the role that DeLay took in trying to direct the work of the committee: "Constantly Hastert and DeLay were making demands on [the appropriations process]." Bill Young (R-FL), who was followed by Jerry Lewis in the position, would necessarily have to allow more leadership involvement in the Appropriations process than their predecessors, and certainly more than the Appropriations Committees of the 1960s, 1970s, and 1980s.

In more recent congresses, the shift toward partisan control of the process has not abated. According to a very senior Appropriations staffer, "Mr. Boehner and Mr. Cantor have very successfully taken over the Appropriations process. In fact, Mr. [Hal] Rogers (R-KY) would not have gotten the chairmanship if he had not agreed to that scenario." Describing his role in negotiations in a Continuing Resolution for the last six months of Fiscal Year 2013, Hal Rogers tipped his hand admitting that critical decisions about spending priorities were largely in the hands of the president and the congressional party leadership.[8]

One indication of leadership involvement was the use of policy riders on Appropriations bills; in particular, riders aimed at achieving partisan policy goals. Appropriations bills are the only bills that must move through the legislative process, and they became an attractive vehicle for the majority party leadership to pursue their legislative goals. Attaching these riders to Appropriations bills, however, expands the scope of conflict by conflating the core responsibility of the committee—funding government—with contentious policy issues such as environmental regulation and abortion. As David Obey observes, "it is hard enough to do the basic job [of appropriating]...the number one responsibility of Congress is to fund the damn budget every year. That's the minimum requirement that you have, and every time somebody drags another issue in, it makes it harder to meet your basic responsibilities."

Change in the Senate Appropriations Committee has taken a different path but arrived in much the same place as House Appropriations. According to a Senate Appropriations clerk, "[Over] the past several years we have seen the whole committee growing more partisan. It used to be the Appropriators stood together, and they haven't done that for a long time."

Senate leaders exercise less control over the leadership of the Appropriations Committee. Unlike the House, Senate Appropriations Committee and Subcommittee chairs are determined largely by seniority and individual preferences.[9] Likewise, in making committee assignments, the leadership exercises only slightly more control over who is assigned to the committee. Both leaders have the ability to assign new members to choice committees and then defer mostly to the seniority norm, especially on the Republican side (Frisch and Kelly 2006b). As a result, committee leaders have more autonomy in theory than House committee chairs, and the ability of the leadership to add new and more ideologically extreme members to the committee is somewhat attenuated. Even in recent years, the Senate Appropriations has been the province of very senior members such as Robert Byrd (D-WV), Ted Stevens (R-AK), Thad Cochran (R-MS), and Daniel Inouye (D-HI). One staffer characterized it this way: "The desire to complete the Appropriations process and take care of members' interests" prevailed over other concerns.

Senate leaders do have an important power over the Appropriations Committee, however, in the control of scheduling floor time for consideration of bills. According to many inside observers of the Senate process whom we interviewed, Senate Leaders from both parties have become much more involved in the Appropriations process, particularly by refusing to provide floor time for controversial bills, especially those that will force their members to make politically difficult votes. Leaders in both parties (Reid, McConnell, Durbin) are either current or former members of the committee and have also been much more influential in pressuring members to support party priorities, as the anecdote that begins this chapter illustrates.

It was not until the 2000s that the dynamics of the Senate Appropriations Committee took on a more partisan tone. "It started to break down over the war in Iraq where the Republicans circles the wagons around President Bush's policy" says a staffer who has worked with appropriators from both ends of Pennsylvania Avenue. "Senator Stevens, Senator Cochran, Senator McConnell basically did whatever the president wanted and that started the change."[10] It "really came to flower" he continued "after the [2010] elections...the Republicans won and they were feeling more empowered and Senator Cochran followed [McConnell's partisan strategy]." Said another staffer "The leadership in the Republican Party...made it very clear that the sole mission of these last few years is to see that President Obama is not reelected and to do that...the leadership on the Republican side takes everything the Democrats say and puts a 'no' in front of it."[11]

As in the House, Senate Appropriations Committee bills have become targets for partisan attacks. A Senate Appropriations staffer observes that "No one used to pay a lot of attention to Appropriations bills...as partisanship has increased we've become the target [of partisan conflict] through spending, through policy riders." Appropriations bills become another opportunity for partisans to communicate to DC-based constituencies, and activists back in the district. Everything is a "message vote," he observed, "even an Appropriations bill becomes a message vote."

In 2002, Democrats were in the majority and writing FY 2003 Appropriations bills. All 12 of the bills were reported out of the committee, mostly on a unanimous, bipartisan basis. "The Republican leadership decided to kill the process because they anticipated winning the 2002 elections" says a committee staffer. Instead, a Continuing Resolution was passed to fund government through the election. When Republicans assumed the majority in the Senate in 2003, Republican chairman Stevens wanted to finish the Appropriations process.

> [Stevens] literally took the 12 bills...word for word, number for number, earmark for earmark—put them together in a single omnibus bill put a title on the back of the bill that reduced overall spending by $9 billion so that Republicans could show there was a "change in town"...they weren't political, just reductions in spending—he didn't even change the earmark ratio [to reflect Republicans' new majority status]...because bipartisan bills were done in the first place he took the bills, put them all into one [omnibus]...he passed it through the Senate and it went the president and he signed it.

This is in stark contrast to the scene that unfolded in the anecdote that began this chapter wherein an omnibus, negotiated on a bipartisan basis, was scuttled by a partisan minority on the committee.

Distributive Politics, Earmarks, and Collapse of the Committees

Joseph White highlights the central role that distributive politics played in promoting bipartisanship in the Appropriations process up through the 1980s. The distribution of benefits to districts or states united the common interests of appropriators and nonappropriators. Distributive benefits are nonpartisan: "...distributional politics only becomes partisan if the parties decided to go to war as part of some other dispute" (White 1989, 224). Gordon, surveying the Appropriations process a decade later observed that "...by the end of the 1990s there seemed to be an increased desire some partisans to make distributional politics itself partisan" (2002, 195).

Searching for electoral advantage first Democrats and then Republicans launched an attack on one of the primary means at the disposal of committee to build coalitions on the floor: earmarks. Both parties focused attention on abuses in the earmarking process, real or perceived, to cast the opposition as corrupt and spendthrift. The term "earmark"—previously an

inside-baseball term known only to Washington insiders and political scientists—became part of the common vernacular. Their poster child: "The
Bridge to Nowhere." When Republicans surrendered their majority in the
2006 midterm elections, they blamed their loss of fiscal discipline and
the explosion in earmarks (an "explosion" in the number of earmarks and
not so much the total value of earmarks). Democrats promised reforms,
and following a year-long moratorium put into place a series of reforms aimed
at increasing transparency in the process. Earmarks returned the following
year, and Republicans picked up the newly generated public animus toward
earmarks and began using it against Democrats. The antiearmark fervor was
accelerated when staunch earmark appointment John McCain received the
Republican Presidential nomination and used the theme that earmarks are
emblematic of government waste as a major focus of his campaign. When
Republicans returned to the majority in both chambers in 2011, they put in
place a complete moratorium on earmarks that remains in force.

Frisch and Kelly (2013) argued that in the absence of earmarks, Congress
would find it difficult to legislate. Earmarks guaranteed that each legislator
would have some "skin in the game," that is, that members of Congress
might have something to lose by opposing every piece of legislation that
comes to the floor.[12] Former House Appropriator Henry Bonilla (R-TX)
explains: "You wanted those bills to get done...to tout when you go back
home." Former Senate Democratic Leader Tom Daschle (D-SD) relates this
story highlighting the importance of earmarks in the legislative process:

> I asked [former Republican Senate Leader] Howard Baker (TN) once how he
> was so successful getting things done and he said one word: "earmarks." [He
> said] "People feel invested, and if they feel invested in the legislation because
> it brings something to their constituencies they are far more willing to be
> engaged all the way through the process because they want that piece to be
> included."[13]

A point that a Senate Appropriations Committee staffer echoes:

> Earmarks were, in fact, the grease that moved the process along; members
> wanted to get a bill through the Senate because there were things in the bill
> they cared about. In the absence of that there isn't a great deal of incentive
> for the Senate to move Appropriations bills...pile on the fact that we're in an
> environment in which you can't do anything in the Senate unless you have 60
> votes...Appropriations bills don't move.

Asked to explain the dysfunction of the Senate Appropriations Committee
the staffer replied, "loss of the earmark authority, and the change in the
culture."

In short, distributive politics has become a point of contention in itself; it
is not caught up in a fight over some extraneous issue, *it is the issue*. As is the
power and authority of the Appropriations Committee a matter of contention within the institution. Authorizers have historically resented the role of

the Appropriations Committee. Leaders have sought to gain control over the committee to push the party's agenda. Jerry Lewis explains:

> There has been this...confrontation between the Appropriations Committee and people who are outside of the appropriations process. Over the last decade at any rate, there is no doubt that within the leadership on both sides there has been reaction to the fact that the Appropriations Committee has been the place where work actually got done, but the leadership would much prefer to have that authority and that power in their hands rather than somebody else— "just because you put them on a committee called Appropriations shouldn't give them some special level of power."

The last two election cycles have further aggravated the ability of Republicans to build coalitions within their Conference. Newly elected Republicans are considerably less supportive of many of the programs they are asked to support through the Appropriations process. Tea Party supported House and Senate members were elected on a promise to end earmarks and cut federal programs and spending. Opposing Appropriations bills reinforces their electoral message. One Senate Appropriations Committee staffer noted "we have one [Republican] member in particular who hasn't voted for any of the appropriations bills because we weren't cutting enough." The antigovernment consensus that marks the Republican Party in both the House and the Senate is the fundamental issue of the contemporary Congress that divides Democrats and Republicans.

Many new Republicans actively spurn the "Washington culture." A staffer to a senior appropriator explains it this way: "As little as six years ago, maybe eight years ago, you were considered a weird flake if you slept in your office, but this last freshman class all of a sudden people made it a virtue...Now what that tells you is they don't want anything to do with anybody outside of the building. They are coming here to work in the building and then they're going to go home [to their district]." When members reject the institution of which they are a part they are unlikely to feel part of a common cause to govern: *Being an institutional patriot is virtually unpatriotic.*

APPROPRIATIONS TO THE EXTREME

The qualitative data from our interviews suggest that ideological polarization surrounding Appropriations Committee bills has changed over the past 45 years. Using roll call votes on Appropriations votes in the House and the Senate, we explore the nature of this change to determine whether these patterns persist when using objective data on members' behavior.[14]

The House

Figure 1.1 provides a look at variation in interparty and intraparty variation surrounding House votes on Appropriations measures over time. Differences

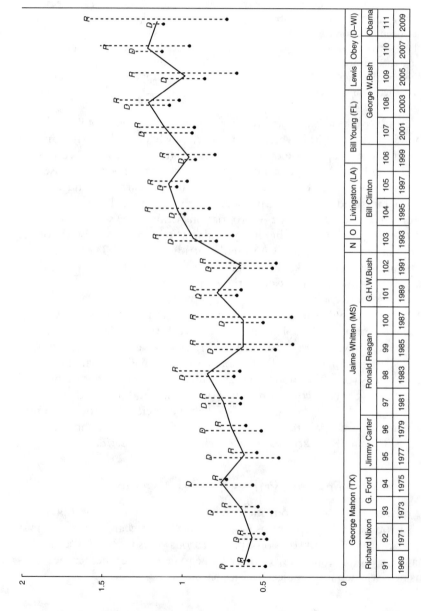

Figure 1.1 Intra- and Interparty Distances on Appropriations Votes in the House.

between the interparty medians for appropriators are represented by the solid line. Between the ninety-first and the one hundred and second Congress, the distance between Democratic and Republican Appropriators on Appropriations-related votes is reasonably constant. This is consistent with both Fenno and White's observations about the essentially bipartisan nature of Appropriations bills. Between the one hundred and second and the one hundred and fifth Congress, interparty distances increase considerably; subsequent to the one hundred and fifth Congress, the general trend is for the two parties to drift further apart on Appropriations matters. This is consistent with the qualitative assessments offered by Appropriations insiders presented above. Under the influence of Newt Gingrich, House Republicans developed a more confrontational approach toward Democrats and the Clinton White House. Seizing control of the House in the one hundred and fourth Congress, House Republicans sought, in almost-parliamentary manner, to render the Clinton White House irrelevant in the policy process. Through the aggressive use of policy and limitation riders on Appropriations bills, the Republican leadership attempted to loosen executive control over the regulatory environment, and press the conservative policy agenda through the Appropriations process. Despite attempts to resist leadership interference, new Appropriations Chair Bob Livingston (and many of the subcommittee chairs) was pressured to incorporate elements of the party policy agenda. Where votes on Appropriations matters were previously largely unhindered by policy matters, bipartisanship on the floor was possible. In the new, more partisan and confrontational environment, appropriators were increasingly washing their "dirty laundry" on the floor.

Figure 1.1 also reflects changes in *intra*party divisions. The dashed, vertical "fish bones" along the solid line represent the distance between the median position of each part and the median position of Democratic and Republican Party appropriators, on Appropriations votes. The distance between the ends of the line indicates the differences within the parties on Appropriations matters; the longer the line, the greater the differences. Between the ninety-first and the one hundred and second congresses, Democratic appropriators were, on average, more distant from their party median than were Republican appropriators. This reflects the breadth of interests represented within the Democratic Caucus during that period; conservative Democrats, especially from the South, created large internal differences within the caucus.

Beginning in the one hundred and fourth Congress, as the Democrats moved into the minority, the committee and party medians tend to converge. In part this reflects the departure of conservative Democrats from the Democratic Caucus, replaced with either Republicans or more liberal Democrats. It also reflects the response of Democrats to the conservative policy agenda advanced by Republicans. The distance between Republican appropriators and their party median began to converge as new, more partisan members were added to the committee, but then increased substantially, especially in more recent congresses.

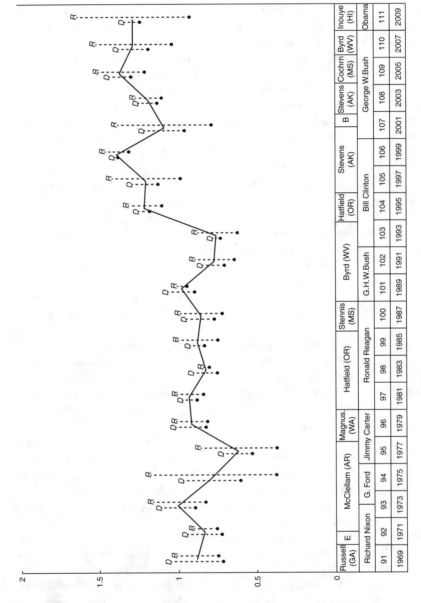

Figure 1.2 Intra- and Interparty Distances on Appropriations Votes in the Senate.

Figure 1.2 illustrates the same results for the Senate. The pattern of interparty polarization surrounding Appropriations is similar to that in the House. Notable, however, is the pronounced increase in the one hundred and fourth Congress. This coincides with an influx of Republican senators who had served with Newt Gingrich in the House and were part of his revolution. Similar to the House, the intraparty distances among Republicans. Intraparty differences likely reflect the fact that sitting members of Senate Appropriations were mostly senior members more accustomed to cutting bipartisan deals, who were encountering a changing Republican Conference composed of members hostile to the work of the committee, that is, the expenditure of funds on a wide swath of federal programs. All indications are that the increased polarization surrounding Appropriations will continue at the same high level.

Conclusions

The last time Congress passed all of the Appropriations bills by the statutory deadline of October 1 was the one hundred and fourth Congress, the year after the infamous government shutdown that resulted from a confrontation between Republicans and Democratic President Bill Clinton (figure 1.3). Between the one hundred and fifth and one hundred and eleventh Congress, only 16 of 186 required bills were completed by the October date; an average of just over two bills per Congress. In the 10 congresses prior to the one hundred and fifth Congress for which we have data, the record of Congress, while not perfect, was substantially better.

Interviews with participants and close observers of the process suggest that increasing ideological polarization and partisanship—within previously bipartisan committees, is to blame for bringing the process to its knees. Former Appropriations Chair Jerry Lewis believes that "There's going to have to be either a rethinking, readjustment...or a brand new ball game" with regard to the operation of the committee.

The clearest example of the failure of the Appropriations Committees to do its work can be seen in the fate of the bill that funds the Departments of Labor, Health and Human Services, and Education in recent years. This bill is the most controversial of all the Appropriations bills as it supports many of the social programs where there is a great disagreement between the parties. It has also frequently been used for policy positioning through the inclusion of limitation riders, many of which are pushed by the more extreme members. In the words of one House Appropriations staffer talking of the staff who work on that bill, ". . .Labor-HHS. I mean, poor guys because they just work so hard to try to put a bill out that balances all the competing interests of the crazies of both parties as well as on their subcommittee and that's about as far as they get, at least the last few years."

The failure of the Appropriations process is more than a political curiosity. It has implications for the power and prestige of the committees, and the power and prerogatives of Congress vis-à-vis the executive branch. But most

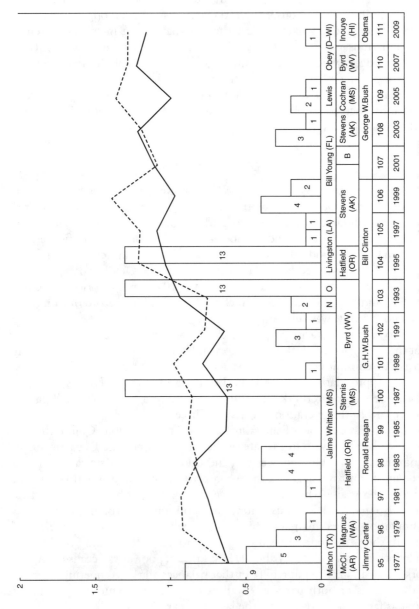

Figure 1.3 Interparty difference in the House and Senate and the Passage of Appropriations Bills.

important, the failure has implications for public policy. Funding decisions made by the Appropriations Committees are among the most important decisions made by government. The Constitution empowers the representatives of the people with the power of the purse. The breakdown of the bipartisan Appropriations process that was described by Fenno has serious implications for the way our nation makes its most fundamental decisions. Without clear congressional direction, thousands of spending decisions are delegated to the executive. The role of unelected bureaucrats in the agencies and at the Office of Management and Budget has been aggrandized at the expense of those elected to represent constituents. Almost one hundred years ago Edward Fitzpatrick (1918) wrote:

> When you have decided on your budget procedure, you have decided on the form of government you will have as a matter of fact. Make the executive the dominating and controlling factor in budget-making and you have irrespective of what label you put on it, an autocratic government. If, recognizing the large part the executive or administration may play in budget- making, you give the dominating and controlling influence in budget-making to the legislature, you have, irrespective or what label you put on it, a democratic or representative actual government.

As the Appropriations process is currently operating—Continuing Resolutions, Omnibus and Minibus bills all devoid of earmarks, the executive has been greatly empowered at the expense of representative government.

NOTES

1. In this chapter, we capitalize on a large number of interviews with current and former appropriators, current and former Appropriations Committee clerks, congressional staff, and lobbyists. Most of these interviews were conducted in person, lasting between 45 minutes and two-and-a-half hours. All interviews with staff were conducted on the promise of anonymity. Only their chamber, seniority, and position are acknowledged, along with the location and approximate date of the interview. Interview with the authors, Washington, DC, November 2011.
2. Interview with the authors, Washington, DC, October 2012.
3. Interview with the authors, Washington, DC, October 2012.
4. Interview with the authors, Washington, DC, November 2011.
5. Telephonic interview with the authors, December 2011.
6. While most of Fenno's book is devoted to the House Appropriations Committee, he does include a chapter on the Senate Committee. Horn (1970) provides a more extended exploration of the Senate Appropriations Committee of the same era.
7. The entire letter is reprinted in Schick (2007, 221).
8. "Four Things to Know about the Next Big Budget Battle," accessed March 7, 2013. http://www.npr.org/blogs/itsallpolitics/2013/03/05/173477979/four-things-to-know-about-the-next-big-budget-battle.
9. For instance, with the death of Senate Appropriations Chair Daniel Inouye (D-HI), Senator Patrick Leahy (D-VT) was the most senior Democrat on the

committee and entitled to assume the Chair. He decided to remain the Chair of
the Judiciary Committee.

10. Interview with the authors, Washington, DC, November 2011.

11. Interview with the authors, Washington, DC, November 2011.

12. On the important role of earmarks in facilitating legislative coalition building,
see also Frisch (1998), Evans (2004), and White (1989, especially Chapter 3).

13. Panel discussion, Commission on Political Reform, Ronald Reagan Presidential
Library, and Museum, Simi Valley, CA, March 6, 2013, accessed March 7, 2013.
http://www.ustream.tv/recorded/29780287.

14. Congressional scholars make extensive use of roll calls to understand the internal
dynamics of the institution. Poole and Rosenthal (2000) developed the NOMI-
NATE algorithm to use roll call votes to estimate legislator "ideal points." In this
chapter, we pool all votes on Appropriations matters for each Congress from
the ninety-first through the one hundred and eleventh, for both the House and
the Senate. We use NOMINATE to create "appropriations ideal points" for each
Congress. Appropriations votes were identified using the Rohde (2010) database subsequently updated through the one hundred and eleventh Congress.
We use the W-NOMINATE algorithm, implemented in R, to calculate members'
two-dimensional "appropriations ideal points." The horizontal axis captures
the left-right ideological dimension, and the vertical access represents members'
"affinity" for the preferences of the Appropriations Committee. Creation of
this second dimension is driven by an a priori assumption—based on the mostly
qualitative empirical evidence developed over the last five decades—that the
Appropriations Committees in Congress represent a unique "center of gravity"
in the legislative process. That appropriations votes are multidimensional (see
Crespin and Rohde 2010). Using data on member ideal points within this two-
dimensional space, we are able to characterize relationships between medians
calculated for the parties, and for partisans on the Appropriations committees,
this two-dimensional space over time. Contact the authors for additional docu-
mentation regarding this approach.

REFERENCES

Aldrich, John H., and David W. Rohde. 2000. "The Republican Revolution and the
House Appropriations Committee." *The Journal of Politics* 62(1): 1–33.

Crespin, Michael H., and David W. Rohde. 2010. "Dimensions, Issues, and Bills:
Appropriations Voting on the House Floor." *The Journal of Politics* 72(4):
976–989.

Evans, Diana. 2004. *Greasing the Wheels: Using Pork Barrel Projects to Build Minority
Coalitions in Congress.* Cambridge: Cambridge University Press.

Fenno, Richard F. 1962. "The House Appropriations Committee as a Political
System: The Problem of Integration." *American Political Science Review* 56(2):
310–324.

———. 1966. *The Power of the Purse: Appropriations Politics in Congress.* Boston:
Little, Brown and Company.

Frisch, Scott A. 1998. *The Politics of Pork: A Study of Congressional Appropriations
Earmarks.* New York: Garland.

Frisch, Scott A., and Sean Q Kelly. 2006a. *Committee Assignment Politics in the U.S.
House of Representatives.* Norman: The University of Oklahoma Press.

————. 2006b. "Committee Assignment Politics in the U.S. Senate: Democratic Leaders and Democratic Committee Assignments, 1953–1994." *Congress and the Presidency* 33(1): 1–23.

————. 2013. "Frisch and Kelly: Lack of Earmarks Makes Congress Harder to Lead." *Roll Call*, January 16. http://www.rollcall.com/news/frisch_and_kelly_lack_of_earmarks_makes_congress_harder_to_lead-220811-1.html?pos=oplyh (accessed March 7, 2013).

Gordon, Joshua B. 2002. "The Power of the Purse Reconsidered: Partisanship and Social Integration in the House Appropriations Committee." PhD Dissertation, University of Florida, Florida.

Horn, Stephen. 1970. *Unused Power: The Work of the Senate Committee on Appropriations*. Washington, DC: The Brookings Institution.

Poole, Keith T., and Howard Rosenthal. 2000. *Congress: A Political-economic History of Roll Call Voting*. New York: Oxford University Press.

Rohde, David W. 2010. "Political Institutions and Public Choice House Roll-call Database." Duke University, Unpublished manuscript.

Schick, Allen. 2007. *The Federal Budget: Politics, Policy, Process*. Washington, DC: The Brookings Institution.

White, Joseph. 1989. "The Functions and Power of the House Appropriations Committee." PhD Dissertation, University of California, Berkeley.

The Gingrich Senators, the Tea Party Senators, and Their Effect on the US Senate

Sean M. Theriault

Most Americans have recoiled at what their Congress has become. After a recent poll showing congressional approval in the single digits, Senator John McCain (R-AZ) concluded that the only congressional supporters these days include "blood relatives and paid staff."[1] In an article titled "Our Broken Senate," Norman J. Ornstein, the dean of political pundits, argued that "the Senate had taken the term 'deliberate' to a new level...In many ways, the frustration of modern governance in Washington—the arrogance, independence, parochialism—could be called 'The Curse of the Senate.'" He concludes that the problem with the Senate is the "the culture" and that "is not going to change anytime soon."[2] This chorus of dysfunction in the Senate is given its clearest voice as senators are on their way out the door. When Senator Evan Bayh, whose father was also a senator, announced his retirement in 2010, he complained:

> For some time, I've had a growing conviction that Congress is not operating as it should. There is much too much partisanship and not enough progress; too much narrow ideology and not enough practical problem-solving. Even at a time of enormous national challenge, the people's business is not getting done...I love working for the people of Indiana. I love helping our citizens make the most of their lives. But I do not love Congress.[3]

Two years later when Olympia Snowe announced that she would retire at the end of 2012, she commented, "Unfortunately, I do not realistically expect the partisanship of recent years in the Senate to change over the short term."[4]

When they were announcing their retirement from the Senate, it is my contention that Bayh and Snowe were criticizing the institution on two different, though related, underlying dimensions. First, the senators serving today are more ideologically polarized than their predecessors. While the Senate has always had both extreme conservatives and extreme liberals, today's Senate seems to have more of them than it did before. As the senators have become more ideologically polarized, the number of senators in the middle has shrunk, which has impeded the ability of the Senate to find compromises necessary for solving public policy problems.

While some may think that the growing ideological divide between the parties is reason enough to criticize the institution, a second complaint seems to bother Snowe, Bayh, their fellow senators, political pundits, and congressional scholars even more. The complaint, while it has its roots in party polarization, is combative in nature and goes beyond the mere casting of roll call votes on the Senate floor. I call this second dimension, partisan warfare. The partisan warfare dimension taps into the strategies that go beyond defeating your opponents into humiliating them, go beyond questioning your opponents judgment into questioning their motives, and go beyond fighting the good legislative fight to destroying the institution and the legislative process in order to serve not only your partisan or ideological goals, but also your electoral goals.

This warfare certainly has party polarization at its roots. Polarization may be necessary for warfare, but it is not a sufficient cause of it. Parties that are divided over policy can have a serious and honest debate, which can even become heated. In the first half of the famous idiom, the opposing sides can "agree to disagree." Quite apart from the serious policy disagreement, though, the debate between the opposing sides can degenerate into a shouting match where the policy proscriptions are lost in a fight over legislative games where the combatants question the motives, integrity, and patriotism of their opponents. Under such a situation, the second half of the idiom—"without being disagreeable"—is never realized.

This partisan warfare dimension is harder to quantify, though it most certainly exists. What I call, "partisan warfare," is what Frances Lee (2009) characterized as "beyond ideology" in her book of the same name. Lee argues that only so much of the divide between the parties can be understood as a difference in ideology. The rest of the divide—by some accounts, the lion's share of the divide—is motivated by some other goal. Lee (2009, 193) defines this behavior as "partisan bickering" and offers the following description:

> If partisanship has roots in members' political interests, then political parties actually exacerbate and institutionalize conflict, rather than merely represent and give voice to preexisting policy disagreements in the broader political environment. In their quest to win elections and wield power, partisans impeach one another's motives, question one another's ethics and competence, engage in reflexive partisanship, and—when it is politically useful to do so—exploit and deepen divisions rather than seeking common ground.

I argue that it is this portion of the divide that causes the angst of those participants and observers of today's Senate. Lee restricts her evaluation of the combat that is beyond ideology to an examination of roll-call votes, which is an appropriate first step. Partisan warfare, though, can operate in contexts beyond the "yeas" and "nays" on the Senate floor. In fact, it is frequently other actions in the legislative and electoral processes that better exhibit partisan warfare.

More often than not, congressional scholars for a couple of reasons have opted to merge these two dimensions. First, there is no doubt that they are related. The distinction between party polarization and partisan warfare can easily be masked as the same or at least similar enough to collapse on to one dimension. Second, the second dimension of partisan warfare, especially in comparison to the first, is much harder to isolate, operationalize, and analyze. Nonetheless, real analytic leverage can be brought to our understanding of how the current Senate operates and how it is evaluated if these dimensions are pulled apart.

In this chapter, I examine these two dimension among three groups of Republican senators—the Gingrich senators, the Tea Party senators, and the other Republican senators. I find that the current polarization in the Senate can chiefly be explained by the increasing numbers and increasingly conservative voting patterns of the Gingrich senators. In the one hundred and twelfth Congress, the Tea Party senators perpetuated polarization even more. Furthermore, I show how the Gingrich senators and the Tea Party senators have conducted partisan warfare on the Senate by focusing on data from First Session of the one hundred and twelfth Congress (2011).

LINKING THE GINGRICH SENATORS TO THE TEA PARTY SENATORS

As Senator DeMint was declaring his intention to make health-care reform Obama's "Waterloo" in July 2009, the script for the 2010 congressional midterm was changing; perhaps, even because of DeMint's declaration. In July 2009, 61 percent of Americans approved of Obama's presidency, and only 32 percent disapproved.[5] Obama's high numbers were reflected in the predictions that Charlie Cook was making at the time. He projected that the Democrats would retain 58 seats in the 2010 election and that an additional six were in the "toss-up" category.[6]

Within six months, the entire political landscape would change. On January 19, Scott Brown (R-Massachusetts) ended the Democrat's filibuster-proof margin when he won the special election to complete Ted Kennedy's term in the Senate. Brown's victory signaled that Democrats were facing mounting and ominous odds in the 2010 elections. Republican believed that if they could win in Massachusetts, they could win just about anywhere. The numbers supported their belief. Those approving of Obama exactly equaled those disapproving and Cook down-graded the Democrat's projection to 51 seats, with an additional 12 in the toss-up category.[7]

No politician encapsulates the narrative for the 2010-midterm elections better than Gingrich senator, Jim DeMint. While it is in unclear if he led the Tea Party movement or simply got out in front of it after it started, few dispute how crucial he was for its success. In fact, the vary definition of what it meant to be a Tea Party candidate according to the *New York Times*, in part, depending upon having his endorsement.[8] While former House Majority Leader (under Gingrich's speakership) Dick Armey (R-Texas) and former Governor Sarah Palin (R-Alaska) also played important roles in the Tea Party movement, both were out of office in 2010 and did not have to walk that fine line between being an outsider, which the Tea Party movement valued, while still operating the levers of government power. DeMint, incidentally, gave up the latter when he resigned his Senate seat in 2012.

Even before his "Waterloo" comment, DeMint had a significant effect on the 2010 election when he endorsed Pat Toomey, a former House member, in the 2010 Republican primary for a Pennsylvania Senate seat. Toomey's opponent in the primary was incumbent Arlen Specter, who, within a week of DeMint's endorsement, switched parties giving the Democrats the sixtieth vote they needed to break Republican filibusters. In making his choice of Toomey, DeMint argued, "I would rather have 30 Republicans in the Senate who really believe in principles of limited government, free markets, free people, than to have 60 that don't have a set of beliefs."[9]

The Toomey endorsement was only the first of many that would cause the Republican establishment—as best articulated by Senator John Cornyn (R-Texas), who was serving as the chair of the National Republican Senate Committee—much heart-ache. The other endorsements of candidates running against establishment candidates included the following:

- Marco Rubio, Florida. On June 15, 2009, a week after his Toomey endorsement was publicly announced, DeMint endorsed Rubio, a former Florida House speaker, over Governor Charlie Crist (R-Florida), who received the National Republican Senatorial Committee (NRSC) endorsement a month earlier. At the time of DeMint's announcement, Rubio was trailing by more than 30 points in the polls—a Quinnipiac poll showed Crist with a 54 to 23 advantage.[10] In May 2010, Crist announced that he was dropping out of the Republican primary and would run for the seat as "a non party affiliated" candidate. He lost the general election to Rubio, by almost 20 percentage points; the Democratic candidate, Congressman Kendrick Meek (D-Florida) finished a distant third with 20 percent of the vote.
- Chuck Devore, California. On November 4, 2009, almost a year before the 2010 elections, DeMint endorsed Devore over Carly Fiorina in the Republican primary race to take on Senator Barbara Boxer (D-California). Although Fiorina had not officially earned the NRSC endorsement, she was the candidate of the Republican establishment. In the same month that DeMint endorse her opponent, Fiorina was the guest of honor at a fundraiser featuring Mitch McConnell (R-Kentucky), Olympia Snowe

(R-Maine), and John McCain, who had named her as one of his chief advisers during his 2008 presidential campaign.[11] Devore finished third in the primary with only 19.3 percent of the vote. Fiorina secured 56.4 percent and former Congressman Tom Campbell (R-California) won 21.7 percent. Fiorina lost in the general election to the incumbent.

- Ken Buck, Colorado. On April 14, 2010, DeMint endorsed Ken Buck, the District Attorney of Weld County, over former Lieutenant Governor, Jane Norton, who was the NRSC preferred candidate. In March, Norton lead Buck 41–13 percent in the polls. In the week after DeMint's endorsement, Buck, for the first time, led the polls, though just by 3 percentage points. Although Buck was outspent and out organized by Norton, he won the primary by 4 points, but lost the general election to Michael Bennet, who was appointed to the seat after Ken Salazar (D-Colorado) became Interior Secretary.
- Marlin Stutzman, Indiana. On April 20, 2010, DeMint endorsed a young farmer and businessman, Marlin Stutzman, over former Senator Dan Coats (a Gingrich senator) and former Congressman John Hostettler (R-Indiana). DeMint's endorsement helped the Stutzman campaign gain traction against Coats, who had the NRSC endorsement. He lost the primary by 10 percentage points to Dan Coats, who easily won the general election. Stutzman would later win a special election to fill the House seat vacancy caused by the resignation of Mark Souder (R-Indiana), who was caught in a sex scandal.
- Rand Paul, Kentucky. On May 5, 2010, DeMint endorsed ophthalmologist Rand Paul over Trey Grayson, the Attorney general, who was backed by Kentucky's senior senator, Minority Leader Mitch McConnell, as well as former Vice President Dick Cheney and former New York Mayor Rudy Giuliani. Paul won the primary by more than 20 points and the general election by more than 10 points.
- Mike Lee, Utah. In the week before the Republican convention on May 8, 2010, DeMint made a video endorsing Mike Lee that was to be played only if the incumbent, Senator Bob Bennett, was defeated in early voting. The contents of the video were leaked prior to the vote. Subsequently, Bennett finished third in a preliminary ballot at the convention, knocking him from contention. Although Tim Bridgewater finished first in the final round of voting at the convention, he did not secure the 60 percent of supporters that would have cancelled the primary. Lee reversed the order in the primary by less than 2.5 percentage points and went on to win the general election in a landslide.
- Ovide Lamontagne, New Hampshire. On September 11, 2010, with less than a week to go before the primary, DeMint endorsed Ovide Lamontagne, over the establishment-candidate, Kelly Ayotte, who was the former Attorney general. The New Hampshire race was the only Senate race where Sarah Palin and Jim DeMint gave contradicting endorsements. Ayotte also had the endorsement of Judd Gregg, whose seat she was seeking, Mitch McConnell, Warren Rudman (R-New Hampshire), and John

McCain. Although Lamontagne trailed Ayotte 34 percent to 15 percent in the polls a week before DeMint's endorsement, he ended up losing the race by less than 2,000 votes out of more than 138,000 votes cast. Ayotte went on to win the general election.

- Christine O'Donnell, Delaware. On the same day as he made his Lamontagne endorsement, DeMint also endorsed Christine O'Donnell over Congressman Mike Castle (R-Delaware). Although he made his endorsement only three days before the primary, it may have made the difference as O'Donnell won the primary by less than 4,000 votes. O'Donnell's primary victory compelled Charlie Cook to shift the seat from "Likely Republican" to "Likely Democrat." She was soundly defeated by Chris Coons (D-Delaware), who was the sitting county executive for New Castle County, in the general election.

The aforementioned candidates are not the only candidates DeMint backed. His endorsements of Ron Johnson (Wisconsin), Dino Rossi (Washington), Tom Coburn (Oklahoma), and John Raese (West Virginia) were not controversial among Republicans. Furthermore, he withheld two endorsements during contested primaries. In Nevada, DeMint found both Sharon Angle and Sue Lowden sufficiently conservative. In Alaska, he respected senatorial courtesy and remained neutral in Joe Miller's challenge to Senator Lisa Murkowski. After the primaries in these two states, he fervently rallied to Miller's and Angle's causes, though both in a losing effort.

DeMint's endorsements, unlike those from almost every other leadership Political Action Committee (PAC), came with more than a just a check from the Leadership PAC. DeMint not only provided funds directly from his Leadership PAC, but also encouraged his followers to contribute to the individual campaigns. While his Leadership PACs gave $135,000, his nationwide network of donors added $6.6 million more through the Senate Conservative Fund (table 2.1 lists the donations DeMint made in the 2010 Senate races).[12]

While Republicans were overwhelmingly pleased with the results on election night, the record in the Senate for the Tea Party and DeMint was more mixed. While they were pleased with the victories by Johnson (Wisconsin), Lee (Utah), Paul (Kentucky), Rubio (Florida), and Toomey (Pennsylvania), they mourned the losses by Miller (Alaska), Angle (Nevada), Buck (Colordao), O'Donnell (Delaware) and, especially, Angle (Nevada), who lost to Majority Leader Harry Reid. While the Tea Party was credited with providing the fuel for the overwhelming Republican victories, their over zealousness in the primaries was criticized for keeping the Senate in Democratic hands. Had Norton faced Bennet in Colorado, Castle faced Coons in Delaware, and Lowden faced Reid in Nevada, the pundits reasoned that the Republicans could have picked up an additional three Senate seats.

Jim DeMint, of course, was not the only Gingrich senator who was involved in the 2010 elections. The Gingrich senators gave more than $2.3

Table 2.1 DeMint Campaign Contributions to Senate Candidates, 2010

Candidate	State	Leadership PACs*	Coordinated through SFC*	State GOP Committees*	Total
General Election Winners					
Marco Rubio	Florida	$10,000	$573,000	$250,000	$833,000
Johnny Isakson	Georgia	$5,000			$5,000
Dan Coats	Indinia	$5,000			$5,000
Jerry Moran	Kansas	$5,000			$5,000
Rand Paul	Kentucky	$5,000	$258,000	$150,000	$413,000
Richard Burr	N. Carolina	$5,000			$5,000
John Thune	N. Dakota	$7,500			$7,500
Rob Portman	Ohio	$5,000			$5,000
Tom Coburn	Oklahoma		$13,136#		$13,136
Pat Toomey	Pennsylvania	$5,000	$304,000	$150,000	$459,000
Jim DeMint	S. Carolina	$5,000		$350,000	$355,000
Mike Lee	Utah	$10,000	$302,000		$312,000
Ron Johnson	Wisconsin	$5,000	$195,000		$200,000
General Election Losers					
Joe Miller	Alaska	$10,000	$570,000	$100,000	$680,000
Carly Fiorina	California	$2,500			$2,500
Ken Buck	Colorado	$10,000	$871,000	$250,000	$1,131,000
Christine O'Donnell	Delaware	$10,000	$505,000	$250,000	$765,000
Sharon Angle	Nevada	$5,000	$682,000	$156,000	$843,000
Dino Rossi	Washington	$5,000	$326,000	$100,000	$431,000
John Raese	W. Virginia	$5,000	$70,000		$75,000
Primary Losers					
Chuck Devore	California	$5,000	$33,776#		$38,776
Marlin Stutzman	Indiana	$5,000	$121,808#		$126,808
Ovide Lamontagne	New Hampshire	$5,000	$1,125#	$100,000	$106,125
Total		$135,000	$4,825,845	$1,856,000	$6,816,845

*Leadership PAC direct contributions from FEC; Coordinated through Senate Conservative Fund (SCF) from the SCF website; State GOP Victory Committee contributions from SCF website.
Coordinated through SCF from the FEC.

million through their Leadership PACs. The other Republicans contributed $3.2 through their leadership PACs. While these amounts are quite
significant, it not equal the $6.6 million that DeMint orchestrated. His
2010 contributions, both directly through his Leadership PAC and indi-
rectly through its website, accounted for 73 percent of the Republican total
and nearly half of the total Senate leadership PACs contributions (including
Democrats!). Whether this form of influencing congressional elections will
catch on among the other Gingrich senators or the newly minted Tea Party
senators, only time can tell. At least one Tea Party senator, Mike Lee, has
fashioned his Leadership PAC in the mold of DeMint's.[13]

THE GINGRICH SENATORS AND TEA PARTY SENATORS AS PARTY POLARIZERS

In the 2010 elections, the Republicans gained 63 seats in the House and 6
seats in the Senate. While Gingrich Senators Sam Brownback, Jim Bunning,
and Judd Gregg were leaving the Senate, six new Republicans with House
experience were elected to the Senate and Dan Coats, who had retired 12
years earlier, was elected again to his old seat. For a list of the Gingrich
senators and the Tea Party senators, see table 2.2. While Gingrich Senators
John Boozman, Roy Blunt, Mark Kirk, Jerry Moran, Rob Portman, and
Pat Toomey were being welcomed to the Senate, they were not the stars of
the show. Republicans and the entire political world were especially eager to
see how the Tea Party senators would adapt to the Senate. Rand Paul, for
his iconoclastic beliefs, and Marco Rubio, for his compelling life story, were
the two newly elected senators who received the most press. In this section,
I describe the voting behavior of the Gingrich senators and the Tea Party
senators.

Since the first of their rank, Phil Gramm, entered the Senate in 1985,
the Gingrich senators have been much more conservative than the other
Republicans. Up through the one hundred and tenth Congress (2007–
2008), Theriault and Rohde (2012) find that the Gingrich senators are
56 percent more conservative than the other Republicans. The distinction
continued seamlessly in the first session of the one hundred and twelfth
Congress (2011). While the other Republicans had a similarly averaged
polarization score of 0.38, the Gingrich senators polarization score was
38 percent higher at 0.53. This distinction is similar to the differences
between the two groups of Republicans over the last few congresses. In
the one hundred and twelfth Congress, the Tea Party senators made their
mark as party polarizers. This new group had a polarization score of 0.80,
which was less than their primary benefactor, Jim DeMint, who had a
0.87 polarization (see table 2.2 for a list of the polarization scores for all
the Republicans in the one hundred and twelfth Congress). The only two
senators more polarizing than DeMint were Rand Paul (1.00) and Mike
Lee (0.99). Figure 2.1 shows the polarization scores for the Democrats

Table 2.2 Polarization Scores for Republicans, 2011

Rank	Name	Score*	Category	Rank	Name	Score*	Category
1	PAUL	1.000	Tea Party senator	25	SHELBY	0.462	Other Republican
2	LEE	0.987	Tea Party senator	26	GRAHAM	0.454	Gingrich senator
3	DEMINT	0.872	Gingrich senator	27	GRASSLEY	0.444	Other Republican
4	COBURN	0.857	Gingrich senator	28	BOOZMAN	0.439	Gingrich senator
5	JOHNSON	0.751	Tea Party senator	29	COATS	0.431	Gingrich senator
6	INHOFE	0.733	Gingrich senator	30	ROBERTS	0.431	Gingrich senator
7	ENSIGN#	0.718	Gingrich senator	31	WICKER	0.428	Gingrich senator
8	TOOMEY	0.641	Tea Party senator and Gingrich senator	32	JOHANNS	0.424	Other Republican
9	VITTER	0.623	Gingrich senator	33	PORTMAN	0.421	Gingrich senator
10	ENZI	0.612	Other Republican	34	MORAN	0.410	Gingrich senator
11	BARRASSO	0.605	Other Republican	35	MCCAIN	0.404	Gingrich senator
12	RISCH	0.599	Other Republican	36	CORKER	0.391	Other Republican
13	RUBIO	0.597	Tea Party senator	37	HUTCHISON	0.383	Other Republican
14	CRAPO	0.592	Gingrich senator	38	COCHRAN	0.343	Other Republican
15	SESSIONS	0.577	Other Republican	39	HATCH	0.342	Other Republican
16	KYL	0.576	Gingrich senator	40	HOEVEN	0.321	Other Republican
17	BURR	0.560	Gingrich senator	41	BLUNT	0.310	Gingrich senator
18	CORNYN	0.551	Other Republican	42	KIRK	0.282	Gingrich senator
19	CHAMBLISS	0.531	Gingrich senator	43	ALEXANDER	0.276	Other Republican
20	AYOTTE	0.521	Other Republican	44	LUGAR	0.237	Other Republican
21	MCCONNELL	0.512	Other Republican	45	MURKOWSKI	0.211	Other Republican
22	ISAKSON	0.481	Gingrich senator	46	BROWN	0.125	Other Republican
23	THUNE	0.479	Gingrich senator	47	SNOWE	0.041	Other Republican
24	HELLER#	0.474	Gingrich senator	48	COLLINS	0.040	Republican

*Polarization Score based on Poole–Rosenthal Common Space DW-NOMINATE Scores for 2011.
#Ensign, a Gingrich senator, was replaced by Heller, a fellow Gingrich senator, when he resigned in May 2011.

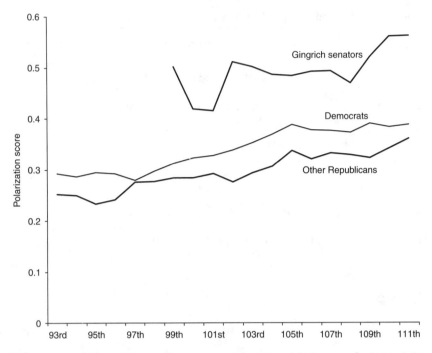

Figure 2.1 Polarization Scores for the Democrats, Gingrich Senators, and the Other Republicans, Ninty-third to One Hundred and Eleventh Congress (1973–2010).

(0.37) as well as the Gingrich senators and the other Republicans from the early 1990s until 2010. Figure 2.2 shows the polarization scores of these groups for the First Session of the one hundred and twelfth Congress (2011). The last bar shows what each of the three groups contributed to Senate party polarization in 2011. Even though the Tea Party senators have the highest polarization score, their overall effect is smaller because they only had five members.[14] The Gingrich senators and the Tea Party senators account for two-thirds of the polarization contributed by the Republicans, even though they are only 55 percent of the conference. Although the two groups were only 26 percent of the entire Senate, they account for 37 percent of the polarization.

The roll-call votes from the First Session of the one hundred and twelfth Congress suggest that the Gingrich senators were every bit the party polarizers that they had been in previous congresses. Their direct descendants—at least Jim DeMint's direct descendants—had even larger polarizing scores.[15] While the Tea Party senators were more polarizing individually, they had fewer than a quarter of the membership of the Gingrich senators. While the future of these Tea Party senators and the Tea Party senator grouping, more generally, is unclear, the roll-call voting analysis from 2011 suggests that the Gingrich senators remain as distinct as ever from the other Republicans.

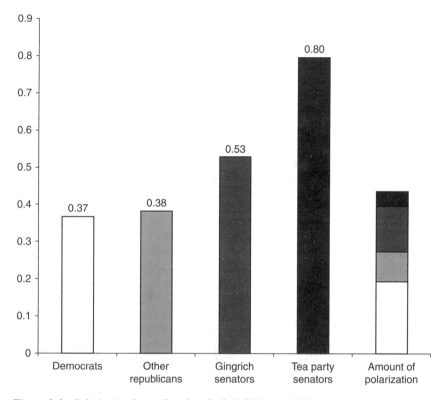

Figure 2.2   Polarization Scores Based on Roll-Call Votes in 2011.

THE GINGRICH SENATORS AND TEA PARTY SENATORS AS PARTISAN WARRIORS

The Gingrich senators as party polarizers did not change as a result of the 2010 elections, as least inasmuch as their roll-call voting behavior in 2011 can attest. Their ranks were increased with the addition of the Tea Party senators, who were even bigger party polarizers. To examine their roles as partisan warriors, I evaluate a variety of evidence—both quantitative and qualitative—because partisan warrior behavior cannot be as easily summarized as polarization scores can summarize party polarizers.

Earmark Ban

The effect of the Tea Party was felt even before the one hundred and twelfth Congress convened on January 3, 2011. Within days of the election, the Republican leaders in the House declared that they would pass a two-year moratorium on earmarks. Jim DeMint and Tom Coburn aimed at getting the Senate Republicans on board with the idea. They faced an uphill battle. Despite an early overture from President Obama, the earmark ban was criticized by Senate Minority Leader Mitch McConnell in a speech two days after the election to the Heritage Foundation. He argued, "Every President, Republican or Democrat, would love to have a blank check from Congress to do whatever he chose to do on every single issue . . . And we'll be discussing the appropriateness of giving the President that kind of blank check in the coming week." He reasoned, "You can eliminate every congressional earmark and you would save no money. It's really an argument about discretion."[16]

On the day before the Senate Republican Conference met for the first time after the 2010 elections, McConnell back-pedalled and supported the earmark ban. On the Senate floor, he offered his explanation:

> Nearly every day that the Senate's been in session for the past 2 years, I have come down to this spot and said that Democrats are ignoring the wishes of the American people. When it comes to earmarks, I will not be guilty of the same thing.
>
> Make no mistake. I know the good that has come from the projects I have helped support throughout my State. I don't apologize for them. But there is simply no doubt that the abuse of this practice has caused Americans to view it as a symbol of the waste and the out-of-control spending that every Republican in Washington is determined to fight. And unless people like me show the American people that we are willing to follow through on small or even symbolic things, we risk losing them on our broader efforts to cut spending and rein in government.
>
> That is why today, I am announcing that I will join the Republican leadership in the House in support of a moratorium on earmarks in the one hundred and twelfth Congress.[17]

The next day, the Republican Conference by voice vote supported the earmark ban.

Two weeks later, in a debate on food safety during the lame duck session to the one hundred and eleventh Congress, Coburn attempted to introduce an amendment that would, in effect, ban earmarks. The procedural motion to bring up the amendment was defeated, 39–56. The Republicans supported the ban, 32–38. The only Gingrich senator to oppose the ban was Jim Inhofe (Sam Brownback was absent). Seven of the 22 other Republicans who voted opposed the earmark ban.[18]

Rather than writing an earmark ban into the rules of the Senate, the Appropriations Committee adopted an earmark moratorium that would last for the entirety of the one hundred and twelfth Congress. Not satisfied with an informal and temporary solution, Claire McCaskill (D-Missouri) and Pat Toomey, who was both a Gingrich senator and a Tea Party senator, introduced, on February 2, 2012, an amendment to the STOCK Act, which would make the earmark ban permanent. Again, the amendment lost, 40–59. All five Tea Party senators supported it as did 17 out of 21 Gingrich senators (Kirk was missing). Twelve out of 21 other Republicans also supported the amendment.[19]

Presidential Support Scores

For every representative and senator since the Eisenhower Administration, Congressional Quarterly has been calculating "Presidential Support Scores," which includes all the roll-call votes in which an "explicit statement is made by the president or his authorized spokesmen."[20] These scores range from 0, if the member never supported the president on one of these votes to 100 if they voted with the president on every single one. Not surprisingly, these votes have become increasingly divided by party in the era of party polarization (see figure 2.3 for the presidential support scores by Democrats, other Republicans, Gingrich senators, and Tea Party senators from George H. W. Bush to Obama).

The differences among the groups of Republicans are especially stark during Democratic administrations. In fact, during Republican Administrations, the presidential support scores for the other Republicans and the Gingrich senators are similar. During Democratic presidential administrations, the difference is large and statistically significant.

The Gingrich senators, combining forces with the Tea Party senators in the one hundred and twelfth Congress, have been leading the charge against the president's public policy agenda in the Senate. Not only is the average for the Gingrich senators lower than the other Republicans, but also the average for the Tea Party senators is much closer to the Gingrich senators than

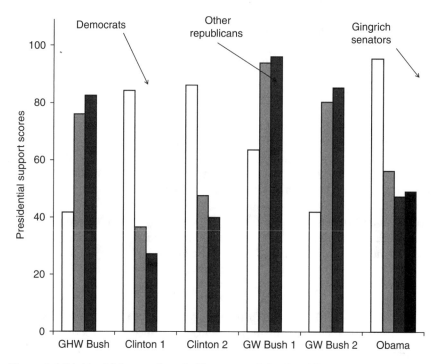

Figure 2.3 Presidential Support Scores of Democrats, Other Republicans, Gingrich Senators, and Tea Party Senators, GHW Bush to Obama (1989–2011).

the other Republicans. During 2011, the anchors of Obama opposition are the Gingrich senators and their descendants. Paul had the lowest score (40.9 percent), followed by DeMint (41.4), Vitter (42.6), Heller (45.1), and Rubio (46.2). Only three other Republicans are among the 15 lowest supporters of President Obama during his third year in office (only Toomey does not make the list among the Tea Party senators).

One way of interpreting these data is that the Gingrich senators are behaving more like the "other Republican" as they accrue more experience in the chamber and as they secure more important positions. An alternative view suggests that just as the Gingrich senators convinced the Republican Conference to ban earmarks, so it is with opposing Obama's legislative initiatives. What at one point in time was a vote based on the substance of the bill or the qualifications of the nominee has become simply a pawn in a larger chess match to win majority party control.

The nomination fight for Obama's choice to lead the Consumer Financial Protection Bureau (CFPB) strongly suggests it is the latter. In 2010, Congress passed and Obama signed into the law the Dodd-Frank Wall Street Reform Bill, which included a provision to establish a CFPB headed by a director. The bill only became law when three Republicans—Brown, Collins, and Snowe—voted with 57 Democrats to both defeat a filibuster and pass the bill.

In an attempt to mollify the Senate Republicans, Obama passed over nominating Elizabeth Warren, who had been a partisan lightning rod, in favor of nominating Richard Cordray, who had lost his Ohio Attorney General reelection bid to Mike DeWine, a Gingrich former senator, in the 2010 election. No one questioned Cordray's credentials to lead the CFPB. Shortly after Obama announced the nomination, Richard Shelby (R-Alabama), the ranking Republican of the Senate Banking Committee wrote Obama a letter stating that 44 Republicans would vote to block any nominee to head the CFPB unless Congress made "reasonable changes" to the law to make it more accountable to Congress.[21] On December 8, 2011, the Republicans held true to their promise when a unified conference—but for Brown—upheld a filibuster to defeat the nomination.[22] Many congressional observers thought that this was the first time a nomination was defeated because of an objection to the underlying law establishing the bureaucratic structure. In a move that escalated the partisan war, Obama made a controversial recesses appointment when he installed Cordray into the position on January 4, 2012. In another unprecedented move in the partisan war, Obama made the recess appointment when it was not clear that the Senate was even in recess.

Amendments on the Senate Floor

On March 24, 2010, Senator Coburn introduced an amendment that prohibited sex offenders from using the health insurance that was being established in Obama's health-care reform package to pay for Viagra. What senator would possibly vote against such an amendment? As it turned out, 55 out of 57 Democrats did.[23] During this particular debate, the Democrats were orchestrating a complex legislative maneuver that could lead to the passage of health-care reform without explicitly overcoming a Republican-led filibuster. By passing the measure through the reconciliation process, the Democrats only needed a majority, but they could not change a word in the bill or the entire process might unravel. As such, the Republicans had the Democrats in the difficult position of voting down amendments that might otherwise seem constructive or reasonable.

In addition to voting down the prohibition of paying for sex offenders' Viagra, the Democrats defeated an amendment by Mike Crapo that would ensure that no individual making less than $200,000 would be subject to a tax increase as a consequence of the legislation. They also defeated an amendment by John Ensign to protect the damages in medical malpractice suits resulting from pro bono cases. By voting against each of these amendments, Democrats could be subject to campaign commercials arguing that they voted to give Viagra to sex offenders, to raise taxes on those making less than $200,000, and to subject pro bono health-care providers to exorbitant malpractice lawsuits. No Democrat disagreed when Senator Max Baucus (D-Montana) called Coburn's amendment, "A crass political stunt aimed at making a 30-second commercial."[24]

Teasing a strategy of electioneering on the Senate floor is difficult. Teasing obstruction on the Senate floor is equally difficult. In an ideal world, we would count the number of holds—or threats of holds—that the Gingrich senators and Tea Party senators have placed on bills or nominations. Regrettably, holds are often secret. No reliable count exists. Nonetheless, we can glean insight of obstructionism by examining the number of roll-call votes that are associated with the Gingrich senators' amendments.

As typified by Coburn's amendment on Viagra, forcing senators to cast difficult or embarrassing votes is a new favorite game of the Gingrich senators. Offering amendments is the easiest way that a senator can get his or her colleagues on the record. Offering amendments serves another purpose as well. It delays action in the Senate. Amendments require debates, motions, and points of order all of which can put otherwise noncontroversial legislation in an endless holding pattern.

As with the introduction of these electioneering amendments, the number of roll-call votes associated with the amendments is a new weapon in the partisan warriors' arsenal. In the one hundred and third (1993–1994) and one hundred and seventh (2001–2002) Congresses, when the Democrats were also a majority, the Gingrich senators, on average, offered amendments with only slightly more roll-call votes than their Republican colleagues (figure 2.4). While the minority party has always offered more amendments resulting in more roll-call votes than the majority, the numbers associated with the Gingrich senators are unprecedented. In the last two congresses, the amendments of 6 Gingrich senator have resulted in more than 20 roll-call votes each. In the previous 7 congresses (1993–2006), only 9 Democrats, 2 non-Gingrich senators Republicans, and 2 Gingrich senators (McCain and Brown in the one hundred and third Congress) have surpassed that benchmark.

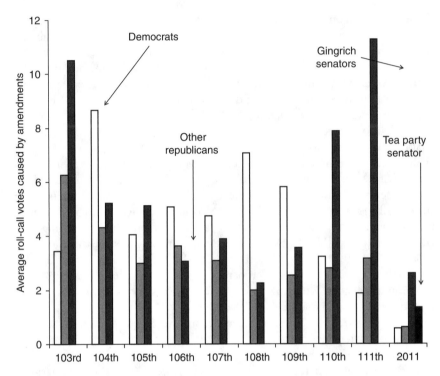

Figure 2.4 Amendments offered by Democrats, Other Republicans, Gingrich Senators, and Tea Party Senators, One Hundred and First to One Hundred and Twelfth Congresses (1993–2011).

The number of amendments that the Gingrich senators have offered has increasingly consumed time on the Senate floor. In the one hundred and tenth Congress (2007–2008), the Gingrich senators amendments resulted in 173 roll call votes, which is 26 percent of the total number of roll call votes that senators took. The top five roll-call producing amendment sponsors were all Gingrich senators: Coburn (34), DeMint (34), Kyl (18), Vitter (17), and Ensign (16). The ranking was only interrupted by Senate Majority Leader, Harry Reid, whose amendments resulted in 15 roll-call votes.

Once the Democratic majority in the Senate was joined with a Democrat in the White House, the number and proportion of votes caused by the Gingrich senators' amendments were even greater. In the one hundred and eleventh Congress (2009–10), the Senate voted 214 times on the Gingrich senators amendments—which accounted for more than 30 percent of the total number of votes! Not surprisingly, the Gingrich senators are at the top of the roll-call amendment sponsor list. Coburn (49), McCain (27), Vitter (23), and Thune (19) were the top four and DeMint (17), Ensign (14), and Kyl (13) were in the top ten.[25] While the Republicans who were not Gingrich senators also faced a majority opposition in the Senate and a Democrat in the White House, their amendments only accounted for 79 roll-call votes, even though they outnumbered the Gingrich senators 25 to 19 in the one hundred and eleventh Congress.

The pattern continued in the First Session of the one hundred and twelfth Congress. Coburn's amendments resulted in the most roll call votes (13), followed by Paul (10), McCain (6), Diane Feinstein (D-California, 5), Vitter (4), and DeMint (4). The other four Tea Party senators offered amendments that resulted in only three additional roll call votes. While the Gingrich senators were responsible for amendments that resulted in 31 roll-call votes, the other Republicans' amendments only contributed 13 roll-call votes. The Democrats, who still enjoyed a majority albeit smaller than their majority in the one hundred and eleventh Congress, offered amendments that resulted in 30 roll-call votes.

The frequency of roll-call votes, alone, does not prove that the Gingrich senators and the Tea Party senators are using the amendment process for obstructionism. What is also true about these roll-call votes is that they are far less successful at securing support for their positions than are even their fellow Republicans. In the one hundred and eleventh Congress, the Gingrich senators won 11 percent of the roll-call votes on their amendments. While we might expect the minority party to have a difficult time getting their amendments adopted, the Republicans who were not Gingrich senators did twice as well—they won 22 percent of the roll-call votes on their amendments. The Democrats, on the other hand, won 62 percent of the roll-call votes on their amendments.

Not only are the Gingrich senators less successful in roll-call votes on their amendments, but also when they fail, they fail miserably. On 22 percent of the unsuccessful roll-call votes associated with their amendments, the Gingrich senators received less than 35 votes. This 35-vote standard is less than the number of Republicans serving in the Senate during the one hundred and eleventh Congress, 15 votes less than the minimum needed to get their amendment adopted, and 25 votes less than the minimum needed to stop a potential filibuster on their particular amendment. Their Republican counterparts do not achieve 35 votes on only 14 percent of the roll-call votes on their amendments. The Gingrich senators do almost 50 percent worse in securing support than their Republican colleagues.

The 2011 Debt-limit Crisis

Even as Congress was trying to avert a government shutdown in April 2011 because it had not yet passed a budget, political and economic experts on Capitol Hill and around the globe feared a much bigger partisan showdown. By July, it was speculated, the federal government would reach its debt ceiling. If Congress did not raise the ceiling, the government was headed not to a shutdown, but a far more drastic outcome: default on its loans. Under the grey clouds that were gathering on the horizon, Senators Mark Warner (D-Virginia) and Saxby Chambliss (R-Georgia), who shared some ideas with one another on the Senate floor, formed a "Gang of Six," who would search for a bipartisan compromise to the impending crisis. They were joined by Dick Durbin (D-Illinois), Kent Conrad (D-North Dakota), Tom Coburn, and Mike Crapo. All three Republican senators participating in the Gang of Six talks were Gingrich senators.

As the drama of the debt ceiling played out over the spring and summer, the stock of the Gang of Six fell and rose and fell again. When talks between the party leaders and the White House faltered, the eyes of the public and the members of Congress switched back to the Gang of Six. In frustration, Coburn quit the group, but then rejoined it a few months later giving it new life. When Biden convened a panel of party leaders for talks over the summer and when Obama and Boehner met in the weeks finally leading up to the compromise package, chatter about the Gang of Six reverted to mere background noise.

The issue that irreparably divided the Gang of Six was on the amount of revenue increases that would be part of the final package. At various times, the participants in the compromise efforts seemed to get close, but they could never reach a final compromise. Most talking heads in Washington, DC, thought that the ground of compromise under discussion in the Gang of Six had more revenue increases than the ground of compromise among the other viable alternatives, which included Biden's working group and the Obama–Boehner talks. While House Republican leaders Boehner and Cantor had been resolute that tax increases could not be part of the package, Chambliss and his fellow Republicans recognized that they had to be part of the solution. Chambliss had argued as such throughout the spring. When word leaked that the Gang of Six was considering tax increases, Grover Norquist, an antitax activist, complained that such tax increases would constitute a breaking of the "Taxpayer Protection Pledge" that all three Republicans in the Gang of Six had signed. Chambliss, Coburn, and Crapo raised the hopes for compromise when they rhetorically sparred with Norquist by releasing a letter that such action would not break their pledge, "but rather affirms the oath we have taken to support and defend the Constitution of the United States against all enemies, foreign and domestic, of which our national debt may now be the greatest."[26]

Rather than enacting a final solution to the problem, Congress passed and Obama signed legislation that would form a Joint Select Committee on Deficit Reduction (a.k.a., "The Super Committee"), which was tasked with coming up with $1.5 billion in deficit savings, either through revenue increases or spending cuts else they would kick-in an automatic trigger mandating across the board cuts, including massive spending cuts in the military. Although few on Capitol Hill were happy that the "can had been kicked down the road," the temporary compromise enjoyed large congressional majorities, including a final passage vote of 74–26 in the Senate. The three Republicans—all of whom were Gingrich senators—who participated in the Gang of Six voted against the final agreement (in opposition to their three Democratic counterparts). They were joined in opposition by the 5 Tea Party senators; the Gingrich senators marginally supported the agreement,

12–10. The other Republicans (16–15) and the Democrats (46–47) overwhelmingly voted for the package.[27]

Each party leader in each chamber named three members to the "Super Committee." Mitch McConnell named Jon Kyl (the Minority Whip), Rob Portman (former director of the Office of Management and Budget for President George W. Bush), and Pat Toomey. All three are Gingrich senators, with Toomey carrying the mantel for both the Tea Party senators and the Gingrich senators. Much like their predecessors, the Super Committee failed and the automatic cuts kicked in.

No Reindeer Games for the Gingrich Senators

The first session of the one hundred and twelfth Congress (2011) was difficult for most senators. Democrats were frustrated that the Republicans made legislating exceedingly difficult. The Republicans were frustrated that the Democrats would not consider important legislation passed by the House. The Gingrich senators and Tea Party senators were frustrated that Obama was still in the White House, the Democrats were still a majority in the Senate, and the budget deficit continued to rise.

Shortly after Thanksgiving, Senator Al Franken (D-Minnesota), who is a Jewish, decided that the Senate needed to institute a new tradition to ease tensions. In conspiring with Senator Mike Johanns (R-Nebraska), he sent an e-mail around to his colleagues asking them to participate in a Senate version of Secret Santa. As Franken explained, "I remember one year [as a child] I picked this kid who used to intimidate me on the playground. Turns out after we got to know each other and we became friends. So, I thought Secret Santa would be a good way to cut through the partisan divide here in the Senate. And who knows, maybe it will create some unlikely friendships."[28] Franken and Johanns set the limit at $10 and picked December 13 as the date that they would exchange gifts.

The trick for the Secret Santa to work, though, was for the senators to participate. They did. At least 58—and, perhaps, as many as 61—senators offered their names up for the possibility of increasing comity (and, perhaps, comedy) in the Senate.[29] The participation rate varied by party. While at least 45 percent of the Republicans participated, 70 percent of Democrats did.[30] The differences among the Republicans groups were remarkable: 67 percent of other Republican senators participated, 40 percent of the Tea Party senators, and 23 percent of the Gingrich senators.[31]

Secret Santa participation cannot be explained by ideology. The other Republicans who participated were slightly more conservative (0.41) than those who did not participate (0.33). For the Tea Party Senators and the Gingrich Senators, the opposite is true, but just barely (0.79 compared to 0.80 for the Tea Party Senators and 0.50 compared to 0.53 for the Gingrich Senators). None of the differences in ideology are close to achieving conventional levels of statistical significance suggest that another dynamic was at work.

Not only was one senator unwilling to participate, but also he ridiculed the entire enterprise. Pat Toomey, who had the unique distinction of being a Tea Party senator as well as a Gingrich senators, scoffed at the gift exchange. When Ginni Thomas, wife of Supreme Court Justice Clarence Thomas, asked him what he would give Majority Leader Harry Reid if he were to have participated, Toomey replied, "I would give him the inspiration to do a budget. I think I would try to inspire him to take responsibility that the majority party in the United States Senate ought to accept, which is to lay out to the American people just what they intend to do with American taxpayer dollars."[32] Perhaps if he had participated, he would have gotten lumps of coal from Senator Joe Manchin (D-West Virginia). Instead, Manchin gave those lumps of coal that were carved into a donkey and an elephant to Senator Chuck Schumer (D-New York).[33]

Appearances on Sunday Morning Talk Shows

Each weekend, while most Americans are sleeping in and going about their normal daily lives, the opinion makers, pundits, politicians, and even political scientists focus their attention on the Sunday morning political talk shows, which includes NBC's Meet the Press, ABC's This Week, Fox News Sunday, CBS's Face the Nation, and CNN's State of the Union. With Obama in the White House and the number of Democrats vacillating around a veto proof margin in the Senate, these talk shows provided the Republicans an outlet to voice their concerns over the direction the Democrats were taking the country.

More often than not, the face of the Republicans in the Senate was represented by the Gingrich senators (and the Tea Party senators in 2011). Although Senate Minority Leader Mitch McConnell alone appeared on the shows 18 times in 2010, the Gingrich senators' appearances still outnumbered the other Republicans' appearances (46–45). The Gingrich senators, on average, were on these shows 2.4 times compared to 1.8 times for the other Republicans—if McConnell's appearances are removed from the total for the other Republicans, they only averaged 1.1 times.[34]

After McConnell, four of the next five Republican senators most likely to make appearances were Gingrich senators (Graham, Kyl, McCain, and DeMint). The only other Republican to break this string was third-ranked John Cornyn (R-Texas), who was the chair of the National Republican Senatorial Committee. The only Democrats to have more appearances than DeMint were Senate Majority Whip Dick Durbin (D-Illinois) and the Chair of the Democratic Senate Campaign Committee Bob Menendez (D-New Jersey). These data suggest that the Gingrich senators are not only leading the war inside the Senate, but also in the media.

In 2011, the Gingrich senators continued to make more regular appearances on the Sunday morning talk shows. They made 65 appearances compared to 30 total appearances for the other Republicans. While there were more than five times as many other Republicans in the Senate as there were Tea Party senators, the latter had about half as many appearances as the former. On average, the Gingrich senators had 3.0 appearances per senator, compared to 2.8 for the Tea Party senators and 1.4 for the other Republicans. In 2011, Gingrich Senators McCain (19) and Graham (18) had more appearances than the elected leader of the Republican Conference, Mitch McConnell.[35]

CONCLUSION

The Gingrich senators have not only been party polarizers, but also partisan warriors. In both quests, they have been joined by another battalion of troops: the Tea Party senators. These first-term senators can trace their election victories to Gingrich Senator Jim DeMint, who was crucial in getting the Tea Party senators elected and acclimated to his style of antiestablishment behavior in the US Senate.

Because of how drastically the Republican Conference in the Senate changed in 2011, Senator Lamar Alexander (R-Tennessee) opted to resign his post as the Republican Conference Chair, the third ranking Republican in the Senate. Rather than continue in the position for the remainder of his term, he stepped down a full year before the Republicans would shuffle their leadership positions as a result of Minority Whip Jon Kyl's retirement. After making the announcement, Alexander claimed that he felt "liberated." According to a knowledgeable Republican lobbyist, "Alexander was frustrated with some of the new tea-party-inspired Members—especially with their impatience, disdain for deal-making and low regard for Senate tradition and protocol. Even less appealing was trying to wrangle that crowd as the Whip." [36]

In an article published two days before Alexander made his announcement, Burr handicapped the impending whip race between Alexander and Cornyn. His observation was astute not only for how he characterized the race, but also for how he depicted the entire Republican Conference in the Senate: "I'd say that the needs we have now and next year are totally different than they were four years ago."[37] Not only were their needs different, but also the entire institution of the Senate was different because of them.

The 2010 elections only exacerbated the party polarization and partisan war in the Senate.[38] While the other Republicans appeared to behave a bit more like the Gingrich senators, the introduction of the Tea Party senators provided reinforcements in the battle. The year 2011 may very well be an inflection point from the Gingrich senators being distinct in the Republican Conference to them taking over the strategy of the conference in an all out battle with Democrats not on substantive grounds, but on partisan grounds. While the Gingrich senators may have led the fight, the Democrats, including President Obama, have shown that they will not back down. The result of which gives credibility to Ornstein's new moniker: "The Curse of the Senate."

NOTES

1. As quoted in Norman J. Ornstein, 2012, "Obama's Tactic Could Yield Political Results," *Roll Call* February 8. http://www.rollcall.com/issues/57_92/obama_tactic_could_yield_political_results-212210-1.html.
2. Norman J. Ornstein, 2008, "Our Broken Senate," *The American: The Journal of the American Enterprise Institute* March/April. http://www.american.com/archive/2008/march-april-magazine-contents/our-broken-senate
3. Quoted in Lynn Sweet, 2010, "Sen. Evan Bayh Won't Run Again," *Chicago Sun Times* February 15.
4. As quoted in Paul Kane and Chris Cillizza, 2012, "Sen. Olympia Snowe Announces Retirement: Can the GOP hold her seat?" *The Washington Post* February 29, xx. http://articles.washingtonpost.com/2012-02-29/politics/35444037_1_fewer-senators-partisanship-moderates-from-both-parties.
5. Data taken from a Gallup Poll as reported by "The American Presidency Project." http://www.presidency.ucsb.edu/data/popularity.php (accessed on March 10, 2012).
6. See http://cookpolitical.com/charts/senate/raceratings_2009–07–15_13–59–09.php (accessed on March 10, 2012).
7. See http://cookpolitical.com/charts/senate/raceratings_2010–01–14_14–48–48.php (accessed on March 10, 2012).
8. See Kate Zernike, 2010, "Tea Party Set to Win Enough Races for Wide Influence," *The New York Times* October 14, A 1.
9. See Timothy P. Carney, 2009, "Did DeMint's endorsement of Toomey set off Specter?" *The Washington Examiner* April. http://washingtonexaminer.com/politics/beltway-confidential/2009/04/did-demints-endorsement-toomey-set-specter/136018 (accessed on March 10, 2012).
10. As reported by Manu Raju, 2009, "Jim DeMint backs Marco Rubio in Florida Governor Race," *Politico* June 15. http://www.politico.com/news/stories/0609/23754.html (accessed on March 12, 2012). Incidentally, the headline of this article is inaccurate—the endorsement was in the Senate race.
11. As reported by Reid Wilson, 2009, "Senator DeMint Bucks Republican Party, Backs Conservative in California Race," *The Hill* November 4,. http://thehill.com/homenews/campaign/66169-demint-bucks-party-backs-conservative-in-california (accessed March 10, 2012).
12. The SCF claimed that DeMint was responsible for raising more than $9.3 million in the 2010 cycle. See http://senateconservatives.com/site/post/692/release-scf-raises-100000-for-mandel (accessed on March 31, 2012). The records filed with FEC shows that DeMint raised less than that amount. As such, it is not clear for whom he raised that much and how it was distributed. In an earlier SCF press release (http://senateconservatives.com/site/post/366/scf-tops-5-million-candidate-goal; accessed on April 3, 2012), $5.2 million of the $9.3 million is accounted. This includes $554,000 to candidates that lost in the primary (the FEC only reports $156,709 of that amount). It also includes $1,856,000 in donations to state GOP victory committees. The same press released announced that he had raised more than $7 million dollars.
13. See Alexander Bolton, 2011, "DeMint's Leadership PAC Battles Leaders in Fight for Future of Senate GOP Caucus," *The Hill* August 4. http://thehill.com/homenews/senate/175397-demints-leadership-pac-battles-leaders-in-fight-for-future-of-senate.

14. This assessment is based on an average polarizing score of the Tea Party senators of 0.80 multiplied by the five senators giving them a total polarizing effect of 3.98. The 22 Gingrich senators had an average polarizing score of 0.53, giving them a polarizing effect of 12.15, which is more than three times larger the effect of the Tea Party senators.

15. Not all the Gingrich senators greeted the Tea Party senators with open arms. In separate incidents, McCain, on the Senate floor, went after Paul on his foreign policy views and Toomey on his budget views. For the former, see Halimah Abdullah, 2011, "D.C. is Big Tea Party for Rand Paul," *The Houston Chronicle* December 11, A38. For the latter, see David M. Drucker, 2011, "McCain Spars with Activists on Debt," *Roll Call* July 29, 3. On the other hand, McCain has become a mentor to Portman, a fellow Gingrich senators. See David M. Drucker, "McCain Coaches Portman," *Roll Call* 2011, 1.

16. See http://www.heritage.org/events/2010/11/mitch-mcconnell (accessed March 13, 2012).

17. *The Congressional Record*, 2010. 111th Congress, 2nd Session, November 15, S7872.

18. The roll-call votes of the Gingrich Senators and the other Republicans are statistically significantly different from one another ($p = 0.010$).

19. The roll-call votes among the Tea Party senators, the Gingrich senators, and the other Republicans are statistically significantly different from one another ($p = 0.042$ for Gingrich senators and other Republicans; 0.013 for Gingrich senators and Tea Party Senators; and 0.000 for Tea Party senators and other Republicans).

20. Quoted from *2006 CQ Almanac*, B-19.

21. See Richard Shelby, 2011, "The Danger of an Unaccountable 'Consumer-Protection' Czar." *The Wall Street Journal* July 21. http://online.wsj.com/article/SB10001424053111903554904576457931310814462.html.

22. While Collins switched her vote to uphold the filibuster even though she voted for the initial legislation, Snowe voted "present" to avoid a potential conflict with her husband's business involving student loans that are regulated by the agency.

23. The floor mechanics on this amendment are a bit tricky. Instead of subjecting Democrats to an explicit vote on the amendment, Senate Max Baucus (D-Montana) offered a motion to table Coburn's amendment. Fifty-five out of 57 Democrats voted for that motion; thus, the amendment was tabled, which in this instance is equivalent to defeating the amendment.

24. As quoted in Chris Casteel,2010, "U.S. Sen. Tom Coburn's Viagra Amendment Fails," *NewsOK* March 25. http://newsok.com/u.s.-sen.-tom-coburns-viagra-amendment-fails/article/3449000 (accessed on December 20, 2011).

25. The other senators in the top ten were Baucus (ranked fifth with 17), Reid (seventh, 15), and Sessions (tenth, 12).

26. As quoted in Jackie Calmes, 2011, "'Gang of Six' in the Senate Seeking a Plan on Debt," *The New York Times* April 16.

27. The roll-call votes among the Tea Party senators, the Gingrich senators, and the other Republicans are statistically significantly different from one another ($p = 0.063$ for Gingrich senators and other Republicans; 0.000 for Gingrich senators and Tea Party senators; and 0.000 for Tea Party senators and other Republicans).

28. As quoted in Jennifer Steinhauer, 2011, "Secret Santa in the Senate," *The New York Times* November 30. http://thecaucus.blogs.nytimes.com/2011/11/30/secret-santa-in-the-senate/

29. On the day of the drawing, 58 senators participated. At the day of the gift exchanged, news accounts indicated that as many as 61 senators exchanged gifts. All news accounts said that either 21 or 22 Republicans participated. Through a extensive search of the internet, including news articles, press releases, and blogs, 21 Republican senators and 29 Democratic senators could be identified.

30. The proportions are statistically significantly different from one another ($p = 0.015$).

31. The Tea Party senators who participated were Rubio and Lee. The Gingrich senators who participated were Boozman, Crapo, Portman, Vitter, and Wicker. The differences in proportions between the Gingrich senators and the other Republicans is statistically significant ($p = 0.001$). The difference in proportions involving the Tea Party senators is not ($p = 0.767$ with the Gingrich senators and $p = 0.135$ with the other Republicans).

32. See http://dailycaller.com/2011/12/24/sen-toomey-on-his-secret-santa-gift-for-sen-reid-video/#ixzz1pNuuu000 (accessed on March 17, 2012).

33. To learn more about the gifts given and received, see Ann Gerhart, 2011, "Senate's Secret Santas Make Their Rounds," *The Washington Post* December 13, xx. http://www.washingtonpost.com/lifestyle/style/senates-secret-santas-make-their-rounds/2011/12/13/gIQAQ0udsO_story.html. Interestingly, the article was published in the Style section, not the Front Page.

34. The difference in appearances between the Gingrich senators and the other Republicans is not statistically significant ($p = 0.317$). When McConnell is deleted from the analysis, the difference nears statistical significance ($p = 0.113$).

35. The difference in appearances between the Gingrich senators and the other Republicans is not quite statistically significant ($p = 0.141$), unless McConnell is deleted from the analysis ($p = 0.051$). The differences in appearances neither between the Tea Party senators and the other Republicans ($p = 0.185$) nor the Tea Party senators and the Gingrich senators ($p = 0.438$) is statistically significant.

36. Quotes from David M. Drucker,2011, "Alexander Takes a Step Back." *Roll Call* September 21, 1.

37. As quoted in David M. Drucker, 2011, "Independence Could Stall Alexander's Rise." *Roll Call* September 19, 1, 12.

38. Through the 2010 elections, the Gingrich senators not only transformed the Senate, but also, as it turns out, the Republican Conference in the Kansas Legislature. Brownback, who was elected its governor in 2010, took the lessons of the Gingrich senators to the state legislature. When Republican moderates, in the tradition of Senators Bob Dole and Nancy Kassebaum dared to cross him, he vowed revenge: "We cannot continue on this path and hope we can move forward and win the future. It won't work. We have to change course, and we're going to have to be aggressive about it or we are doomed to a slow decline." Nine of them faced primary challengers in 2012. Quote from Annie Gowen,2011, "In Kansas, Gov. Sam Brownback Puts Tea Party Tenets into Action with Sharp Cuts," *The Washington Post* December 21, xx. http://articles.washingtonpost.com/2011-12-21/politics/35286057_1_sam-brownback-state-pensions-repealer.

3

THE WEAPONIZATION OF CONGRESSIONAL OVERSIGHT

THE POLITICS OF THE WATCHFUL EYE, 1947–2010

David C. W. Parker and Matthew Dull

During the 2006 election cycle, Democrats campaigned on the promise of returning managerial competence to Washington.[1] Congressional Republicans had been wracked by a series of ethics scandals, while the Bush administration had to deal with charges of maladministration in the handling of Hurricane Katrina's aftermath and the postwar reconstruction of Iraq. Democrats complained loudly that congressional Republicans, serving as handmaidens for the administration and leery of possible political fallout, turned a blind eye to the serious allegations of administrative failings. Not only was the one hundred and ninth Congress notable for its relative lack of legislative productivity, it paid scant attention to executive oversight.[2] House committees held only 960 hearings during the two year session—200 less than Democrats held during unified government under President Bill Clinton between 1993 and 1994. Senate Democrats, frustrated with Republican unwillingness to examine seriously the Bush Administration's policy in Iraq, resorted to holding their own hearings on prewar intelligence (Pincus 2006). Democrats campaigned throughout the summer and fall on the promise to exercise increased oversight of the executive branch, with Minority Leader Nancy Pelosi notably pledging to "drain the Republican swamp" if voters threw out Republicans and gave them the majority (Espo 2006). Voters threw Republicans out, and the Democratic majority made good on their promise: At the conclusion of the one hundred and tenth Congress, the House conducted more than 1,400 hearings. Congressman Henry Waxman (D-CA), the new chair of the House Committee on Oversight and Government Reform, alone held 203 hearings during the last two years of the Bush administration (Sherman and Cohen 2010).

Fast forward four years. Congressional Republicans focused their campaign for the majority on policy-oriented complaints, most notably the economic stimulus plan and the Obama administration's health-care reform. Republicans charged that the stimulus plan did not noticeably improve the nation's economy, and that the Affordable Health Care Act represented an unprecedented grab of federal power intruding into the private lives of Americans. What was relatively absent was a call for increased oversight of the executive branch. Republicans managed in an historic election to recapture their lost House majority. Given the relative lack of attention to oversight, Representative Darrell Issa (R-CA)—the incoming House Oversight and Government Reform Committee Chairman—made an interesting pledge after the election. He promised to launch more investigations than his predecessor, Henry Waxman, saying he would like to hold seven hearings a week—a goal of more than double the number of hearings (Sherman and Cohen 2010). The Chairman's investigation into an alleged cover-up involving a high-profile Bureau of Alcohol, Tobacco, and Firearms (ATF) scandal and the subsequent refusal by the Obama administration to turn over subpoenaed Justice Department documents led to an unprecedented House floor vote holding Attorney General Eric Holder in civil and criminal contempt, a first for a sitting cabinet official. Only 17 Democrats joined nearly all House Republicans in voting to hold Attorney General Holder in contempt of Congress (Weisman and Savage 2012). Issa's aggressive oversight was critical in the pursuit of Holder and the pinnacle of a series of investigations he held to root out allegations of waste, fraud, and abuse in the executive branch.

"If any realm exists in which [Congress] can be autonomous and consequential," writes one of the foremost experts on Congress, "it is in the realm of investigation" (Mayhew 2000, 89). Committee hearings and investigations are perhaps the most important tool Congress has to check the authority of the executive branch, and both parties have claimed that the other—when serving in the majority—failed to exercise this critical responsibility. Implicit in the argument is that the lack of oversight is related to political considerations: Congressional majorities did not want to embarrass friendly administrations in unified government for fear of hurting the party brand. Although the claim has been made before by some political scientists that investigations are inviting tools for political combat (Ginsberg and Shefter 2004), until recently, the notion that investigations are launched or not because of partisan considerations has met with resistance by the discipline (Mayhew 1991; 2005). Oversight and its vigorous exercise are discussed in terms of constitutional responsibilities, the pursuit of "good" and efficient government, and the incentives faced by individual members of Congress. We contend that the when, how, and why of congressional oversight is little understood by congressional scholars. In this chapter, we discuss the purpose of congressional investigation, some of the reasons advanced by political scientists explaining why Congress investigates and oversees administrations, and finally, shed light on an increasingly apparent development in the politics of congressional oversight: the "weaponization" of congressional investigations. To weaponize a biological agent is to develop a strain of the agent that is highly contagious and deadly while creating a delivery device that maximizes the spread of the disease for the greatest destructive effect. In the same sense, we conceive of how Congress has done the same to the process of investigation. We do not use this term lightly. We explain how congressional investigations have changed in the era of the partisan Congress, and how an ostensibly good practice—of making sure the executive branch is doing its job and carrying out congressional mandates—has become an activity motivated in large part by politics and the needs of partisan majorities.

OVERSEEING THE EXECUTIVE BRANCH

Committees are the workhorses of Congress, and the key place where committees work is hearings. As a *Congressional Research Service* report summarizes, "congressional hearings are the principal formal method by which committees collect and analyze information in the early stages of policy making. Whether legislative, oversight, investigative, or a combination of these, all hearings share common elements of preparation and conduct" (Carr 2006). Although the power of Congress to hold hearings and investigate the executive branch is not clearly defined in the Constitution, Congress has launched inquiries into the activities of the executive branch from the earliest days of the Republic. In 1792, a select committee was established by the House of Representatives during Washington's administration to examine defeats during a military expedition to the Northwest Territories (Harris 1964). The Legislative Reorganization Act of 1946, which streamlined committee jurisdictions in both the Senate and the House and provided appropriate staff resources, contains statutory language exhorting committees "to exercise continued watchfulness over the implementation of laws by the executive branch" (Deering and Smith 1990, 29). Hearings have two general functions: fact finding, to aid in the production of public policy, and investigative, to oversee and check the executive branch as it interprets and carries out the laws written by Congress. In this chapter, we focus most directly on Congress' role as an investigator of executive branch wrongdoings and misdeeds.

Political scientists generally talk about congressional investigations and oversight using three particular lenses: the Constitution, the pursuit of "good government," and the individual needs and incentives facing individual members of Congress. As every student of the American system of government knows, the Founders established a system of elaborate checks and balances to allow—in the famous words of James Madison—ambition to counter ambition. The Founders feared concentrated governmental authority in the hands of an overreaching and dominant executive. The best way to prevent this abuse of political power at the hands of a tyrant was to spread power among three different branches with each in charge of a fundamental governing function. A legislative branch would create the laws to be executed by an executive and interpreted by a judiciary. Fundamental to this design, however, was not just separating these powers but incorporating in each branch a bit of the other branches' "action". That is to say the executive branch, while not preeminent in lawmaking, has the power to make law—by suggesting it in the State of Union address or blocking its implementation with a veto. Conversely, Congress can check the execution of law by refusing to appropriate money or by holding hearings questioning the conduct of executive branch officials in the implementation or interpretation of statutes. Investigations of the executive branch sit at the nexus of this carefully balanced system and are part of the "invitation" of the branches to "struggle" outlined by presidential scholar Edwin Corwin (1957, 171). In short, because of the Constitution's separation of powers and checks and balances, we should expect Congress to guard its legislative priorities by aggressively overseeing and investigating the executive branch. The Constitution establishes a constant push and pull between the branches, so one might expect a constant vigilance through hearings, which is not affected by external political factors, the individual incentives of members of Congress, or the political strength of a particular president.

Another motivating factor behind congressional investigation is the pursuit of "good government." In the late nineteenth and early twentieth centuries, progressive reformers—beginning at the level of municipalities—began to push for government to be run more efficiently on scientific principles. Much of the impetuous for the reform movement lay with the business elite and upper-middle class managers who, in implementing scientific principles in the operation of their businesses, were dismayed by the rampant cronyism and inefficient delivery of services provided by political machines dominating local and state governments throughout the nation (Schiesl 1977). Progressive reformers felt through the application of science, government could be run more efficiently, cheaply, and "correctly." Woodrow Wilson, a political scientist and a progressive politician, wrote in *Congressional Government* of the importance of investigations in the production of good government: "The informing function of Congress should be preferred even to its legislative function. The argument is not only that a discussed and interrogated administration is the only pure and efficient administration, but, more than that, that the only really self-governing people is that people which discusses and interrogates its administration" (1885, 303). Investigations serve not only an important constitutional mandate, but they also help achieve the *ideal* government. In both the case of the Constitutional and Good Government models, one would expect a constantly vigilant Congress that conducts many hearings and investigations of the executive branch, looking both for efforts to usurp legislative authority and for ways to better operate the machinery of government.

Unfortunately, Congress is not necessarily as watchful or as jealous of its constitutional prerogatives as one might like or hope. Scholars of public administration and Congress have long bemoaned congressional inattention to oversight and investigation (Scher 1963; Ogul 1976; but see Aberbach 2002). Given the lack of attention to this essential activity by Congress, political scientists have sought to understand why the constitutional or good government motives do not explain Capitol Hill hearing activity. One predominant theory is that members of Congress simply do not have the appropriate incentives to monitor continuously the executive branch. The argument of Thomas Schwartz and Mat McCubbins (1984) goes something like this: Members of Congress have lots of competing pressures for their time. Given that resources are scare, members direct their attention to activities that provide them the most return on their investment—the return being reelection and the advancement of their careers. Exercising aggressive oversight and investigating the executive branch can provide substantial payoffs—if the member uncovers a scandal, for example, it can raise their profile substantially and may vault them to a higher elected office.

More often than not, however, the pursuit of vigorous oversight is a losing proposition for individual members of Congress. Vast amounts of resources can often be spent searching for possible problems and, if no problem is unearthed, then the time and effort are wasted with no clear benefit to the member. Time spent on a fruitless investigation out of the public eye could have been spent raising money, traveling home, writing legislation, or doing media interviews—all of which directly support the reelection motive of members. McCubbins and Schwartz argue that the oversight anticipated by the constitutional and good government schools—police patrols walking a beat and looking for crime—are not the preferred way members conduct congressional hearings because they are inefficient and produce a low return on investment. Instead, members of Congress rely upon a fire alarm style of investigations to keep the executive branch in check. Congress legislatively mandates the creation of fire boxes that other actors—interest groups, lobbyists, or citizens interested in particular policy areas—can pull when they witness an abuse by the executive branch. Congress will then react like firemen—hoisting the ladders, pulling out the truck, and putting out the fire that has received attention and publicity. Individual members of Congress win because they expend fewer resources rooting out problems, while receiving credit for responding to concerned citizens worried about a specific abuse by government. To summarize, the Fire Alarm Model of investigations suggests that the willingness of Congress to investigate is not constant, is subject to the incentives faced by individual members, and relies upon the actions of external political actors who make Congress aware of waste, fraud, and abuse.

What is conspicuously lacking from these models is an accounting for how the external political environment and the institutional incentive structure shapes the willingness of Congress to initiate and sustain oversight of the executive branch. The Constitutional and Good Government Models assume a sustained desire to investigate, but fueled by different motivations. The Fire Alarm Model assumes that the incentives faced by individual members dominate the decision of a committee to investigate. In reality, all three are gross simplifications of the logic of congressional oversight. Take, for example, the Fire Alarm Model. A fire alarm is pulled by an interest group, perhaps Congress does respond, but it may take its time. Perhaps it gets up, has breakfast, grabs some coffee, and then loads the fire truck—and by the time Congress gets underway, the building has already burned down. Perhaps Congress and its individual members are unable to pass substantial legislation due to gridlock and polarization, so they instead utilize the only power they have, the hearing, to show their constituents they are working. Perhaps in walking the beat, members of Congress chose to make political hay over a relatively minor incident in the hopes of scoring political points with fellow partisans. Investigations are shaped by the broader political environment (the popularity of a president, the presence or absence of divided government) and the institutional context (the role of the committee in Congress and its jurisdictional mandates). The watchful eye of Congress is not always fixed or attentive. Congress does not always aggressively pursue allegations of wrongdoing, but it does not always sit on its hands waiting for a fire alarm to be pulled.

Congress does not abdicate oversight, but its motivations for oversight are neither driven by a desire to produce efficient and effective governance nor a need to counter executive branch ambition due to constitutional design alone. Congressional oversight in the form of fire alarm-style investigations serves a variety of purposes, including the creation of better public policy, the advancement of partisan and member agendas, the protection of the legislature's constitutional prerogatives, and the contestation of the state's capacity and direction. In short, the willingness of Congress to utilize its investigative function is contingent on various and sometimes competing incentives and opportunity costs that are a function of the institution of Congress, individual committee prerogatives, the needs of individual members, and the external political environment. In following analysis, we focus on two external factors that have an enormous consequence for the conduct of congressional investigations: divided government and the rise of party polarization in the post-Watergate Era. Congressional investigations in the era of party polarization are as much, if not more, about scoring partisan points and protecting party reputations as they are about pursuing effective and efficient government or checking real executive abuses. Investigations, on average, have become shorter in both divided and unified government during the era of the polarized Congress, while at the same time have become far more frequent. We explain why and how these changes have occurred, and the implications for future congresses.

DIVIDED WE QUARREL. STILL

Pundits and the popular press often bemoan the consequences of divided government on the productivity of Congress. The following refrain is common: Congress is unable to pass legislation, and often gets wrapped up in investigations charging executive branch skullduggery. The Whitewater investigations by the House and Senate charging the Clintons with financial improprieties involving Arkansas real-estate transactions before achieving the presidency are often cited as an example of a congressional majority seeking to use political power to unnecessarily sully an administration to gain a partisan advantage. Prominent political scientist David Mayhew (1991; 2005), however, found in his own analysis of congressional investigations that partisan context and divided government had little effect on congressional propensity to investigate the executive branch. Restricting his analysis to congressional committee-based charges of executive branch wrongdoing appearing on the front page of *The New York Times* for at least 20 days, Mayhew found that the House and the Senate together were equally willing to investigate the president for charges of wrongdoing regardless of whether party control of government was divided. Specifically, he found 15 high publicity probes occurred under divided government and 15 under unified government between 1947 and 1990 (1991). In an updated version of his study, he found three more high publicity probes—all of which took place during the Clinton administration. Two probes occurred during divided control, and one during unified control of government. During the first two years of George W. Bush's administration and the final two years of George H. W. Bush's administration, he found no additional high publicity probes.

We have challenged Mayhew's findings and approach elsewhere (Parker and Dull 2009). We found that congressional investigations of the executive branch were indeed more common in divided government in the House of Representatives but not in the Senate. They are also more intensive—longer in days and in pages produced by the committees in the aggregate. A complimentary article (Parker and Dull 2013), which looks at the House of Representatives only and utilizes committee hearings as the unit of analysis, supports these findings concerning the relationship between divided government and the willingness of committee chairs to charge and investigate the executive branch with malfeasance. Both of these analyses examined investigatory activity between 1947 and 2004. Here, we extend the analysis by incorporating the last four years of the George W. Bush administration and the first two years of the Obama administration, adding a total of two unified congresses and one divided congress to the mix. Given recent developments and the continued growth of polarization, do we still find that the external political environment affects congressional willingness to launch and sustain an investigation alleging executive branch malfeasance?

To evaluate the relationship between divided government and congressional investigations, we first had to establish the universe of congressional investigations. We focused particularly on fire alarm-style investigations akin to the high publicity probes outlined by David Mayhew in *Divided We Govern*. We use the *Congressional Information Service* (CIS) Index to develop a measure of fire alarm investigations initiated by House and Senate committees between 1947 and 2010. We focus on the substantive charge emanating from the congressional committee, using David Mayhew's definition of a congressional "exposure" probe as a guide. Like Mayhew, we were interested in identifying a committee-based charge of executive branch malfeasance.

An electronic sweep of the CIS Index resulted in a large list of hearings, which were then coded based on the following decision rule: A hearing is included if the CIS Index record includes reference to violation of law, mismanagement, or abuse of discretion in current or past conduct in one or more federal agency or an organization tasked with carrying out agency functions. Violation of law refers to activities that contradict formal discretion as interpreted by Congress, the judiciary, a specified investigator, or a hearing witness. Mismanagement is included if reference is made to specific added costs, delay, poor planning or analysis, inconsistency, improper influence, or negligence in the administration of agency mandates. This includes inadequacies in agency procurement and contract management or any of the above resulting from deficiencies in intergovernmental coordination. Mismanagement is not included if it is attributed to the structure of formal discretion or if the reference is ambiguous, such as a reference only to "improving efficiency." Abuse of discretion refers to specific accusations that the agency or organization under scrutiny engaged in improper, covert, or deceitful activities in defiance the congressional wishes—even if a specific violation of law is not alleged.[3] Unlike Mayhew, we do not rely on media attention for our measure of investigations. Although high publicity probes reported by the press certainly have the potential to damage an administration's reputation, addressing a less public probe still drains administrative energy and attention that might be utilized more profitably pursuing other key objectives. The cumulative effect of addressing many smaller and less visible investigations can be just as troublesome as a major probe in the limelight.

RESULTS

Our analysis yields a total of 1,137 investigations conducted by House and Senate committees from 1947 through 2010. Figure 3.1 shows the number of investigations undertaken by chamber in each congressional term. Four trends are worth noting. First, the House and Senate generally undertook the same number of investigations until the ninety-fourth Congress (1975–1977). After that, the House becomes the dominant investigator of executive branch malfeasance. Second, although the House investigates more than the Senate in the post-Watergate, polarized era, the ebb and flow of investigatory activity in each chamber seems related: Both the Senate and the House mirror the other during periods of high and low investigatory activity. Third, although not definitive, it appears that—particularly in the post-Watergate, polarized era—there is a relationship between divided government and the willingness to investigate the executive branch for wrong doing. The top three congresses for investigation in the House were all during periods of divided government: the ninety-seventh Congress during Ronald Reagan's first term generated 73 separate investigations, the one hundred and tenth Congress during the final two years of the George W. Bush administration produced 47, and the ninety-eighth Congress during 1983 and 1984 yielded 41. In the Senate, two of the top three investigation

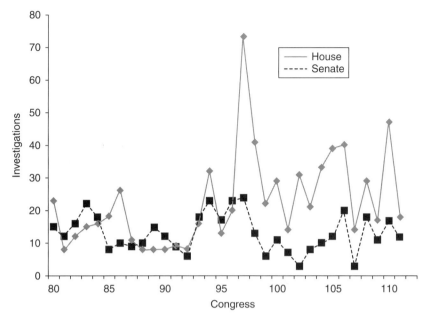

Figure 3.1   Congressional Investigations by Chamber, 1947–2010.

Congresses occurred under divided government: the Senate launched 24 investigations of the Reagan administration in the ninety-seventh Congress, and 23 investigations in both the final two years of Jimmy Carter and Gerald Ford's terms of office (in the ninety-fourth and ninety-sixth Congresses, respectively). Finally, the number of investigations in the House is on an upward trajectory, while in the Senate the trend is flat throughout the time period.

If investigations of executive branch malfeasance are becoming more frequent in the House, what about the intensity of those investigations? We created two additional variables measuring investigatory intensity: *Investigation Days* and *Investigation Pages*. *Days* is simply the number of days on which investigations occurred, and *Pages* sums the total page count for all published hearing volumes and appendices. Figure 3.2 plots the variations in investigation length by chamber while additionally providing the majority parties controlling each chamber. Chambers opposing the president are highlighted in gray. First, note how days and pages closely track each other in both chambers. Longer hearings in days generate more testimony and more hearing pages. Second, the relationship between divided government and hearing intensity seems chamber specific. Peaks in the page series are often associated with divided government in the House, but not in the Senate. Third, the overall trend in both chambers is toward shorter hearings. Hearings in both the House and Senate occupy fewer days, and fewer pages in the Senate. Page production in the House, on the contrary, is essentially flat throughout the period. Combining the findings from figure 3.1 with figure 3.2 leads

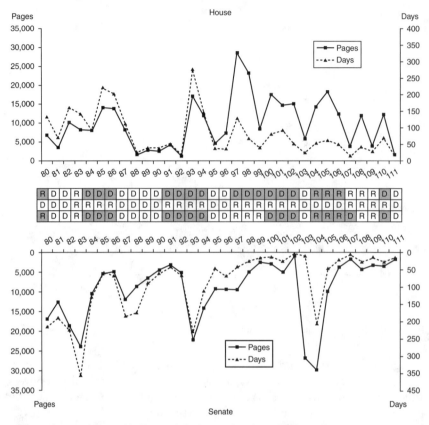

The top row reports the party of the House majority, the second row the party of the president, and the final row the party of the Senate majority.

Figure 3.2 Congressional Committee Investigations, Days, and Pages by Chamber, 1947–2010.

to the conclusion that committee investigations alleging government waste, fraud, and abuse are becoming more common while simultaneously becoming shorter on average.

Table 3.1 makes the point about the relationship between divided government and committee investigations clear.[4] We report the average number and length of congressional investigations in divided and unified government by chamber in the cells of the table. The numbers in parentheses represent the years of divided and unified government in each chamber between 1947 and 2010. In the House, the average congressional session held during divided government featured twice as many committee investigations charging executive branch malfeasance when compared to congresses meeting during unified government (29 versus 14). They also are nearly twice as long in days (102 versus 56), and more than twice as long in pages (13,400 versus 5,400) under divided government. In the Senate, there are actually more investigations of the executive branch under unified

Table 3.1 The Mean Number and Intensity of Congressional Investigations in Divided and Unified Government, 1947–2010

	Investigations	Days	Pages
House			
Divided Government	28.72	101.97	13,393.44
	(38)	(38)	(38)
Unified Government	14.42	56.21	5,414.75
	(26)	(26)	(26)
Senate			
Divided Government	11.88	79.91	8770
	(32)	(32)	(32)
Unified Government	14.25	96.75	9919
	(32)	(32)	(32)

government (14) than divided (12) on average, and those investigations are slightly more intense (97 versus 80 days and 9,900 versus 8,770 pages). The presence of divided government seems to be a contributing factor to the number and intensity of committee investigations of the executive branch in the House, but not in the Senate—and this is the case throughout the entire time period.

Congress, of course, has undergone a number of important changes affecting the way in which it does business. These include the well-documented rise in partisan polarization spurred in part by congressional redistricting, residential mobility, and the Republicanization of the South; the reform of House rules shifting power to the chamber's party leadership; and the substantial growth of committee resource capacity that provided far more staff for newly empowered subcommittees to launch more investigations (Sinclair 2006; Polsby 2004; Mann and Ornstein 2008; 2012). Add to this the rise of investigative journalism post-Watergate (Armao 2000, 40; Aucoin 1995) and the culture of mistrust in government, and the incentive structures for pursuing vigorous oversight of the executive branch significantly change both for individual members and partisan majorities. Although these various forces are hard to disentangle, it is clear that by the mid-1970s, the resource environment facing Congress and the external political environment had changed substantially. To provide a rough proxy for these important changes, we divide our data using the ninety-fourth Congress as a point of demarcation for the bipartisan, accommodating, and "compromise" Congress witnessed by early scholars of the legislative process like Richard Fenno (1973), and the new polarized, winner-take-all Congresses featuring sharp partisanship and polarization in the new technology age. Do we see any difference in the relationship between divided government and committee investigations before and after the Watergate era?

Table 3.2 presents the same data as table 3.1 but with the additional variable of pre- and post-1975 included. Looking at the Senate on the right-hand side of the table, one sees no growth in the number of investigations post-1975 and, if anything, the Senate is slightly more likely to initiate investigations on average during unified government. Investigations are also less intensive—far less time is spent per investigation in the Senate in terms of days and pages after 1974. While the Senate generates more hearing days during divided government in the polarized era, page production between divided and unified government is essentially the same (7,207 versus 7,977).

The House data tell a different story. Unlike the Senate, the House witnesses a rather substantial growth of investigations of the executive branch in the polarized era under both divided and unified government. The number of investigations pursued by House committees doubles on average under divided government between the consensus and polarized era (19 versus 37) and almost doubles under unified government (10 versus 19). Although the number of days devoted on average declines markedly in the partisan era when compared to the consensus era, the difference between hearing days in divided and unified government grows in the era of polarized parties. To be precise, hearing days under unified government before 1975 represented 58% of the hearing day activity, on average, under divided government

Table 3.2 Divided Government, Watergate, and the Effect of Increasing Committee Staff on Congressional Investigations, 1947–2010.

	House		Senate	
	Divided	*Unified*	*Divided*	*Unified*
(A) *Number of Investigations*				
Pre-1974	18.5	10	13.75	13.71
	(14)	(14)	(16)	(14)
Post-1974	36.90	18.90	10.38	14.67
	(24)	(12)	(16)	(18)
(B) *Number of Investigation Days*				
Pre-1974	142.94	83.57	115.56	182.86
	(14)	(14)	(16)	(14)
Post-1974	69.20	28.90	44.25	29.77
	(24)	(12)	(16)	(18)
(C) *Number of Investigation Pages*				
Pre-1974	9598	5257	10,333	12,415
	(14)	(14)	(16)	(14)
Post-1974	16,429.50	5572.71	7207	7,977
	(24)	(12)	(16)	(18)

during the same period. That percentage drops to 42% in the polarized era. In simple terms, while the House spends less time as measured in days on each individual committee investigation, the difference in hearing activity between unified and divided government becomes greater during the era of party polarization. The relationship is similar in terms of pages produced by committees, although hearings in the polarized era produce—on average—more pages than in the consensus Congress period. Again, while House committees generated more pages of testimony on average under divided government in both eras, the gap between hearings conducted during divided versus unified government grows during the era of polarization: unified pages represent 54% of the average page production of hearings in divided government before 1974, and only 33% after. To summarize, the relationship between committee investigatory intensity and divided government has become sharper in the era of polarized parties: Hearings in unified government are shorter than ever on average, and while hearings in divided government are shorter on average, too, they are much longer on average when compared to unified government hearings in the partisan era.

Before considering the implications of these findings, it is worth considering the high publicity probes of executive branch malfeasance as defined by David Mayhew (1991; 2005), which serves as the basis for his findings that divided government does not affect the conduct of congressional investigations. If we update his analysis and consider investigatory intensity, do we see a relationship between divided government and high publicity probes—particularly in the era of the polarized Congress? Mayhew's analysis ended in 1990, but he updated his data set through 2002 in a subsequent edition of *Divided We Govern*. We, in turn, updated his list of congressional probes through 2010. Using a search logic, we queried *The New York Times* in *LexisNexis* for articles mentioning committee-based charges of waste, fraud, and malfeasance appearing on the front page for more than 20 days.[5] Between 2003 and 2010, we found exactly one: a series of House and Senate investigations into the partisan-motivated firings of US Attorneys and widespread politicization in the Department of Justice during the Bush administration, featuring the testimony and eventual resignation of Attorney General Alberto Gonzales. These hearings appeared on the front page of *The Times* for 24 nonconsecutive days and occurred during divided government in the last two years of George W. Bush's administration.

In figure 3.3, we plot the total number of days that the Mayhew-defined high publicity probes received coverage on the front page of *The New York Times* between 1947 and 2010. The dark solid line represents the ninety-fourth Congress—or the demarcation between the polarized Congress and the consensus Congress. Gray bars represent periods of divided government. First, note the great decline in attention to high publicity style probes by *The New York Times* post-1974. Second, there seems to be a relationship in the era of party polarization between the amount of coverage received by committees investigating charges of executive waste, fraud, and abuse and divided government—a relationship that is not present prior to 1974. Table 3.3 helps

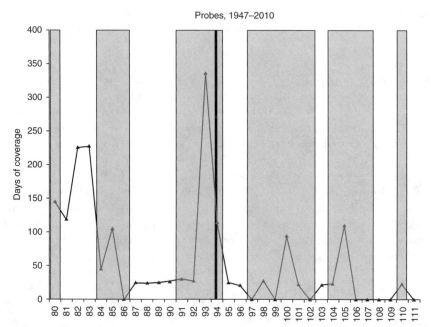

Figure 3.3 *The New York Times* Coverage of High-publicity Congressional Committee Probes, 1947–2010.

put these findings into clearer relief. Part A reports the average number of days *The New York Times* reported high publicity probes pre- and post-1974 in both unified and divided government. Before 1974, the number of days was no different (99 versus 97). The amount of attention paid to high publicity probes was far greater as well: nearly three times as many days in divided government pre-1974 compared to post-1974, and almost ten times the attention in unified government pre- and post-1974. Most important, however, is the difference between divided and unified government after 1974 to the attention received by high publicity probes in *The New York Times*: Probes during divided government drew three times the coverage when compared to unified government (35 versus 11.5 days). Part B reports the average number of high publicity probes conducted by Congress each session. Although the differences are likely not significant, before 1974 unified governments averaged two high publicity probes per congress and 1.4 per congress in divided government. After 1975, the average number of probes was .75 per congress in divided government and 0.5 in unified government. The high publicity probes noted by Mayhew have seen better days and are clearly in decline, but more importantly the high publicity probes that still receive the notice of the mainstream press are more likely to emerge in divided rather than unified government during the period of polarized parties.

Table 3.3   High-publicity Congressional Probes in Divided and Unified Government, Pre- and Post-1974

Party Control of Government		
	Divided	Unified
(A) *Days of Coverage in The New York Times*		
Pre-1974	99.00	96.71
	(14)	(14)
Post-1974	35.00	11.50
	(24)	(12)
(B) *Number of Investigations Receiving Coverage in The New York Times*		
Pre-1974	1.43	2.00
	(14)	(14)
Post-1974	0.75	0.50
	(24)	(12)

DISCUSSION

Many of changes in the era of polarized parties have led to what we term the *weaponization* and *politicization* of congressional investigations. Weaponization involves transforming committee investigations into a tool of political combat, and politicization concerns a movement away from the constitutional or efficiency rationale to investigate toward an impetus to investigate (or not) based upon partisan considerations. This weaponization and politicization is rooted in two related developments. First, in the electoral arena, investigations present useful opportunities for position-taking during divided government when legislative options may be limited. Divided party control obscures the already difficult task of assigning accountability for policy success and failure. It muddles fragmented lines of authority over administrative processes, hindering congressional efforts to steer agency policy-making. It is difficult for parties and their candidates to run on their legislative accomplishments when there are fewer to tout. Other ways are needed to differentiate themselves to various constituencies, and investigations are an easy way to draw a bright line in the political sand. In this context, investigations also allow partisan congressional majorities to differentiate themselves from the president and the opposition party (Cox and McCubbins 1993; Parker 2008).[6]

A second factor contributing to the politicization of congressional investigations is the significant expansion of congressional capacity occurring particularly in the 1970s, but continuing in some forms to the current day. Committee staff and hearing days more than doubled between 1969 and 1977, before leveling off in the 1980s and 1990s (Aberbach 1990;

2002). The General Accounting Office expanded its evaluation capacity
and the offices inspectors general were established in the executive branch
agencies by statute (Oleszek 1996; Light 1993). New management laws
mandating standardized public reporting of information regarding agency
financial and program status have proliferated (Brass 2004). Congress now
has more tools and information available with which to launch investigations. Successful probes help validate the establishment of new instruments
of congressional control, similar to the role scandals have long played in
the development of regulation (Kemp 1984). Expanded resources and new
sources of program and agency evaluation also help to hone the strategic
use of oversight.

On the electoral side of the equation, investigations need not capture the
attention of *The New York Times* to be useful as shapers of individual or party
reputations. Parties and Members of Congress serve multiple constituencies
(Fenno 1978), and investigations may simply be aimed at the reelection or
activist constituencies rather than the public at large. Across institutions,
investigations erode agency reputations and limit bureaucratic autonomy
(Carpenter 2000; 2001). They also signal to bureaucratic actors the potential costs of diverging from committee wishes. These strategic probes drain
resources, centralize decisions, distort the flow of information, and degrade
morale within targeted agencies. A congressional party opposed to values
embedded in agency policies and structure might seek simply to the obstruct
agency from functioning.

Finally, changes in technology and political culture in the period since
Watergate have also altered the ways Americans think and talk about politics.
A "culture of mistrust" has emerged, making politics by allegation not only
advantageous, but also an established part of the rules of the game (Garment
1991; deLeon 1993). The sources of this development defy simple explanation, but changes in the news media and the reemergence of investigative
journalism in the early 1970s play a role (Armao 2000, 40; Aucoin 1995).
Media consolidation and increased competitive pressures have placed greater
emphasis on breaking attention-grabbing news stories. The result has been
an erosion of the traditional norms guiding journalists and the rise of a new
symbiosis between journalists looking for and politicians hoping to benefit
from scandal (Sabato 1991; Witcover 1998). Ultimately, political coverage
has become increasingly interpretative, negative, and less policy oriented
(Patterson 1993; Daniel 2000; Starobin 2001). These factors, combined
with expanded congressional institutional capacity and extended periods of
divided party control, have led to investigations framed by alleged negligence, abuse of power, violation of law, and ethical misconduct becoming a
critical venue in the competition over the direction of government policy.

The politicization of congressional investigations emerged neither from
one source nor all at once. Newt Gingrich's entrepreneurial leadership and
the rise of House Republicans, however, provide an illuminating chapter.
Written off as a permanent partisan minority in the early and mid-1980s, a
group of Republicans coalesced around Gingrich with the goal of winning

back the House. The group developed a range of grenade-tossing tactics designed both to obstruct chamber business and to degrade public support for House Democrats. In 1988–1989, they pushed ethics charges against Democratic Speaker Jim Wright, ultimately forcing his resignation. Citing these tactics in his analysis of congressional institutional innovations, Eric Schickler writes, "The ethics fight showed Republicans that making the House and its Democratic majority look bad could propel the GOP to power" (2001, 243–246).

In 1994, Gingrich and the Republicans succeeded in taking control of the House after 40 years in the minority. Unsurprisingly, the party carried many take-no-prisoner tactics into leadership. Among other inquiries, Republican-controlled committees initiated probes of the Clintons' involvement in the Whitewater Development Corporation, the White House Travel Office firings, and the ATF's actions during the standoff in Waco. An internal GOP memo leaked to *Roll Call* in April 1996 sheds light on this pattern. The memo, marked "urgent," instructed committee staff to search their files for information in three areas of interest: "Waste, Fraud and Abuse in the Clinton administration," "Influence of Washington Labor Bosses/Corruption," and "Examples of dishonesty or ethical lapses in the Clinton administration" (Chappie 1996). Democrats took note, and when the shoe was on their foot, pursued their own aggressive investigations of the executive branch when they held the majority. Thirteen years after the Gingrich Revolution, Republicans chafed at Representative Waxman's various investigations into prewar Iraq intelligence, postwar reconstruction contracts, the friendly fire death of National Football League (NFL) star Pat Tillman in Afghanistan, and White House contacts with disgraced lobbyist Jack Abramoff (Badkhen and Sterngold 2007). Republican Congressman Patrick McHenry complained that "oversight committee hearings are reduced to Bush-bashing press conferences" (Badkhen and Sterngold 2007). As the Representative Issa's recent investigations into Solyndra, Fannie Mae, the Food and Drug Administration (FDA), and the Justice Department signify, the pattern of weaponized, partisan-motivated committee investigations is not going away anytime soon (Negrin 2012).

CONCLUSION

The Weekly Standard, noting our findings concerning the relationship between divided and unified government, applauded the increased oversight accompanying divided government (Andres 2009). Although divided government is associated with more investigations, we do not agree with the conclusion that more investigations in the polarized party era is a good thing. While the raw number of committee-based investigations charging executive branch waste, fraud, and abuse is increasing in the House—and especially under divided government—the average hearing has become less intense in terms of the days produced. Two critical developments drive this change. First, investigations initiated under unified government, we suspect, have become largely cursory affairs. The investigation is necessary to avoid the appearance of partisan favoritism, but it is kept short and sweet to protect the administration from undue political harm. Alternatively, investigations are launched willy-nilly on the pretext of slim evidence in the hopes of drawing the attention of the press with the specific desire to harm and undercut a hostile administration in divided government. As a recent story on Congressman Issa's chairmanship notes, the so-called Fast and Furious investigation of the Department of Justice appears to be "the would-be scandal that Issa was hoping for, and ...should guarantee him the attention he wants" (Negrin 2012). These trends in investigatory behavior go beyond ambition countering ambition as outlined by Madison. Instead, ambition is tempered when it is good for the party in unified government and excited and exploited under divided government. If there is a silver lining in this era of polarization politics, it is the Senate, which seems to have been somewhat immune from developments metastasizing in the House. Although the Senate has become a more partisan chamber during this period (Theriault and Rhode 2011), it is still far harder for partisan majorities to work their will in that chamber than it is in the House. Perhaps this is a positive outgrowth of the filibuster and the need to obtain supermajorities to conduct business in the Senate. Both make it harder to initiate an investigation appearing to be largely motivated by partisan considerations.

The relationship between divided government and the rise of party polarization also serves to change how we think of the police patrol/fire alarm dichotomy so prevalent among political scientists studying congressional oversight. The reason why members of Congress prefer fire alarm to police patrol is one of incentives and costs: police patrols are expensive to conduct and may not yield benefits to members. Fire alarms, on the other hand, help members appear responsive to constituents while building individual reputations for addressing unpopular waste, fraud, and abuse in government. Our data, alternatively, show that external political considerations matter for when and how congressional committees chose to investigate the executive branch for wrongdoing. Party control matters, with partisan majorities choosing to pull fire alarms and walk jurisdictional beats aggressively in divided government while staying at home in bed when loud alarms are sounded during unified government. Explaining a preference for fire alarm oversight by resorting to the individual preferences of individual members alone does little to explain the variation observed in congressional attention (or lack thereof) to the executive branch.

However, in another way, the fire alarm model of oversight is vindicated by our findings. The high publicity probes noted by David Mayhew may have fallen out of favor, but this is very different from saying that fire alarm style investigations are disappearing. If anything, the decline of the high publicity probe suggests both the success of the fire containment systems developed by Congress and the evolving way in which congressional investigations are used by members of Congress, partisan majorities, interest groups, and the press. Congress has outsourced the work of police patrols by expanding the investigatory role and resources of the General Accounting Office and by creating offices of inspectors general in each executive agency. These agencies look for problems of waste, fraud, and abuse and shine the flashlights into the dark corners members of Congress do not have the time or inclination to examine. When these agencies produce reports, they set off fire alarms for Congress that then holds investigatory hearings and to play the heroes of efficiency and frugality. As these agencies have already done the heavy lifting and produced extensive reports, Congress can hold not only hearings for fewer days on average per investigation—saving time—but also producing less for the mainstream media to report. Perhaps as important, however, is the changing nature of the media and technology in disseminating the results of these investigations and continuing the attack on the executive branch after hearings conclude. Before the Internet and the widespread rise of investigative journalism, committees had to hold long hearings to sustain attention to their allegations of executive branch abuse. Now, Congress can take a GAO report, hold a short hearing, and external allies can continue to lob allegations and aspersions from the blogosphere. The days of the long investigative hearing broadcast on television may be over, but the effect on executive branch capacity and resources may be just as great if not greater in the age of party polarization. As recent events demonstrate, interest groups can exploit hearings for their own political ends. The National Rifle Association pressured Democratic members to hold Attorney General Eric Holder in contempt for refusing to respond to a subpoena from the House Committee on Oversight and Government Reform requesting documents for investigation into the department's gun-smuggling investigation known as Operation Fast and Furious (Weisman 2012; Serrano 2012). The National Rifle Association's (NRA) actions provide further evidence of the complex role investigations play in a polarized and fragmented political system that belie simplistic explanations grounded in individual member incentives.

Finally, it is worth considering how weaponization and politicization of congressional investigations affects the body politic. John Hibbing and Elizabeth Theiss-Morse (1995) have argued dislike of Congress stems from public distaste of quarrelling politicians and the mechanics of the democratic process (also Hibbing 1999). Public approval and support for Congress has declined substantially in recent years. In August 2012, Congress tied an historic low with only 10% of Americans approving of the job Congress is doing in the Gallup poll (Newport 2012). Considering the widespread concern with public disgust with Congress, it is surprising more political scientists have failed to either take note of or explore the linkage between trust and the politics of investigations. Investigations are an important institutional tool available to Congress, and a necessary one in a democratic system predicated on accountability to its citizens. Nevertheless, if the public has a marked distaste for political conflict, the increased scope and intensity of congressional investigations of executive branch malfeasance in the post-Watergate era does little to increase public confidence in Congress while simultaneously eroding support for the presidency. The temporary advantages gained both institutionally and electorally by Congress in its jousting with the president and the executive branch may, over the long haul, come at the cost of increased public apathy.

NOTES

1. There are many people we should acknowledge for their continued support. We would like to first thank our colleagues at Montana State and Virginia Tech, respectively, for providing great working environments. Second, thanks to Sean Kelly, Scott Frisch, and California State University Channel Islands for inviting us to Camarillo to share our thoughts on congressional investigations in a polarized era. Many others have helped us along the way, including Robert Van Houweling, Craig Goodman, David Canon, Wade Cole, Anne Khademian, Rachel Girshick, Patrick Roberts, Mike Franz, Karen Hult, Hilary Parker, Jeffrey Lazarus, Pavielle Haines, John Coleman, Mike Franz, Byron Shafer, Graham Wilson, Patrick Roberts, David Canon, Ken Mayer, Sam Kernell, Sarah Binder, David Nickerson, David Campbell, John Griffin, Peri Arnold, Christina Wolbrecht, and Mike Keene. Finally, we would like to thank David Mayhew, whose book *Divided We Govern* inspired the whole intellectual endeavor. All provided feedback, criticism, and constructive suggestions during this project, which has produced four publications to date. Any errors or omissions that remain are ours alone.

2. The 109th Congress passed 482 bills into public law. In the previous Congress, 498 bills became public law. It is notable that legislative productivity, in general, seems to be on a downward trend. The 110th Congress with Democrats in control in the final two years during the Bush administration only passed 460 laws. See the Congressional Resume of Activity, http://www.senate.gov/pagelayout/reference/two_column_table/Resumes.htm.

3. See Parker and Dull (2009) for the syntax employed for investigations through 2004. After 2004, we had to adopt a new syntax due to the new interface provided by *ProQuest* when CIS was transferred from LexisNexis. That syntax is (Fraud OR corrupt! OR brib! OR conflict OR illegal OR ethic! OR espion! OR incrimin! OR alleg!) OR (Influe! OR loyal! OR sabotage! OR impropriety! OR favorit! OR affair OR abus! OR impeach) AND (Executi! OR commiss! OR federal OR serv! OR agency OR depart! OR administrat! OR militar OR counc!). Given the number of hits produced before our initial sweeps and our rules for discarding oversight hearings, we have no reason to believe we missed any investigations.

4. We ran the same negative binomial models reported in Dull and Parker (2009) and the results again show that divided government and the post-Watergate variables are positive and significant predictors of the initiation of House hearings and their intensity. Results available on request.

5. We searched *The New York Times* in LexisNexis. After a series of attempts using various search logics to find the stories Mayhew uncovered about Whitewater appearing on the front page of *The New York Times*, we settled on the following syntax using the advanced search function in LexisNexis: SECTION("pg. 1" OR "page 1" OR "p. 1") AND SECTION("Section A" OR "Section 1") AND committee AND (Congress OR House OR Senate OR Congressional) AND (hearing OR oversight or investigation OR inquiry) AND DATELINE(Washington)

AND NOT SECTION(foreign desk OR metropolitan desk OR "Section E"). We ran this search on each year, and then read each article and discarded those that did not appear to represent a committee-based charge of executive branch malfeasance. Mayhew's updated data and the actual stories he uncovered using his approach are available at his website http://pantheon.yale.edu/~dmayhew/data3.html.

6. This portion of the chapter draws upon an earlier paper we gave at the American Political Science Association's annual meeting in 2003. See Parker and Dull (2003).

REFERENCES

Aberbach, Joel. 1990. *Keeping a Watchful Eye: The Politics of Congressional Oversight.* Washington: The Brookings Institution Press.

———. 2002."What's Happened to the Watchful Eye?" *Congress and the Presidency* 29(1): 3–23.

Armao, Rosemary. 2000. "The History of Investigative Reporting." In *The Big Chill: Investigative Reporting in the Current Media Environment,* edited by Marilyn S. Greenwald and Joseph Bernt, 35–50. Ames: Iowa State University Press.

Andres, Gary. 2009. "The Accountability Gap." *The Weekly Standard Blog* September 17. http://www.weeklystandard.com/Content/Public/Articles/000/000/016/964nlyxl.asp.

Aucoin, James L. 1995. "The Re-emergence of American Investigative Journalism, 1960–1975." *Journalism History* 21(1): 3–15.

Badkhen, Anna, and James Sterngold. 2007. "Thorn in the Side of GOP Says He's Just Doing His Job." *San Francisco Chronicle* May 28.

Brass, Clinton P. 2004. "General Management Laws: Major Themes and Management Policy Options." *Congressional Research Service Report RL32388,* May.

Carpenter, Daniel P. 2000. "State Building through Reputation Building: Coalitions of Esteem and Program Innovation in the National Postal System, 1883–1913." *Studies in American Political Development* 14(2): 121–155.

———. 2001. . *The Forging of Bureaucratic Autonomy: Reputations, Networks, and Policy Innovation in Executive Agencies, 1862–1928.* Princeton: Princeton University Press.

Carr, Thomas P. 2006. "Hearings in the House of Representatives: A Guide for Preparation and Procedure." *Congressional Research Service Report RL30539,* Washington, DC, June 13.

Chappie, Damon. 1996. "GOP Leaders Ask Panels to Dig Up Information on Clinton, Unions." *Roll Call* April 29.

Corwin, Edwin S. 1957. *The President: The Office and Powers.* 4th revised edition. New York: New York University Press.

Cox, Gary W., and Mathew D. McCubbins. 1993. *Legislative Leviathan: Party Government in the House.* Berkeley: The University of California Press.

Daniel, Douglass K. 2000. "Best of Times and Worst of Times: Investigative Reporting in Post- Watergate America." In *The Big Chill: Investigative Reporting in the Current Media Environment,* Edited by Marilyn S. Greenwald and Joseph Bernt, 11–33. Ames: Iowa State University Press.

Deering, Christopher J., and Stephen S. Smith.1990. *Committees in Congress.* 2nd Edition. Washington: CQ Press.

deLeon, Peter. 1993. *Thinking About Political Corruption.* Armonk: M. E. Sharpe.

Espo, David. 2006. "Pelosi Says She Would Drain GOP 'Swamp.'" *The Associated Press* October 6.

Fenno, Richard F., Jr. 1973. *Congressmen in Committees*. Boston: Little and Brown.

———. 1978. *Home Style: House Members in Their Districts*. Boston: Little and Brown.

Garment, Suzanne. 1991. *Scandal: The Crisis of Mistrust in American Politics*. New York: Random House.

Ginsberg, Benjamin, and Martin Shefter. 2004. *Politics by Other Means: Politics, Prosecutors and the Press from Watergate to Whitewater*. New York: W.W. Norton.

Harris, Joseph P. 1964. *Improving Control of Administration*. Washington: Brookings Institution.

Hibbing, John R. 1999. "Appreciating Congress." In *Congress and the Decline of Public Trust*, edited by Joseph Cooper, 43–64. Boulder: Westview Press.

Hibbing, John R., and Elizabeth Theiss-Morse. 1995. *Congress as Public Enemy: Public Attitudes Toward American Political Institutions*. Cambridge: Cambridge University Press.

Kemp, Kathleen A. 1984. "Accidents, Scandals, and Political Support for Regulatory Agencies." *The Journal of Politics* 46(2): 401–427.

Mann, Thomas E., and Norman J. Ornstein. 2012. *It's Even Worse Than It Looks: How the American Constitutional System Collided with the Politics of Extremism*. New York: Basic Books.

———. 2008. *The Broken Branch: How Congress is Failing America and How to Get it Back on Track*. Oxford: Oxford University Press.

Mayhew, David R. 2000. *America's Congress: Actions in the Public Sphere, James Madison Through Newt Gingrich*. New Haven: Yale University Press.

———. 1991. *Divided We Govern: Party Control, Lawmaking, and Investigations, 1946–1990*. New Haven: Yale University Press.

———. 2005. *Divided We Govern: Party Control, Lawmaking, and Investigations, 1946–1990*. 2nd edition. New Haven: Yale University Press.

McCubbins, Mathew, and Thomas Schwartz. 1984. "Congressional Oversight Overlooked: Police Patrols versus Fire Alarms." *American Journal of Political Science* 2(1): 165–179.

Negrin, Matt. 2012. Darrell Issa Fashions Crown Jewel to Investigate White House. ABCNews.com. http://abcnews.go.com/blogs/politics/2012/06/darrell-issa-fashions-crown-jewel-to-investigate-white-house/.

Newport, Frank. 2012. "Congress Approval Ties All-Time Low at 10%." *Gallup Politics*. http://www.gallup.com/poll/156662/Congress-Approval-Ties-Time-Low.aspx.

Ogul, Morris. 1976. *Congress Oversees the Bureaucracy: Studies in Legislative Supervision*. Pittsburgh: University of Pittsburgh Press.

Oleszek, Walter J. 1996. *Congressional Procedures and the Policy Process*. 4th Edition. Washington: Congressional Quarterly Press.

Parker, David C. W. 2008. *The Power of Money in Congressional Campaigns, 1880–2006*. Norman: University of Oklahoma Press.

Parker, David C. W., and Matthew Dull. 2003. "Divided We Quarrel: Institutional Conflict beyond the Legislative Arena." Paper presented at the annual meeting of the American Political Science Association, Philadelphia, September.

————. 2009. "Divided We Quarrel: The Politics of Congressional Investigations, 1947–2004." *Legislative Studies Quarterly* 34(3): 319–345.

————. 2013. "Rooting Out Waste, Fraud, and Abuse: The Politics of House Committee Investigations, 1947–2004." *Political Research Quarterly* 66(3): 630–644.

Patterson, Thomas J. 1993. *Out of Order*. New York: Alfred P. Knopf.

Pincus, Walter. 2006. "Analyst Says He Warned of Iraqi Resistance; Danger Was Clear Early, White Said." *Washington Post* June 27. WashingtonPost.com: http://www.washingtonpost.com/wpdyn/content/article/2006/06/26/AR2006062601306.html.

Polsby, Nelson W. 2004. *How Congress Evolves: Social Basis of Institutional Change*. Oxford: Oxford University Press.

Sabato, Larry J. 1991. *Feeding Frenzy: How Attack Journalism Has Transformed American Politics*. New York: Free Press.

Scher, Seymour. 1963. "Conditions for Legislative Control." *The Journal of Politics* 25(3): 526–551.

Schickler, Eric. 2001. *Disjointed Pluralism: Institutional Innovation and the Development of the U.S. Congress*. Princeton: Princeton University Press.

Schiesl, Martin J. 1977. *The Politics of Efficiency: Municipal Administration and Reform in America, 1880–1920*. Berkeley: University of California Press.

Serrano, Richard A. 2012. "House Panel Recommends Holder be Found in Contempt of Congress." *Los Angeles Times* June 20.

Sherman, Jake, and Richard E. Cohen. 2010. "Darrell Issa Plans Hundreds of Hearings." *Politico* November 18. http://www.politico.com/news/stories/1110/44850.html.

Sinclair, Barbara. 2006. *Party Wars: Polarization and the Politics of National Policy Making*. Norman: University of Oklahoma Press.

Starobin, Paul. 2001. "A Generation of Vipers." *Columbia Journalism Review* 40(4): 118–120.

Theriault, Sean M., and David W. Rhode. 2011. "The Gingrich Senators and Party Polarization in the U.S. Senate." *Journal of Politics* 73(4): 1011–1024.

Weisman, Jonathan. 2012. "Democrats Feel Pressure from Gun Lobby on Contempt Vote." *The New York Times* June 26.

Weisman, Jonathan, and Charlie Savage. 2012. "House Finds Holder in Contempt Over Inquiry on Guns." *The New York Times* June 28.

Wilson, Woodrow. 1885. *Congressional Government: A Study in American Politics*. Boston: Houghton and Mifflin.

Witcover, Jules. 1998. "Where We Went Wrong." *Columbia Journalism Review* 36(6): 18–26.

4

Taking Incivility Seriously

Analyzing Breaches of Decorum in the US Congress (1891–2012)

Lawrence C. Dodd and Scot Schraufnagel

Even casual observers of the US Congress have heard about the heated exchanges, name calling, booing and hissing, and other uncivil breaches of decorum that have occurred in the House and Senate chambers in recent years. One has only to recall the shout from the floor of the House chambers, "You Lie!," by Congressman Joe Wilson (R-SC) in September 2009, when President Barak Obama was explaining his national health-care plan to a joint televised session of Congress. The list of anecdotes and illustrations of norm-breaking and personal incivility are numerous, with most Congresses having at least one or two publicized uncivil acts as well as many less visible ones. But what are we to make of such actions?

Certainly few of them—maybe one every century or so—will ever rise to the momentousness of the 1858 caning of Senator William Sumner by Congressman Preston Brooks (D-SC) in the Senate chambers. Enraged over Sumner's support of the abolition of slavery, including his personal attacks on several senators who supported slavery, Brooks entered Senate chamber and virtually beat Sumner to death. This event, which greatly enraged the Northern public and rallied support for secession in the South, is often cited as a factor leading to the Civil War. In the twentieth century, the most momentous such uncivil behavior came with the sustained and unsubstantiated attacks by Senator Joseph McCarthy (R-WI) on the patriotism of a wide array of government, military, and political figures of both parties. The attacks, coming in committee hearings and speeches on the Senate floor, maintained that communist infiltration of government was responsible for such developments as the fall of China to the communists and Soviet success in testing an atomic bomb. Despite his lack of proof, such accusations destroyed careers and fueled the "Red Scare" of the early 1950s. His attacks and breaches of decorum, which virtually brought the Eisenhower administration to a standstill in the spring and summer of 1954, eventually led the Senate to censure him for bringing the institution "into dishonor and disrepute."

With the exception of such rare events, uncivil behavior in Congress, as with the Wilson shout, tends to be dismissed as part of the normal conflict associated with highly partisan battles over public policy in Congress, having little if any independent effect on policymaking. Seen in this manner, uncivil acts are useful in providing "color" to our discussions of party conflict, but add nothing to the explanation of political and policy outcomes on Capitol Hill. The real explanation of policy outcomes in this view is the polarization over policy between the major parties, as measured by roll-call votes in Congress, with high polarization undermining policy productivity. Uncivil behavior is simply a momentary side-effect and gauge of such conflict, it is asserted, not an independent factor with consequences of its own.

There is, however, an alternative perspective. Perhaps uncivil breaches of decorum arise for a wide variety of reasons, with high levels of polarized conflict between the two major parties being only one basis for the generation of uncivil behavior. Moreover, once they occur, perhaps uncivil acts take on "a life of their own." In doing so, they may spark discussion of issues that were previously unmentionable, pushing the legislative process forward. Or, at the opposite extreme, they may generate such hard feelings among individuals and groups involved that no fruitful discussion of policy issues can occur at all, even in situations where grounds appear to exist for dialogue and compromise.

In politics as in private life, in other words, incivility may affect human deliberations and decision-making in very special, complicated, context-specific, and consequential ways. Even when such acts are not of such severity and visibility as the caning of Sumner or the character assassinations of McCarthy, they can shake up the daily legislative grind on Capitol Hill in ways that have significant consequences for the fate of critically important legislation. Seen in this manner, incivility could be conceptualized as a separate kind of conflict, distinct from partisan polarization and critically important to an accurate understanding of congressional decision-making.

This chapter seeks to explore this latter possibility. It proposes that we take incivility on Capitol Hill seriously as a political phenomenon, capable of having real and measurable consequences for congressional policymaking. The chapter opens in part one by discussing in greater depth why and how incivility can play a significant role on the Hill. This discussion introduces a series of theoretical arguments about the distinctive ways incivility might matter across polarized and depolarized Congresses. Part two presents strategies of theory-testing, proposing ways to measure incivility and also ways to test its influence on congressional policymaking. Part three presents initial statistical analysis that examine when and how incivility can matter in enactment of major landmark legislation.

PART ONE: UNDERSTANDING HOW AND WHY INCIVILITY MATTERS

DEVELOPING AN EXPLANATORY THEORY

In making the case for incivility as a separate form of conflict distinct from roll-call party polarization, we start by noting that roll-call votes capture conflict among legislators on those policy issues that party and committee leaders are willing to bring to the floor of a chamber. As a result, roll-call polarization can miss some of the most egregious policy conflicts within, between, or across parties, conflicts whose existence can have substantial consequences for the willingness of members to work together on those issues that do come to the floor. Thus in the 1990s, Republican Party leaders often sought to keep votes on abortion or gay rights away from the House floor, because they could create animosities within their conference or coalition supporters (Oldmixon 2005), just as Democratic leaders in the 1940s and 1950s sought to avoid votes on civil rights legislation (Thurber 2004; 530).

In contrast to roll-call behavior, uncivil breaches in decorum can occur on any issue and in public or private settings on the Hill far from the floor of a chamber, as well as on the floor. Thus, committee and party leaders are less able to control or regulate their occurrence. This fact provides uncivil behavior substantial capacity to shape policymaking in ways quite separate from traditional roll call voting.

Seeing Incivility as a Separate Form of Conflict

Because leaders are less able to control the occurrence of uncivil behavior, such action can provide members with autonomous ways to seek to influence policy debate on the Hill. Thus by engaging in breaches of decorum, members can highlight how serious their concerns are about certain issues, perhaps thereby bringing attention to policy issues leaders would prefer to ignore. Alternatively, members opposed to legislation may act in uncivil ways precisely to create interpersonal animosities that will limit the capacity of Congress to act on certain policy issues. Seen in these varied ways, uncivil behavior can be calculated and tactical, related to policy issues or to other political concerns such as leadership races.

Additionally, uncivil breaches may result from and highlight personal conflicts among members. Such personal conflicts can occur because specific members simply do not like each other. They can also occur because an individual or individuals have difficult personalities, drinking problems, physical or emotional problems, class, gender, ethnic/racial or other prejudices, limited socialization into professional life and norms of public decorum, and the like. Uncivil behavior can occur as well because legislative politics is a difficult and tedious enterprise in which almost any human being can at times experience deep frustrations that pour forth in spontaneous uncivil statements or behavior. In conditions in which all of these various problems are present more or less simultaneously, personal battles can sabotage healthy political debate of important issues owing to a blanket inability of colleagues in the congressional workplace to get along with one another.

With their occurrence, whether intended or spontaneous, uncivil actions can affect the operations of a legislature just as they can affect other human enterprises. In particular, from the perspective of the research we present, uncivil acts can affect the willingness of members to talk about policy problems and negotiate their resolution.

At times, particularly in periods when leaders are imposing strong constraining norms on members that inhibit their discussion of a nation's policy problems, uncivil acts that highlight such policy problems may serve to bring them to public attention. Aroused public concern may then foster open discussion within Congress, perhaps with time leading to legislative action. In other words, incivility may not always be a negative thing, from the perspective of policy productivity, but in fact may help bring neglected issues to the fore and garner supportive attention to them that forces the legislature to respond. Moreover, such positive effects could come even if the individual or individuals engaged in them had acted spontaneously out of real frustration and anger over efforts to silence discussion, or even as a result of personality disorders, rather than through careful, premeditated, and calculated intent.

At other times, particularly in periods when intense, public and polarized differences on issues already exist, adding uncivil behavior into the mix may upend any opportunity that might otherwise exist to break deadlock and move the Congress forward toward issue resolution. Such disruptive behavior as we have noted may be calculated, designed to sabotage compromise and policy enactment. However, such action can have similar effects even if it is not calculated. In times of great polarization, members' strong personal feelings and tension may get the best of them and lead them to strike out at one another, even when they may be committed to finding a solution to policy deadlock, inadvertently creating animosities that undercut negotiation and compromise. This is one of the reason leaders can give so much attention to instilling norms of civility in members in periods of high polarization, and also try to avoid roll-call votes in the evening period in order to avoid the possibility that exhaustion and drinking among members may foster spontaneous and destructive explosions.

Seen in these ways, uncivil member behavior is a phenomenon that is conceptually distinct from—though at times overlapping with—partisan battles over the substance of competing public policies. In embracing this view, we differ from contemporary scholars such as Sinclair or Uslaner, who tend to see incivility as a direct product of high levels of partisan difference or party polarization (Sinclair 2000; Uslaner 2000). Instead, we will argue that incivility—in various guises—can influence policy productivity in Congress in ways that are distinct from party polarization while occurring in interplay with varying levels of party system polarization. Moreover, as suggested above, it is possible that uncivil breaches of decorum could aid policy productivity under some partisan conditions, focusing attention on neglected or taboo topics; however, it could undermine productivity under other partisan conditions by upending efforts at policy compromise. Attention to incivility could aid statistical explanation of congressional policymaking in ways that move us beyond the causal models currently prevalent in the literature, which stress party polarization as the sole dimension of conflict influencing productivity (Coleman 1997; Binder 1999; 2003; Groeling and Kernell 2000).

The challenge in studying incivility in Congress comes in developing a conceptual approach to seeing and studying its effects that (1) treats incivility as a phenomenon distinct from high polarized party conflict but (2) is sensitive to the ways in which incivility interplays with the varying partisan contexts of conflict in Congress. In addressing this challenge, we propose a simple starting point.

CONCEPTUALIZING THE INTERPLAY BETWEEN PARTY SYSTEM POLARIZATION AND MEMBER INCIVILITY

We propose that the discussion of and arguments about incivility should be divided according to the depolarized or polarized context of Congress. To aid the reader in understanding our argument, we ask that you see Congresses as spread out across time on a continuum from low or depolarized interparty conflict on roll-call votes to high or polarized interparty conflict on roll-call votes. At the center of this continuum, as illustrated in figure 4.1, we can imagine an analytical tipping point—a "T" point—where Congresses move away from more depolarized settings to more polarized ones. Those Congresses to the left of this point we will treat as depolarized and those to the right we will treat as polarized. The relationship between incivility and policy productivity in the two different contexts, we argue, differs in significant and consequential ways.

Incivility in Depolarized Congresses: In the discussion above, we have noted that there are times when norms of silence suppress debate and action, so that breaking them aids productivity. Such behavior is likely to occur often and consequentially, we suggest, in depolarized Congresses on the left of figure 4.1.Moreover, we propose, *it is moments of uncivil breaches of decorum within parties during depolarized periods that are most important in aiding policy productivity*.

As a general rule, periods of low conflict between political parties—depolarized periods—tend to occur, at least in part, because there are a number of serious issues that divide each party internally—particularly the majority party—and that the leaders seek to avoid discussing, lest such issues tear apart the coalitions that underlie their party (Zelizer 2004, 42–46; Cox and McCubbins 1993, 271). In such settings, as witnessed in leadership behavior within the Democratic Party during its dominance of the textbook era of congressional politics from the late 1930s into the 1970s, party and committee leaders seek to impose norms of silence on their party members that constrain them from raising such divisive issues in Congress or introducing controversial legislation that addresses them. Such norms can be imposed even if a large plurality or majority of members within the party is in agreement on such divisive issues, owing to the consequences such discussion could have for the party. Civil rights is one obvious example, from the textbook era, but so too are such issues as federal aid to education. The latter raised concerns about whether or not such aid should go to parochial schools, a prospect that would have divided Democrats in that period. The immediate result was a failure of the party to bring such legislation to a vote, with the House Rules Committee and Senate cloture rule playing a critical role in this delay.

The broad result of constrained conflict during depolarized periods can be the abdication by parties and leaders of their normal roles in fostering debate on the major policy issues of the day and in addressing the issues through appropriate legislation. The great concern in such situations then is how best to move the parties forward and provide policy leadership to the nation in the face of such passivity. This was certainly a critical issue in the 1940s and 1950s. There was broad agreement in the scholarly community of the period that "responsible parties" were needed that took seriously their policy roles. In doing so, they would provide point/counterpoint debates in order to clarify alternative left/right perspectives on issue resolution and then would engage in negotiation and compromise to enact acceptable policies and move the country forward (Beck and Sorauf 1988, 426–454). But how does one jump-start the parties into action in light of the constraining norms of such an era?

One way forward toward increased party attention to pressing policy problems in such depolarized periods can be the willingness of activist members to break the constraining norms dominant in Congress at the time, speaking out on issues and even doing so quite forcefully from the perspectives of such norms. Sometimes this can mean that activist members themselves use inflammatory language breaking civil norms of decorum; other times it can mean that their actions in breaking the silence on issues such as civil rights, while stated in mild language, serve to enrage their opponents who then cross lines of civility in denouncing the activists. Either way, enhanced and public conflict by members of Congress on neglected policy issues can rally citizen support that pressures leaders to allow debate and policymaking to go forward on such topics (Zelizer 2004, 47–62).

Seen in this manner, a willingness to challenge norms of silence during a depolarized era, even doing so in ways that generate uncivil breaches decorum, can be a way to garner attention to neglected policy areas and push congressional parties to act in more responsible ways, addressing critical policy issues of the day. Moreover, because the norms of silence are generally imposed by party and committee leaders on their own party members, particularly within the majority party, the most effective breaches of decorum in a depolarized era will involve intraparty incivilities more than interparty incivilities. It is through intraparty assertiveness, which includes a willingness to engage in or elicit uncivil breaches in prevailing norms of decorum, that members of a party challenge the silence imposed on them with respect to explosive policy problems. In doing so, they raise issues to public awareness that then may activate support from the party's national electoral base, forcing leaders to move toward debate and action even when a minority in the party opposes such action. As political parties address issues that have fostered norms of silence within Congress, they open up the possibility for Congress to then debate a broad range of other issues that have lain dormant during the period of constrained civility and "silence." This debate then allows the natural conflicts over policy between the leftist and rightist parties to emergence, facilitating the rise of "responsible parties" and a move away from low conflict and toward more moderate interparty conflict in roll-call votes in Congress.

In depolarized periods, then, we expect the emergence of incivility to generate increases both in polarization between the political parties and in policy productivity by Congress. In particular, we expect intraparty incivility to generate increases in productivity by challenging and ultimately sweeping away constraints on debate in ways that enhance the ability of parties to address a wide range of issues. In this sense, we can think of incivility, particularly intraparty incivility, as jarring the system of silence loose and fostering policy deliberation across the array of issues that have been suppressed by prevailing norms. In the process, one party then can begin to tilt in one direction on issues and another in the other direction, creating more overt interparty conflict. As Congress then moves from low conflict between parties on policy issues to moderate levels of conflict, leaders of the majority party can push forward legislation the majority of its members support and the leaders of the minority will organize the loyal opposition to challenge the majority. With these developments, extensive policy debate can occur. In the moderate levels of conflict that then emerge, where the two parties are relatively close to one another ideologically, the two parties become "responsible" actors in legislative policymaking.

Thinking in statistical terms, incivility in depolarized periods should be positively related to policy productivity, rather than negatively related. This positive association should be particularly evident with respect to intraparty incivility. In addition, the interparty polarization that incivility can help generate in depolarized eras could also be positively associated with policy productivity. In other words, as intraparty conflict helps each party address internal policy differences on taboo topics that leaders are trying to avoid through the use of highly constraining norms, the two parties should begin to engage in more overt left/right conflict between them on a vast array of policy matters. The consequent emergence of responsible and moderately polarized parties should aid congressional consideration of long-neglected policy issues and lead to successful mediation of interparty differences on the issues.

In other words, as Congresses in the depolarized side of figure 4.1 move from the far left of the continuum toward the middle, growing interparty conflict should produce enhanced levels of productivity in Congress. Both the growth in interparty conflict and the enhanced levels of productivity will have been activated by intraparty conflicts, including uncivil breaches in the norms of decorum dominant at the time, thereby freeing Congress to engage in interparty contestation over policy.

Incivility in Polarized Congresses: In contrast to depolarized politics, there are times when Congress faces policy deadlock not because the parties are internally divided and unable to address policy issues but because they are so unified internally in opposition to each other that it becomes difficult to find ways to marshal viable and sustainable policy majorities across the House and Senate. *In such polarized settings, the emergence of significant incivilities between members of the two parties is likely to exacerbate interparty animosities and misunderstandings so that the parties cannot cooperate even on procedural issues, insuring policy deadlock.* This pattern of behavior is most prevalent and consequential in the polarized settings as shown on the right-hand side of figure 4.1.

Periods of high roll-call polarization between the two parties comes when they are in internal agreement on salient policy issues but insubstantial disagreement with each other (Rohde 1991; Poole and Rosenthal 1997; Theriault 2008). In other words, the two parties are experiencing great intraparty cohesion on issues but are far apart from each other in ideological terms on the issues. The members of each party in such periods will generally be free to speak their mind, with limited norms within their parties constraining them, and will be encouraged to take part in debates with the opposition. In such settings, as witnessed in the late nineteenth and early twentieth centuries and again in the last two decades or so, almost any kind of uncivil behavior between members of the two parties may produce tensions and animosities that can harm the building of legislative majorities and enactment of legislation. This is particularly the case when the two parties are so close in size that alienating just a few members in the opposite party can derail the building of a viable majority on critical procedural votes or policy enactment.

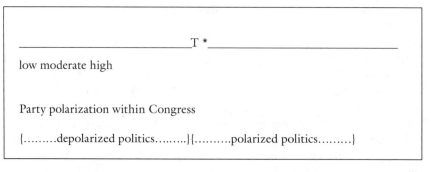

Figure 4.1 Party Polarization and the Differentiation between the Depolarized and Polarized Spectrums of Conflict.

*T designates the critical tipping point at which the dominant style of policy conflict shifts from intraparty difference to inter-party difference.

In such periods of polarized politics, moreover, it can be uncivil hostilities between members of the two parties that lead to increased interparty polarization, rather than growing polarization leading to increased incivilities. The one hundredth and one hundred and first Congresses, coming in the late 1980s, illustrate our point. When we look at "party votes," or the percentage of roll-call votes in a Congress where 90 percent of one party votes in opposition to 90 percent of the opposing party (Lowell 1902), the latter Congress (1989–90) witnessed a 20 percent decline in conflict in the Senate and a more than 35 percent decline in the House of Representatives. In other words, interparty polarization appeared to decline from the one hundredth to the one hundred and first Congress. On the other hand, the one hundred and first Congress witnessed a considerable increase in personal clashes between the two parties. This increase came as Newt Gingrich (R-GA) led Republicans in a no-holds-barred struggle to topple House Speaker Jim Wright (D-TX) from power, doing so to undermine the hold of Democrats on control of the House of Representations. Simultaneously, anger and acrimony in the Senate over the nomination of former Texas Senator John Tower to become Secretary of Defense tried the patience of previously collegial colleagues.

The evidence from the late 1980s suggests that incivility was spiking precisely at a point when partisan roll-call conflict was declining somewhat. This period of incivility and upheaval in the late 1980s then laid the foundations for the "take no prisoners" strategy Gingrich brought to his growing leadership role within the party during the early 1990s. The result was the Republican Revolution of 1994, the great polarization it brought to Congress thereafter, and the associated gridlock that enveloped Congress (Zelizer 2004, 233–262). The willingness of members to engage in boisterous and uncivil interparty conflict in the late 1980s was arguably a decisive development leading to subsequent party polarization. Thereafter followed a decade and a half of policy gridlock during which major policy issues festered unaddressed in the nation, including such vital concerns as immigration policy.

At issue in polarized periods is how to offset highly destructive consequences polarized conflict can have for policy productivity, and whether increases in civility might be an answer. In this regard, one can look at the one hundred and seventh Congress and the momentary regeneration of collegiality and civility that came in the aftermath of the terrorist attacks of September 11, 2001. Partisan conflict measured by roll-call behavior actually increased in the House (party votes in the House increased from 16.5 percent of all votes in the one hundred and sixth to 17.5 percent in the one hundred and seventh) and remained high by historical standards in the Senate. The increase suggests more party polarization. However, media accounts of the legislative process in the one hundred and seventh notes that members were more likely to get along in the aftermath of the foreign threat. Such signature achievements as No Child Left Behind and the enactment of the Bush Tax Cuts that came in the period following 9/11 and amid increased incivility on the Hill, even though polarization remained high.

Such historical examples suggest that increased incivility in polarized eras can increase roll-call polarization and reinforce gridlock, whereas the emergence of civility amid polarized party conflict can lessen animosities and enhance cooperation and productivity. In particular, it is interparty civility that would seem to aid cooperation and policymaking; in contrast, interparty incivilities are likely to create animosities across parties that harm interparty cooperation.

On the flip side, it is possible that intraparty incivility in such periods—as in conflict on the distribution of resources and over leadership positions and power within each party—may break down party cohesion and lead dissidents within parties to reach out to members of the other party in ways that might actually aid policy productivity. The alliance between Progressive Republicans and Democrats during the highly polarized 1909–1910 period in the House of Representatives would seem to exemplify such a development. This alliance involved extended intraparty animosities within the House Republican conference. Out of these conflicts came the upending of the speakership of "Czar" Joseph Cannon and increased policy activism in the subsequent decade in Congress. In other words, as in depolarized periods, it is possible that uncivil intraparty conflict can aid policy productivity in polarized periods. It can do so by jarring internal party "dictatorship" apart in ways that foster growing interparty cooperation, the moderation of polarized conflict, and the increased policy productivity that can result from cooperation and moderation.

Thinking in statistical terms, incivility in polarized periods should have complex and potentially quite consequential roles in shaping interparty conflict and policy productivity. Increased interparty incivility should serve both to increase roll-call polarization between the parties and decrease policy productivity. In the process, it helps to foster and enhance a negative relationship between increased polarization and policy productivity. Intraparty incivility, in contrast, could lead potentially to decreased polarization and increased productivity.

PART TWO: LOOKING FOR EVIDENCE TO TEST THE THEORY

MEASURING AND CHARTING INCIVILITY

To explore the utility of our theoretical arguments, our strategy in this chapter will be to look at the simple statistical relationships between member incivility, party polarization, and landmark legislation. The most difficult task we have confronted in this effort has been to find a systematic and replicable way to measure the occurrence of uncivil behavior by members, Congress by Congress, a topic largely ignored by students of Congress, at least in terms of the direct measurement of incivility. Additionally, we need a strategy for separating out polarized and depolarized Congresses and for measuring the policy productivity of Congresses.

Measuring Incivility, 1891–2012

Our strategy for measuring incivility is a simple, if time consuming, one. As noted at the outset, newspapers have published articles about uncivil behavior in Congress throughout American history, providing the fodder for the colorful stories about legislators and legislative policymaking that proliferate in books on Congress. We propose that newspaper coverage of highly visible acts of incivility also provides a direct way to measure the salient acts of uncivil behavior that characterize a Congress, just as newspaper coverage can be used to gauge landmark or salient laws addressed by Congress. In the past, it has been a daunting and ultimately impossible task to find and read all such articles on incivility published by a newspaper—particularly when one is seeking to measure the level and type of incivilities occurring within polarized and depolarized Congresses across a century in time. Today, however, with the advent of electronic search engines, it is possible to find such articles through word searches of a newspaper. By reading and coding them, we can turn articles about uncivil acts by members of Congress into data about the level and character of incivilities occurring within specific Congresses and thus across Congresses.

Specifically, we gauge the level of member incivility Congress by Congress according to the percentage of articles published on Congress by the *New York Times* and the *Washington Post* that discuss incidents of incivility or the breaking of civility norms occurring on Capitol Hill when Congress is in session. We assume in doing so that a larger number of articles devoted to incivility indicate greater uncivil conflict in a Congress—taking into account the overall level of coverage the *Times* and *Post* devote to articles on the Congress year by year. To find such articles, we rely on the search engine provided by *Pro Quest* that has historical online archives for both newspapers. Our initial search used the terms "Congress," "House of Representatives," and "Senate" in the full text with any of the following terms: "rancor," "comity," "civility," "incivility," "courteous," "courtesy," "discourteous," "discourtesy," "trust and anger," "discord," and "collegiality"; also, in the full text. A second search specified that "Congress," "House," or "Senate" had to appear in the title and that any of the following terms needed to be in the full text: "personalities," "grudge," "raucous," "insolence," "contempt," "amity," "lack of good will," "impertinence," "brash," "audacious," "hotheaded," "heated," "disrespect," "lack of respect," and "discordant."

In the time period we report on here (1891–2012), there were 459 *New York Times* articles and 367 *Washington Post* articles that mention incivility in the US legislative process.

We use only articles that call attention to these behaviors when the legislators are acting in their official capacity as members of the contemporaneous Congress in the nation's capital. We do not count stories about incivilities by members when they served in an earlier Congress, incivilities that occur while they are visiting their districts, or incivilities in election campaigns.

The articles are further broken down and it is determined that 207 *Times* articles (45 percent) and 181 *Post* articles (49 percent) deal with conflict between individuals from different political parties. Correspondingly, we find 141 *Times* articles (31 percent) and 105 *Post* articles (29 percent) deal with norm-breaking incivilities involving members of the same political party. Last, 192 *Times* articles and 128 *Post* articles dealt with hostility by a single individual or made mention of incivility in Congress as a whole, without any partisan context being provided in the article. When an article made a mention of multiple conflicts and the partisan character of the conflict differed, these were counted in multiple categories. Hence, summing the total articles by partisan context (including *no partisan context*), one obtains a value of 540 for the *Times* and 414 for the *Post*. In the *Times*, the 540 mentions of uncivil conflict were found in 459 articles and in the *Post* the 414 mentions of uncivil conflict were found in 367 articles.[1] In an attempt to provide a "best" single measure of overall incivility, interparty incivility, and intraparty incivility, we use an average score for each, summing the number of articles on the specific form of incivility from the two newspapers and taking the average.

Figure 4.2 presents the pattern of variation in member incivility that characterizes Congress from 1891 to 2012, together with the contrasting pattern of variation in party polarization. Party polarization is defined as the absolute value of the difference in median first Dimension DW-NOMINATE scores for the first and second largest political parties (which is always Democrats and Republicans for the time period analyzed). Both data series have been standardized so that they can be displayed in a sensible manner in figure 4.2. The figure indicates that Congress has varied across time quite extensively in the level of member incivility that characterized it. Incivility and polarization are significantly correlated ($r = 0.53$, $p < 0.001$) and this is obvious by high levels of both types of conflict in the early and late years of the time series.

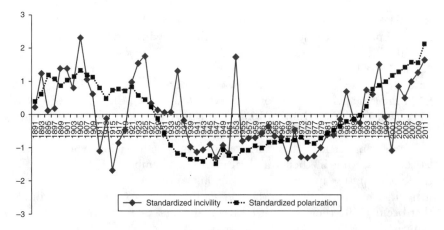

Figure 4.2   Incivility and Party Polarization over Time: $r = 0.58$, $p < 0.001$.

We are not surprised by this, but we are also confident that the two types of conflict are not one and the same. The distinctive character of incivility is seen, for example, in the way it spikes up even in when polarization is low, and its decline even amid high polarization.

Charting Incivility among Polarized and Depolarized Congresses. Looking across time in figure 4.2 gives us a general sense of the interplay between all acts of incivility and party polarization. Yet we have argued in part I that to truly understand how incivility interacts with party polarization we must differentiate between the manner in which incivility affects policy productivity in depolarized Congresses as opposed to polarized ones. This requires a strategy for separating out depolarized and polarized settings. In this endeavor, we rely on the work of David Rohde (1991) who suggests that the logic of politics in the House of Representatives shifted subtly but rapidly during the 1980s, following incremental shifts over the previous several decades. The easiest way to think of the shift from depolarized to polarized Congresses in the modern era, in Rohde's terms, is to see it as move from the textbook-era of Congress, which was characterized by committee government, to a period of conditional party government characterized by some substantial party polarization and party government. While the shift in logic is evident throughout the 1980s, the breakpoint appears to come with the Wright Speakership in the one hundredth Congress. With this Speakership, the thrust toward party government and party responsibility becomes the centerpiece of congressional politics, a legitimate goal as well as a byproduct of incremental changes in polarization and member behavior.

For analytic purposes in theory testing, we use the absolute value of the difference of the two-party aggregate DW-NOMINATE score during the Wright Speakership (one hundredth Congress) to estimate the tipping point at which we divide Congresses into depolarized and polarized groups. This value equals 0.64 and we treat all Congresses below this as depolarized (seventy-first–one hundredth; $n = 30$) and all Congresses at or above 0.64 on the scale (fifty-second–seventieth and one hundred and first–one hundred and twelfth; $n = 32$)as polarized.[2] In the analysis that follows, we will attempt to gauge the effect of incivility on landmark legislative achievements, Congress by Congress. Because the measure of legislative productivity we employ only runs through the one hundred and third Congress, the sample size will be limited to 52 Congresses (30 depolarized and 22 polarized Congresses).

To explore incivility within depolarized and polarized contexts, we produce figures 4.2 and 4.3. Figure 4.2 contrasts the percentage of articles focused on the different forms of incivility by partisan context in polarized and depolarized periods. It demonstrates that interparty incivilities are higher in the polarized Congresses and lower when Congress is depolarized. In other words, uncivil breaches are particularly prone to occur between members of the different parties when the parties are experiencing polarized conflict between one another. Uncivil breaches of decorum are more likely to occur within parties in periods when conflict between the two parties is low and diversity in ideological perspective is pronounced within them.

These findings have considerable face validity and bolster our confidence in the measurement strategies employed. At the same time, the existence of all varieties of incivility in all partisan settings makes clear that incivility and party polarization are distinct phenomena, so that intraparty incivility occurs amid polarization and interparty incivility occurs amid depolarization. If during charged polarized periods there are still reports of intraparty uncivil conflict the normal conceptions scholars have held about conflict in Congress, and polarized political parties in general, begins to break down.

We produce figure 4.3 to provide additional context to incivilities in the legislative process. When tracing uncivil encounters, we learn that the era of depolarized Congresses, often referred to as a period of committee government, is more likely to witness personal battles within committee settings. In the depolarized era, a full 33 percent of all articles discussing incivilities occur during committee deliberations when compared to 21 percent of articles in polarized Congresses. Chamber rules, such as debate in the Senate over filibuster reform, are what instigate 18 percent of the personal fights mentioned in newspaper reports in depolarized Congresses and only 13 percent in polarized Congresses. Both the committee and chamber rule changes are statistically significant. We can also note, in figure 4.3, that there is slightly higher incivility born out of leadership battles in the polarized Congresses, although the difference does not reach standard levels of statistical significance. Last, we examine incivilities born of nomination battles.[3] In both polarized and depolarized Congresses, incivilities that begin as a debate over judicial and cabinet appointments have always been about 6 percent of news reports.

We provide this brief look into the context of reported incivilities primarily as a means of helping the reader better understand what our measurement

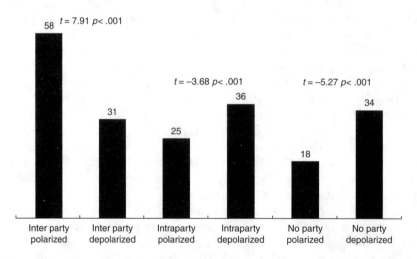

Figure 4.3 Percent of Articles on Incivilities by Partisan Context: Different Polarization Scenarios. *Note*: t-Statistics represent a difference in means test for the two polarization scenarios; *p*-values represent a two-tailed test.

strategy is capturing.[4] However, the central issue is whether incivility is related to policy productivity in the ways we have hypothesized.

Measuring Landmark Legislation. To test our hypotheses, we need a way to measure landmark legislation across the time period of our study. We are fortunate to have available excellent studies of landmark or salient legislation to learn from, build on, and utilize in assessing our own measure (Mayhew 1991; Binder 2003; Heitschusen and Young 2006; Clinton and Lapinski 2006; 2007). In our case, we envision landmark laws as those enacted statutes that have withstood the test of time as significant efforts by Congress to address issues of national import, thereby receiving attention in scholarly works across the years and decades following the Congress in which they were enacted. This perspective leads us to engage in content analysis of 15 relevant and reputable scholarly works that cover the time period under study (1891–1994) but were published following the last Congress (the one hundred and third) in that period. This strategy is analogous to David Mayhew's effort to identify significant actions in the public sphere by individual members of Congress by relying on content analysis of book-length works on Congress and American history (Mayhew 2000).

To estimate landmark laws, we draw, specifically, on seven histories of Congress, the presidents, or the United States and six encyclopedias on the same topics, and then add two encyclopedias on American public policy.[5] We draw on multiple and varied sources to provide a robust check on the landmark status of each law. The public availability of the sources aids replication of our analysis. The histories are read page by page and all new *laws* are noted. Only the indexes are consulted with the encyclopedias; again, each new law is noted. All entries in this database have been independently confirmed via multiple listings in the varied sources, or by searching *Statues at Large* to ensure that the entry represents an enacted law. There are no treaties or independent executive branch actions included in the database.[6] There are 1,649 public laws or joint resolutions mentioned in the 15 sources consulted for the relevant time period, with 709 mentioned only once. Only the Civil Rights Act of 1964 is mentioned in all 15 sources.[7]

Utilizing this data, we code all laws according to the number of references that mention them, in ways described in detail elsewhere (Dodd and Schraufnagel 2012). Those laws mentioned in four or more sources are the ones we refer to as Landmark Laws, so long as at least one of them was in a Congress-specific publication. We require that at least one Congress-specific source mentions a law to ensure that it has support from scholars of the institution. We require four total sources to ensure that a law has broad visibility as a significant enactment. There are 295 landmark laws.

During the time period we study, the two most productive Congresses are the seventy-third, which is President Franklin Roosevelt's first "New Deal" Congress (1933–1935), and the eighty-ninth, which is President Lyndon Johnson's Great Society Congress (1965–1966).Using our measurement strategy, each Congress enacted 17 pieces of landmark legislation. Looking beyond these two Congresses, both widely recognized as historic in nature, the distribution of Congresses with high and low landmark productivity is spread broadly across the 11 decades under study here: Congresses with nine or more landmark laws range across the presidencies of Wilson, Franklin Roosevelt, Lyndon Johnson, Nixon, and Carter. Congresses with three or fewer landmark laws range across the presidencies of Harrison, Cleveland, McKinley, Theodore Roosevelt, Coolidge, Hoover, Franklin Roosevelt, Eisenhower, Reagan, and George H. W. Bush.

Part Three: Exploring the Evidence at Hand

Initial Research Findings and Concluding Remarks

In arguing that incivility is a phenomenon distinct from high party polarization in Congress, we propose that one must distinguish both between the polarized or depolarized character of a Congress and between the types of incivility one is assessing. We expect that interparty incivility matters most in polarized Congresses, depressing landmark productivity, but that it is intraparty incivility that matters in depolarized Congresses, where it enhances productivity. The question is whether there is evidence at hand supporting this argument in ways that could induce students of Congress to think more carefully about the role incivility plays in Congress, leading to more extensive and systematic study of it. We believe there is. To underscore our point in clear, simple, and easily comprehensible ways, we focus here on the bivariate relationship between the forms of incivility and landmark productivity in polarized versus depolarized settings.

Table 4.1 presents our bivariate correlations. Looking first at the top portion of the table focused on Polarized Congresses, the largest correlation is between interparty incivility and landmark productivity and, as expected, it is negative. It also approaches statistical significance, which is

Table 4.1 Bivariate Correlations between Three Forms of Incivility and Landmark Productivity in Polarized versus Depolarized Congresses, 1891–1994

	Landmark Productivity	n-Congresses
Polarized Congresses		
All incivilities	$r = -0.27; p < 0.24$	22
Interparty incivilities	$r = -0.34; p < 0.13$	22
Intraparty incivilities	$r = -0.09; p < 0.69$	22
Depolarized Congresses		
All incivilities	$r = 0.21; p < 0.28$	30
Interparty incivilities	$r = -.23; p < 0.23$	30
Intraparty incivilities	$r = 0.41; p < 0.03$	30

noteworthy in light of the small number of polarized Congresses in the study ($n = 22$). The correlations with landmark productivity for all incivility (i.e., all acts of incivility) and for intraparty incivility are lower and also negative among polarized Congresses. These finding suggest that interparty incivility is the form of incivility most relevant for the enactment of landmark legislation in polarized settings and that it does in fact depress the landmark productivity.

In contrast, looking at the bottom portion of the table focused on Depolarized Congresses, we see that the largest correlation is between intraparty incivility and landmark productivity and, as we have proposed, it is in fact positive. We note that it is also statistically significant ($p < 0.03$; two-tailed test), in a sample that includes 30 depolarized Congresses. The correlation with landmark productivity for all incivility is not only smaller but also positive. The correlation between interparty incivility and landmark productivity is smaller and negative. These findings suggest that intraparty incivility is the form of incivility most relevant for the enactment of landmark legislation in depolarized settings and that it does in face enhance landmark productivity.

We acknowledge, of course, that studies of the role of incivility must go well beyond the bivariate statistical analysis reported here, exploring how well our arguments withstand extensive multivariate analysis and advanced tests of statistical significance. We have pursued these avenues in other studies of our data (Dodd and Schraufnagel 2012) as well as in unpublished analysis. In such work, it appears that the most critical "conflict variable" shaping landmark productivity is the multiplicative interaction between party polarization and uncivil breaches in decorum—so long as one attends to the distinctive way in which this interaction works in depolarized and polarized settings. Additionally, unpublished work also indicates that one can generate high correlations between party polarization, interparty incivility, and landmark legislation across all Congresses if one is willing to ignore the ways in which extreme outlier Congresses drive such correlations. Moreover, such correlations are essentially irrelevant for the depolarized Congresses that constitute roughly half of all Congresses since the enactment of the Reed Rules in 1891. In our various statistical explorations, these Congresses always return positive correlations between intraparty incivility and productivity.

We believe strongly that the nuanced approach introduced here, which seeks to differentiate the role of incivility according to partisan context, holds the greatest long-term value in improving the depth, breadth, and long-term explanatory relevance of our understanding of the role incivility and legislative conflict play in Congress. In doing so, it yields a perspective on the role of incivility that makes considerable sense out of the history of Congress and landmark policy productivity over the past 120 years or so.

During the polarized period from the late nineteenth century to the early 1930s, and then starting again in the late 1980s, the struggle over landmark policies depended more on the outcomes of conflict between the two parties than on resolution of differences within them. During this period, when conflict during a Congress involved highly salient and uncivil breaches of decorum between members of opposite parties, those actions are associated with lower landmark productivity, relative to other polarized Congresses. During polarized periods, then, uncivil interparty breaches in decorum hurt productivity, perhaps by creating such deep animosities between members of the different parties that opportunities for compromise are greatly decreased.

We are currently living in such a period and thus naturally see issues of incivility and policy productivity, at least initially, through the lenses of our own time. The task of systematic analysis of Congress, however, is to look beyond the immediate moment and see what we can learn about the institution by studying it in a broader and more historically informed perspective. In doing so, we see the role of incivility in Congress in more complex and context-specific ways, with the logic of conflict in depolarized periods yielding a different perspective on the role of incivility in policy productivity.

In the depolarized period from the early 1930s to the late 1980s, the struggle over landmark policy activism depended more on resolving conflicts within the two major parties in Congress, particularly within the Democratic Party that dominated Congress in this period, than on struggles between the parties. When such intraparty conflict became so pronounced that it involved uncivil breaches of decorum by members of the same party, those actions were associated with higher landmark productivity, relative to other depolarized Congresses. Seen in this manner, uncivil intraparty breaches of decorum did not hurt productivity and appear to have enhanced it, perhaps by raising the public salience of long-neglected issues such as Civil Rights and forcing one or both parties to confront them.

Particularly when studying Congress amid the polarized conflict of the contemporary period, it is quite easy to imagine how incivility or the flouting of courtesy and reciprocity norms can poison the legislative environment and prompt policy stalemate. However, least we forget, history also tells us that the imposition of too much collegiality, thereby suppressing policy conflict through highly constraining norms of civility, can also corrupt the legislative process. Such heightened civility can unduly silence attention to major issues of an era in ways that allow them to fester and policy problems to mount. In such settings, the courage to challenge norms of silence and raise issues to the fore that leaders would prefer to ignore may be a necessary aspect of representative governance, even when such efforts involve or elicit uncivil behavior.

Uncivil breaches of decorum in depolarized periods may play a role within representative assemblies, particularly in depolarized settings, that is analogous to the role civil disobedience can play within society. Citizens use civil disobedience to raise to the fore long-festering and ignored social problems that "normal politics" is seeking to suppress. Analogously, forceful and even uncivil speech in Congress can raise to the fore policy problems that parties within the legislature seek to suppress (figure 4.4).

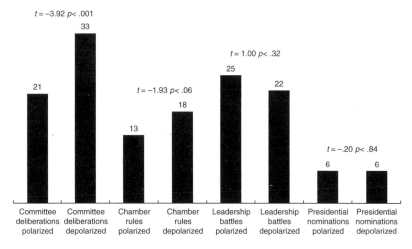

Figure 4.4 Percent of Articles on Incivilities by Topic: Different Polarization Scenarios.

Seen in this manner, reforms or institutional changes designed to foster civility between congressional parties in a polarized era should be undertaken in a careful, balanced, and reasoned manner. Improvement in civil relations between members of the different parties may well enhance policy productivity, as our data suggest. However, such efforts should be alert to the risks involved in embracing hasty and ill-conceived reforms. The ability of legislators to focus attention within their parties on vital and long neglected issues is an essential part of representative democracy, and can enhance policy productivity in depolarized periods, even when members do so in forceful ways that risk breaching civil norms of decorum within the parties. Reforms designed to enhance civility *between* parties should not impose new and restrictive norms of silence so severe and all-encompassing in nature that they inhibit the ability of members to initiate debate *within* their parties on the pressing policy problems of an era.

NOTES

1. We use newspaper coverage (mentions) to gauge "the level of incivility" rather than determining the precise number of acts of incivility that occur in a given Congress. Hence, included in the database are multiple mentions/articles that focus on a single incident, on the assumption that especially serious acts of incivility will generate multiple news stories. This, in effect, creates a weighting factor into our analysis that serves to provide a comparative estimate of the level of serious incivility that is occurring in each Congress. We do not give numerical weights to acts of incivility according to our personal judgments of their severity. Let us also note that when we move to our statistical analysis we control for changes in the coverage of Congress in newspapers by dividing the number of articles mentioning incidents of incivility by the number of articles published in the *New York Times* and *Washington Post* during a specific Congress that

contained the words "Congress" and "United States" and then multiply by 1,000. The resultant variable ranges from "0" in the sixty-fourth Congress (1915–1917) to 1.91 in the fiftieth Congress (1905–1907). We use the precise start and end date for each session of Congress when calculating the denominator.

2. We do not pretend this coding decision is beyond reproach, but significant time is spent testing alternative rules and our findings are not particularly sensitive to the coding decision.

3. There were incivilities reported late in the one hundred and twelfth Congress regarding President Barack Obama's possible nomination of Susan Rice to be Secretary of State, and these are counted in the one hundred and twelfth Congress total.

4. At this date, our analysis of leadership battles is incomplete because we have mixed both floor leadership and committee leadership battles in this category, which might explain the lack of statistical significance.

5. The list of sources is available from the authors upon request; all should be available in university libraries.

6. The vast majority of the entries are public laws; however, we also include joint resolutions that propose amendments to the Constitution. Admission of new states and declarations of war are also included if they are mentioned in the sources consulted.

7. An additional 12 pieces of legislation are mentioned in either 13 or 14 of the 15 sources.

REFERENCES

Beck, Paul Allen, and Frank J. Sorauf. 1988. *Party Politics in America*, 7th edition. New York: Harper Collins.

Binder, Sarah. 1999. "The Dynamics of Legislative Gridlock, 1947–1996." *American Political Science Review* 93(3): 519–536.

———. 2003. *Stalemate: Causes and Consequences of Legislative Gridlock, 1947–96*. Washington, DC: Brookings.

Clinton, Joshua, and John Lapinski. 2006. "Measuring Legislative Accomplishment, 1877-1994." *American Journal of Political Science* 50(1): 232–249.

———. 2007. "Measuring Significant Legislation, 1877–1948." In *Party, Process, and Political Change in Congress*, Volume 2, edited by David Brady and Mathew McCubbins. Palo Alto, CA: Stanford University Press.

Coleman, John J. 1997. "The Decline and Resurgence of Congressional Party Conflict."*Journal of Politics* 59(1):165–184.

Cooper, Joseph. 1970. *The Origins of the Standing Committees and Development of the Modern House*. Houston, TX: William Marsh Rice University Press.

Cox, Gary, and Mathew McCubbins. 1993. *Legislative Leviathan: Party Government in the House*. Berkeley, CA: University of California Press.

Dodd, Lawrence, and Richard Schott. 1979. *Congress and the Administrative State*. New York: John Wiley and Sons.

Dodd, Lawrence C., and Scot Schraufnagel. 2012. "Congress and the Polarity Paradox: Party Polarization, Member Incivility and Landmark Legislation, 1891001E1994." *Congress and the Presidency* 39(2): 109–132.

Groeling, Tim, and Samuel Kernel. 2000. "Congress, the President, and Party Competition via Network News." In *Polarized Politics*, edited by Jon Bond and Richard Fleischer. Washington, DC: CQ Press.

Heitschusen, Valerie, and Garry Young. 2006. "Macropolitics and Changes in the U.S. Code: Testing Competing Theories of Policy Production, 1874–1946." In *The Macropolitics of Congress*, edited by Scott Adler and John Lipinski. Princeton, NJ: Princeton University Press.

Lowell, A. Lawrence. 1902. "The Influence of Party upon Legislation in England and America." *Annual Report of the American Historical Association for 1901*, Washington, DC, 321–543.

Mayhew, David. 1991. *Divided We Govern*.New Haven, CT: Yale University Press.

———. 2000. *American's Congress*. New Haven, CT: Yale University Press.

Oldmixon, Elizabeth. 2005. *Uncompromising Positions: God, Sex and the U. S. House of Representatives*. Washington, DC: Georgetown University Press.

Poole, Keith T., and H. Howard Rosenthal. 1997. *Congress: A Political-Economic History of Roll Call Voting*. New York: Oxford University Press.

Rohde, David. 1991. *Parties and Leaders in the Postreform House*. Chicago, IL: University of Chicago Press.

Sinclair, Barbara. 2000. "Individualism, Partisanship, and Cooperation in the Senate." In *Esteemed Colleagues: Civility and Deliberation in the U. S. Senate*, edited by Burdette Loomis. Washington, DC: Brookings.

Theriault, Sean M. 2008. *Party Polarization in Congress*. Cambridge: Cambridge University Press.

Thurber, Timothy N. 2004. "The Second Reconstruction." In *The American Congress*, edited by Julian E. Zelizer. New York: Houghton Mifflin Company.

Uslaner, Eric M. 2000. "Is the Senate More Civil than the House?" In *Esteemed Colleagues: Civility and Deliberation in the U.S. Senate*, edited by Burdett A. Loomis. Washington, DC: Brookings Institution Press.

Zelizer, Julian. 2004. *On Capitol Hill: The Struggle to Reform Congress and Its Consequences, 1948–2000*. Cambridge: Cambridge University Press.

5

Let's Play Hardball

Congressional Partisanship in the Television Era

Douglas B. Harris

> Hardball is clean, aggressive Machiavellian politics. It is the discipline of gaining and holding power, useful to any profession or undertaking, but practiced most openly and unashamedly in the world of public affairs.
>
> Christopher Matthews, *Hardball: How Politics Is Played*

> Congressional elections are the ultimate in hardball politics. Members of Congress and those who want to join their ranks must compete for a limited number of positions, and there can be only one winner at the end of each campaign.
>
> Paul S. Herrnson, *Playing Hardball: Campaigning for the U.S. Congress*

The Machiavellian aim of "gaining and holding power" by winning a majority of legislative seats is a key aim, arguably the primary purpose, of legislative parties (Kolodny 1998). To be sure, legislative parties also play important roles in building legislative coalitions, passing policy, and organizing the chamber, but each of these legislative roles hinges on gaining or maintaining majority control. In this respect, contemporary parties fit well Anthony Downs' definition of a political party as "a team of men [and women] seeking to control the governing apparatus by gaining office in a duly constituted election" (1957, 25). Still, what it takes to win enough offices to control the legislature has changed significantly in the last half century, particularly as Congress became more polarized in the post-Reagan era.

Although congressional party polarization seems the norm, the degree of partisanship in Congress has varied greatly throughout congressional history. In the mid-twentieth century's "textbook Congress," for example, party outliers—southern Conservative Democrats and Rockefeller Republicans—were numerous, occupied important positions of influence, and frequently held sway in what were comparatively broad and internally divided congressional parties. Typically blurring partisan lines, cautious, pragmatic, and permissive "middlemen" legislative leaders such as Sam Rayburn (D-TX), Joe

Martin (R-MA), and John McCormack (D-MA) were personally popular and uniquely situated to reach out to all elements of their parties (as well as to the opposing party) to strike bargains for policy passage (Truman 1959; Cooper and Brady 1981).

If low levels of congressional partisanship and the decline of these internal House party organizations resulted from low levels of district-based partisanship outside of Congress (Cooper and Brady 1981), renewed district-based partisan polarization and a better regional and ideological "sorting" of liberals and conservatives into the Democratic and Republican Parties in the 1970s and 1980s served as the bases for increased prerogatives, activism, and overall influence of party organizations and leaders in the current era (Rohde 1991; Aldrich and Rohde 1997–1998; Sinclair 2006). No longer "middlemen," beginning in the 1980s and 1990s, House leaders were increasingly drawn from their parties' ideological extremes (Harris and Nelson 2008) and use their renewed resources to drive party agendas and sharpen interparty differences.

These contemporary congressional leaders were not only more partisan and ideological but they were more public and media oriented, too (Sinclair 1995; Harris 1998). Although "taciturn" Speakers Rayburn, Martin, and McCormack avoided the media limelight that was likely to endanger the bargains necessary for passing legislation, more recent leaders such as Tip O'Neill (D-MA), Newt Gingrich (R-GA), Nancy Pelosi (D-CA), and John Boehner (R-OH) were/are mainly ideological and "public Speakers" who seek out media attention to shape their parties' national "brand names" and publicize party positions on legislative issues in overall efforts to excite party activists and outside groups, thus deriving sources of party discipline from outside the chamber.

Although the congressional polarization story is frequently told, congressional leaders' media efforts *and the contributions of those efforts to polarization* have received considerably less attention. Drawing on both internal documents uncovered in House party leaders' archival collections and interviews with congressional staff,[1] this chapter examines the impact of congressional party messaging on polarization. First, I argue that party media strategies intentionally propel polarization enhancing extreme voices and leaving behind moderate party outliers. Second, I consider how the already difficult position of moderate members in Congress is made even more tenuous because of the rise of congressional party media strategies. That is, not only has the decline of moderates enhanced polarization but also, given the contemporary media landscape, that polarization, in turn, has further propelled the disappearance of moderate members.

POLARIZATION AND THE PARTY BRAND

Contemporary congressional leaders are *public congressional leaders* who are more media active and savvy than their predecessors in their efforts to develop and promote party images (the party "brand"), to use media to build legislative coalitions, and to connect their legislative efforts with their electoral strategizing. There are three primary elements of this public congressional leadership style:

1. Public congressional leaders seek an increased presence for themselves and their ideas in the mass media, appearing more frequently in the media, devoting more attention and resources to press outreach, and delivering more high-profile speeches.
2. Public congressional leaders and their attendant leadership organizations have become a clearinghouse of political information and resources that seeks to connect more deeply the legislative realm with public opinion and electoral politics.
3. Public congressional leaders work to promote and coordinate the media messages carried by rank and file members and other close political allies.

The institutional development of the public congressional leadership style is a relatively recent occurrence and is quite a departure from the past practices of "taciturn" leaders of the "textbook Congress." Although it had antecedents in the 1960s and 1970s, the public Speakership emerged in full form in 1981 as Speaker Tip O'Neill and other House Democratic leaders sought to revamp internal party operations to cope with and counter Ronald Reagan's successful "going public" strategies (Sinclair 1995; Harris 1998; 2005a).[2] In subsequent years, House leaders built upon these initial innovations and public congressional leadership became a routine and pervasive force in both legislative parties reaching a crescendo, of course, during the Gingrich Speakership but nevertheless persisting in important respects to present day.[3]

In their broadest efforts, public congressional leaders seek to influence press and public perceptions of the party's "image" or "brand name" for both legislative and electoral effect (Cox and McCubbins 1993). Legislative leaders increasingly adopt poll-tested party themes and named agendas—the "Contract with America," Dennis Hastert's "BEST Agenda," Richard Gephardt's "Families First" agenda, and Nancy Pelosi's "Six for '06"—as the basis of both their reelection messages and their policy agendas. Although these agendas sometimes are aimed at "taking the partisan edge off" as the electoral context might demand, internal party documents uncovered in archives reveal that Democratic and Republican leaders develop party images (including shaping the other party's image) often with the explicit intention of sharpening distinctions between the two parties and exciting party activists.

Framing Party Conflicts

The development of party agendas and the consequent efforts at image making are efforts to employ what political communications scholars call "conflict framing," wherein political elites seek to divide partisan "protagonists into 'us' and 'them'" (Neuman et al. 1992, 62, 64–66).[4] Determined to influence how the American press and public perceive each party and the differences between them, party communicators look to draw the lines of partisan difference in ways that impel independents and moderates to choose them over the opposition. For example, in a 1988 strategy session, Newt Gingrich outlined a strategy to use a series of legislative battles as a backdrop for redrawing images of and the lines between the two parties:

> We need to build a simple clear case which the news media and the voter finds true and compelling the longer it is studied. The following three themes meet that goal: 1) a humanitarian Republican Party . . . 2) there is a loony left; . . . [3] The U.S. House of Representatives has been stolen from the American people by an increasingly corrupt left wing machine."[5]

In this instance, defining the "loony left" and the "corrupt[ion]" of the Democratic "machine" was just as essential to Republican efforts to woo voters as was explaining how "humanitarian" and "solution-oriented" the House Republicans had become. To be sure, both parties engage in these efforts at conflict framing. As Democratic strategist Paul Begala, then-advisor to House Majority Leader Dick Gephardt, put it, "How do we re-draw the lines between Us and Them? That's the essence of message-making."[6]

Conflict frames challenge, if not preclude, coalition-building efforts to bridge partisan divides and to make cross-partisan or bipartisan coalitions. These "us versus them—which side are you on" rhetorical frames force members of Congress to choose sides and impose electoral penalties for members who seek to cross those divides to compromise. Moreover, these polarized characterizations of "us versus them" set the frame in which public relations battles regarding specific legislation are fought. Within this context, congressional leaders deploy issues—commonly referred to as "magnet" and "wedge" issues—designed either to attract independent and moderate support to one's own party base or to drive a "wedge" between centrist opinion and the opposition's party base.

As public congressional leadership strategies first took shape in the early 1980s, House leaders deployed "wedge issues" to polarize by casting aspersions on the opposition. For example, even as President Reagan successfully used media strategies to advance his budget and tax-cutting agenda in the ninety-seventh Congress, Speaker O'Neill and other House Democrats began using the mass media to frame legislative debates and policy outcomes so that negative public reactions to Reagan era budget cuts might harm House Republican members. Believing that Reagan's "Teflon" popularity insulated him from the negative fallout of his own policies, Democrats nevertheless thought they could force Republican House members to choose between party support and their constituencies back home. Pollsters and consultants told Democratic leaders "let's not be too smart by half. It's Republican economics, not Reaganomics which scare people. Reagan, personally, is more popular than the Republicans, so we should talk about Republican economic policies, rather than Reaganomics."[7] Two years later, continuing to believe that "Reagan's affable personality and easy manner serve[d] to mask public concern about the [Republicans'] elitist, party of privilege image," the . Democratic Congressional Campaign Committee (DCCC) aimed to attack Reagan's policies not so much in the hopes of "lower[ing] his personal popularity ratings" but to "increas[e] public concern about the undue influence of the wealthy and large corporations over the Republican party" and to tie less well-known and less personable congressional Republicans to that negative party image.[8] When O'Neill was asked about losing impending legislative battles, he revealed his intentions to gain in the electoral realm what he might lose legislatively; he said, "Wait till Middle America realizes what's happened with these budget cuts...Am I going to get some Republican scalps down the road? You bet I am" (Ajemian 1981, 17).

Minority party Republicans found mass media a powerful polarizing force, too. As leader of the Conservative Opportunity Society, Newt Gingrich sought to stoke the emergent partisanship by organizing one-minute and special orders speeches, carried on C-SPAN, to criticize the Democratic leadership. Describing House Republicans' early use of one-minute speeches in the late 1970s and early 1980s, a Democratic leadership adviser from the era said, "Bob Bauman, [Bob] Walker, and Gingrich...used [C-SPAN] really to polarize. A lot of polarization is due to the media and the way they used it." In a 1982 "Dear Republican Colleague" letter, Gingrich presented an analysis of Democrats' and Republicans' appearances on television talk shows in which he found that although Republican "talkers" were much more likely to speak favorably of their Democratic colleagues, but "Not one time," he explained, "did a Democrat praise or otherwise speak highly about a Republican." Exhorting his colleagues to stop accommodating majority party Democrats and to join the battle, Gingrich concluded, "The Democrats are being partisan about blame...[whereas] Republicans tend to be bipartisan about credit."[9]

As his influence increased in the 1980s and 1990s, Gingrich's "bomb-thrower" and blame attribution tactics aimed to take nearly every legislative opportunity to heighten congressional partisanship. For example, in the ninety-eighth Congress, Gingrich outlined his plans to try to use wedges to force vulnerable House Democrats to take difficult votes where they would have to choose between party loyalty and voter sentiment; his explicit aim was to set up key votes in the House "to maximize public understanding of our positions, public anger with the Democrats and the likelihood that the voters will defeat Democratic incumbents to punish them for voting with the national party and against the beliefs of the American people."[10]

These are but a few early instances of this new model of party leadership politics that would proliferate in subsequent years in which partisan polarization is not merely a consequence but the avowed aim of leaders' media efforts. Public congressional leaders aim to polarize by polishing their own brand, disparaging the opposition, and manipulating the policy content of the legislative agenda to win the favor of moderates and independents. These glimpses into strategy and intent are put into a more meaningful context by examining who carries the party media messages.

Who Carries the Message? Ideological Tilts in Congressional Communications

Although a great deal of public congressional leadership involves top party leaders seeking national press and media attention, the latest wave of party communications involves aggressive and formalized attempts to get individual members to carry party messages in their press releases and town hall meetings, back home to local and regional press, on the House floor, and when they appear on television. As one Republican communications aide put it, "Members have to be a critical, critical part of any message effort"; message success is determined by whether "it's something members talk about at home." Still, if this talking points-based communications strategy is essential to success, enlisting member support and participation is not easy and is best understood as a collective action problem for the legislative parties: collective party messages are more likely to get coverage to the extent that leaders can get as many members as possible "on message," but individual members have incentives to convey their own messages (or to engage in some other activity—legislative work, constituency casework, etc.—entirely) at the expense of the contributing to collective party efforts (Sellers 2000; Harris 2005b).

To encourage member participation in party media efforts, staff members in the top party leadership offices, especially the Democratic Caucus and the Republican Conference, offer numerous media services to party members that "subsidize" media activities on particular topics. With extensive press and communications staffs in party leadership offices, Democrats and Republicans alike regularly provide their members with talking points on salient issues as well as sample press releases and op-ed templates designed so that members' staff can "plug in [the] member's name" and "tailor it to your district." According to one Republican leadership communicator, these and other "member services" constitute a "heavy part" of what the Conference communications staff does. One staffer said, "Republican Policy Committee and the Republican Conference send talking points all the time . . . leadership was always good at making sure that what they wanted to be said [to the press and the public] was said."

To be sure, the content and tone of party media messages hinge importantly on what members participate in these collective efforts. Who contributes to the party effort to control debate in the House and on television? What types of members carry party messages? The following examines the "ideological tilt" in two kinds of member media participation: (1) participation in internal party message organizations; and (2) appearances on cable talk programs like *Hardball with Chris Matthews*.

Party Message Organizations. Although party leadership efforts to coordinate messages are ongoing and pervade most aspects of the legislative process, two organizations—the Democratic Message Board (DMB) and the

Republican Theme Team established in the one hundred and first and one hundred and second Congresses, respectively—were among the most organized/institutionalized manifestations of parties' internal communications efforts in this contemporary era.[11] Organizing messages and participation in "non-legislative debate" opportunities (Rocca 2007) during "one-minute" and "special orders" speeches, the DMB and the Theme Team sought to attract both a direct audience through C-SPAN and, more importantly, the attention of the congressional press gallery and broader media. Inasmuch as unity of message is key to achieving that broader press and media attention (Sellers 2000), the DMB and Theme Team stress message coordination and repetition of key party themes, and engage in extensive organization and efforts, first, to persuade members to participate and, second, to get them "on message" (Harris 2005b).[12]

After their creation in the late 1980s and early 1990s, the DMB and Theme Team became central operating arms of both parties' overall communications efforts. "A way to assign [and] to look to different groups of members and empower them to drive the message," the stated purpose of the Theme Team was "to present to the American people a unified message on certain Republican themes."[13] Similarly, one Democratic leadership aide described "the Message Group formula" of "communicating the House Democratic Agenda to the living rooms of Middle America" as part of an overall communications plan to "defin[e] a cohesive national Democratic perspective."[14] Moreover, the groups' duties include not only the daily delivery of messages but also the development of party themes. As one Republican leadership document suggested, the Theme Team "ideally" would "develop ideas and phrases to be used by all Republicans."[15] To the extent that the DMB and Theme Team both develop and give daily voice to party messages, their memberships become important factors in how each party presents itself to the press and the public.

Who, then, are the members of the DMB and Theme Team that help direct and deliver the parties' messages? Although both parties initially stressed the need to achieve broad ideological participation in these message organizations, the participating membership was largely determined by individual members' self-selection likely promoting more ideological and confrontational members over more moderate and less ideological voices. Indeed, one Republican planning document suggested that the message group would "consist of members who by nature are willing to take on the Democrats in one minutes and special orders" and willing to "counte[r] the Democrats' themes on a daily basis."[16] Inasmuch as it is difficult to obtain complete membership lists of the Message Board and the Theme Team (politicians frequently hide their media planning efforts), such lists were retrieved for the DMB in the one hundred and first Congress and the Theme Team during the one hundred and third, one hundred and fourth, and one hundred and sixth Congress.[17]

Using DW-NOMINATE ideological scores of each member of the Democratic Caucus in the one hundred and first Congress and the

Republican Conference for the one hundred and third, one hundred and fourth, and one hundred and sixth Congresses, we can analyze the ideological composition of these House message organizations.[18] Figures 5.1 and 5.2 break down the House Democratic Caucus and the Republican Conference into ideological deciles again following the traditional liberal left-conservative right orientation; the most liberal tenth of the Democratic Caucus is the first decile, whereas the most moderate (or conservative) tenth of the Caucus is the tenth decile; however, for Republicans, the most moderate (or liberal) members of the Conference represent the first decile, and the most conservative members of the Conference are in the tenth decile. Consistent with our expectations and despite the efforts of both parties' leadership to try to get broad participation from throughout the Caucus/Conference, both Democrat and Republican message organizations tend to draw disproportionately from the parties' more extreme wings, though the ideological tilt is more pronounced among Republicans than among Democrats. These ideological tilts with regard to the members who make and carry the party messages, presumably, work to highlight and sharpen, rather than blur, the divisions between the two parties. Not surprisingly, scholars have noted an increase in partisan rancor and a decline in civility in one-minute and special orders speeches (Jamieson 1997).

Hardball Appearances. Not only do parties try to coordinate floor messages but they also seek to encourage members to take party messages to the airwaves and into the "living rooms of Middle America."[19] By the 1990s, both parties' leadership staffs also offered "booking" or "referral" services, wherein they would try to "place" appropriate members on Sunday talk

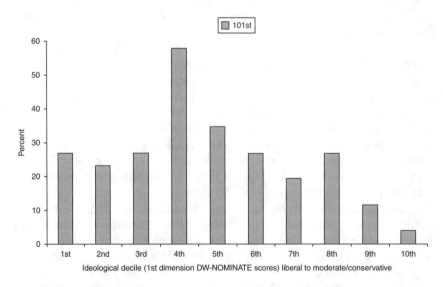

Figure 5.1 House "Democratic Message Board" Membership by Ideological Decile, One Hundred and First Congress.

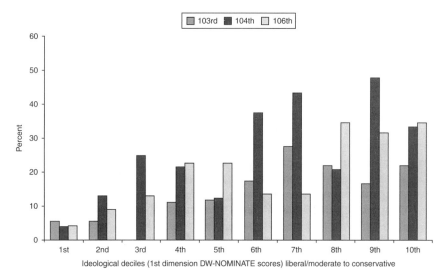

Figure 5.2 House Republican "Theme Team" Membership by Ideological Decile, One Hundred and Third, One Hundred and Fourth, and One Hundred and Sixth Congresses.

programs and, more regularly, cable television talk shows.[20] Facing the same collective action dynamics cited above, again, there is a disparity in what types of members are likely to appear on television. Which members, for example, are most likely to "play *Hardball*"?

Hardball, hosted by Chris Matthews, is one of the longer running cable television public affairs programs with frequent participation from members of Congress. Using *Lexis-Nexis* transcripts of the program, I analyzed the guest lists for every broadcast in 2007 to determine which members appeared on that program. That year, 56 House members appeared on MSNBC's *Hardball with Chris Matthews* 124 times.[21] A relatively small proportion of each legislative party appears on the program; 13.6 percent of the Democratic Caucus and 11.8 percent of the Republican Conference appeared as guests on the program that year. Figures 5.3 and 5.4 break down both House parties' *Hardball* guests into ideological deciles/tenths with Democrats' moderate members as shown on the right-hand side of figure 5.3 and Republicans' moderates as shown on the left-hand side of figure 5.4 and show the percentage of House Democrats and Republicans, respectively, in each. As expected and more or less consistent with the data on DMB and Theme Team memberships, there is an ideological tilt among both House Democrats and House Republicans in who appears on *Hardball*. For Democrats, although *Hardball* appearances are distributed more widely throughout the Caucus than in the Republican Conference, the liberal tilt is clear: the four most liberal tenths of the Caucus (along with the somewhat moderate eighth ideological decile) have a higher percentage of *Hardball* guests than the Caucus as a whole, members in the party's middle fifth–seventh deciles are slightly less likely to appear, and, predictably, the 20 percent of the Caucus that is

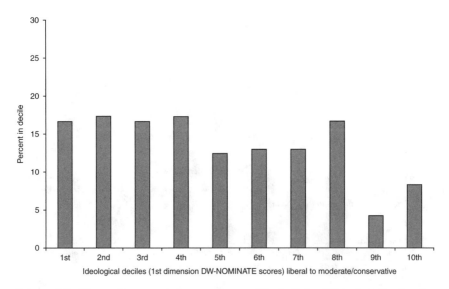

Figure 5.3 House Democrats' Appearances on Hardball by Ideological Decile, One Hundred and Tenth Congress.

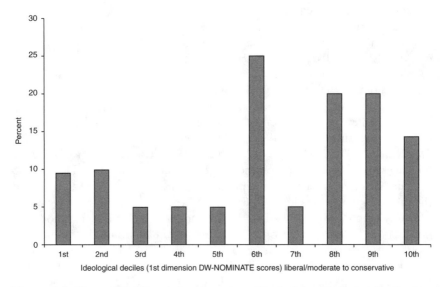

Figure 5.4 House Republicans' Appearances on Hardball by Ideological Decile, One Hundred and Tenth Congress.

most "moderate-to-conservative" is far less likely to appear on the cable news program. As was the case with Theme Team membership, the ideological tilt in the House Republican Conference is even greater: the most moderate half of the Conference is far less likely to appear on *Hardball*, whereas four of the party's five most conservative "tenths" are overrepresented.

Not only is it the intent of party leadership media efforts to polarize, but also the behavioral reality of who carries the message is likely to tend toward the extremes adding rhetorical fuel to the partisan fire. If the emphasis, heretofore, has been on how polarized party communicators are, the other way of looking at this is to note that moderate participation in message efforts is disproportionately low. Both Democratic and Republican congressional moderates are less likely than their more ideological colleagues to "go public" both in terms of who carries (and helps to formulate) the parties' messages for one-minute and special order speeches inside the House and who takes to cable TV to give voice to party messages on *Hardball*. Interpreted either way, the ideological "bias" is clear. Importantly, if these figures are representative indicators of the distribution of congressional voices on C-SPAN and in other mass media, this means that, although it is most certainly the case that the contemporary Congress is polarized on a partisan basis, the public is seeing, hearing, evaluating, and perhaps echoing a more polarized Congress than even exists as ideologues shout louder and moderates lay comparatively low.

CONGRESSIONAL MODERATES IN A POLARIZED ERA

The increased polarization—and public polarization at that—of American politics poses distinct and acute challenges to the survival of the some few moderates who remain in American national politics who are marginalized by partisan efforts to frame ideological and policy conflicts and who are targeted by the opposition for electoral defeat. In this way, the impetus toward polarization feeds back on itself. If the rise of partisan polarization and public congressional leadership tactics were consequences of the declining importance of partisan moderates on both sides of the aisle, it is also true that the rise of media-based polarization had a reciprocal impact making surviving as a moderate all the more difficult.

Surviving as a moderate in the polarized era is no meager feat. Not only are moderates uniquely vulnerable in that they are more likely than other members to face a difficult general election fight but, as outliers within their own parties, they are also increasingly likely to "get primaried" by an ideologically driven intraparty challenge from the party's "base." Moderates—Main Street Republicans, Blue Dog Democrats, and New Democrats—tend to be vulnerable in general elections in that they live in "purple" swing districts and states that represent the greatest potential for electoral gains for the opposing party. Still, as moderate as these outlier purple districts and states may be, they have not been spared the polarization at the elite, activist, and primary electorate level where money is raised and party nominations are won. If balancing centrist voters against the base is a problem for most contemporary politicians, the problem is all the more acute for party moderates. To the activist elements of both parties, the absence of moderate members of party loyalty makes them RINOs (Republicans in Name Only) and even "Bush Dogs" as many Blue Dogs came to be known in the last decade.

If such ideological activists are generally out of place in purple districts, they nevertheless disproportionately constitute primary voters, the net-roots, and campaign donors. Still, any efforts to placate those activists might alienate the bulk of their moderate constituents.

These twin electoral challenges lead partisan moderates to adopt unique "representational styles that personalize rather than partisanize elections and localize rather than nationalize issues" (Harris and Fried 2010, 105). Having banded together in intraparty caucuses (Hammond 1997; Kolodny 1999), these "Blue Dogs, New Democrats and Main Street Republicans are all likely to stress their 'independent' voices, their pragmatism and their personal representation of the district" (Harris and Fried 2010, 105) running away from the national party brand.

If congressional moderates are correct that avoiding stances on national issues and de-emphasizing party and ideology are key to survival in outlier districts, public congressional leadership is bad news for the moderate members of Congress who remain in two chief respects. First, public congressional leadership efforts to forge a cohesive party voice and to sharpen distinctions between the parties pose obvious challenges to moderate members for whom association with their party's brand might put them at odds with their outlier districts and, increasingly, force them to choose between partisan activists and centrist voters. Second, given the "purple" nature of their districts, moderates are more electorally vulnerable than most and, given public congressional leadership's fusing of electoral and legislative House politics, they are most likely to be targeted by the opposing party for electoral defeat.

National Party Image and the Marginalized Moderates

Public congressional leaders' efforts to develop national party images, frame conflict, and to discredit the opposition make bipartisanship increasingly difficult and compel moderates to declare which side they are on. Although public congressional leadership tactics may be valuable "services" to most party members, the House parties' efforts at one-size-fits-all "branding" are less applicable and pose distinct challenges to moderate members for whom unqualified acceptance of party stances on most issues might put them at odds with their outlier districts where the "brand" is less popular. Admittedly all congressional districts are different, but these cookie-cutter messages fit least in outlier districts. To be sure, this was a problem confronted by Boll Weevil and Blue Dog Democrats in the Reagan era harmed as they were by a "liberal" Democratic national brand. More recently, it has become more pronounced for northern and other Republicans representing moderate districts in recent years. As Republican Main Street Partnership (RMSP) member and former NRCC Chairman Tom Davis (R-VA) warned Republicans in 2008:

> Tom Davis's brand is not Jeb Henserling's (sic) or Joe Barton's brand. I run as a friend of federal government employees and contractors—not making

government smaller, but making it work...I run as a moderate and thoughtful doer who supports the GOP on trade and taxes, but takes a more libertarian approach on gays, stem cell research, etc.

That branding doesn't work for most in our conference, but if we don't want our numbers to sink to 180, we have to have a party reputation that allows us to compete nationally and especially in swing districts. Democrats have gone out of their way to attract the pro-gun, pro-life candidates where it suits them" (Davis 2008, 20).

To be sure, the increasingly strident conservatism of the Gingrich-Armey-Hastert-DeLay era forced many northern Republicans to choose between party fidelity and district representation. As one Main Street affiliated Republican put it, the national "stance of the party definitely hurt these moderate members...[who have a] very broad constituency." Another echoed this sentiment saying, "New England, especially, but the entire Northeast—the [Republican] brand is entirely damaged."

For these and other reasons, moderate members are less likely to avail themselves of party messaging services and, more generally, to participate in party-coordinated media efforts. The staffer for one moderate Democrat said that although the leadership produces "a lot of talking points...a lot of sample op-eds," "we don't use any of it." A Main Street-affiliated Republican argued that "Conference [messaging] was too national...trying to get a national message out without paying enough attention to district needs." Leadership communicators agree that the "stuff out of a can" can be "discordant" with many moderate districts and that moderate members are less likely to avail themselves of these media services. One Republican leadership staffer said, "Chris Shays doesn't call as much as I'd like him to." A Democratic leadership aide cited Pennsylvania Blue Dog Tim Holden as an example, "I can't see his office using a lot of our stuff." One Republican leadership press aide who devotes a lot his day to writing press materials seemed certain that the "30 to 40 members in marginal districts ... take our messages and just delete them," and he added, "They wouldn't be around very long if they used them."[22]

Not only do party "branding" efforts not help moderates as much as other members but they also actually may complicate the balancing act moderates have to perform back home. In a legislative world increasingly dominated by "us versus them" fights, moderates must make the difficult choice of declaring which side they are on putting them between a base excited and activated by party messages and a more centrist electorate just as likely to be turned off by rank partisanship. Although in an increasingly partisan and polarized America, articulating conflicts as battles between "us and them" advanced the goals of most House members, it nevertheless exacerbated the dilemmas cross-pressured moderate members face back home: if middle-of-the-road voters are likely to be turned off by bitter partisanship, many of the more extreme party activists on both sides of the aisle are more likely to be aware of and more likely to be excited by these messages. The activists, then, are more likely to demand of their representatives in Congress: which side are you on?

It is also worth pointing out that such "conflict frame" and "wedge" political techniques are antithetical to the avowed philosophy of moderate groups committed to pragmatic approaches and consensus policies. If, as interviews suggest, many Blue Dogs and Main Street Republicans join moderate groups because of their policy commitments and their beliefs that the center is "where policy is made" and "compromise is how to get policy done," intentionally polarizing legislative politics hinders policy advances in favor of maintaining the kinds of "magnet" and "wedge" issues important to accomplishing partisan and political goals (Gilmour 1995). Main Street Partnership Chairman of the Board John "Jock" McKernan said, for example, that the group's "message" is "one of quiet diplomacy, rather than wedge politics."[23]

Marginalized Moderates Are Likely Targets for Electoral Defeat

If it is true that moderates are ignored or even harmed by the new public congressional leadership, perhaps even more challenging to them is the fact that they are the most vulnerable electoral targets of the opposition's framing and electoral messaging strategies. Indeed, a notable irony of both parties' electoral targeting efforts is that, in targeting moderates, they target for defeat those members of the other party with whom they share the most in common and with whom they are most likely (under other circumstances) to cooperate legislatively.

Public congressional leadership's fusing of legislative and electoral politics both polarized Congress and imperiled moderates. In the 1970s and 1980s, both the DCCC and the NRCC's traditional campaign activities were innovated and integrated more than previously with the activities of the formal legislative party leadership (Kolodny 1998, 214–215) in the House. Blurring the twin activities of governing and electioneering, some of the very earliest public congressional leadership media efforts were tied to targeting members of the opposing party, especially moderates in vulnerable seats, for electoral defeat. During the ninety-fifth Congress, when three class of 1976 Democratic Freshmen (two of whom had won what previously were Republican districts) "expressed concern" to the Speaker that "The Republicans have a very impressive apparatus to get Republican propaganda into Democratic districts where it can most seriously hurt the Democratic Member," O'Neill assured them that Majority Whip John Brademas (D-IN) was working on "a PR counter-attack" program where "Democratic propaganda" would be "systematically filtered" into districts "to hurt Republican members."[24] Indeed, Brademas had reported to O'Neill months before that the focus was on providing "general communications services[to]district Democrats [in] Republican-held districts in which a reasonable chance exists" for Democratic victory.[25]

It was the ninety-seventh Congress, the first of the Reagan era, when the greatest innovations took place. Although the DCCC previously had lagged behind Republicans in terms of modernizing its campaigning

(Menefee-Libey 2000), new Chairman Tony Coelho (D-CA) modeled recent NRCC tactical innovations in fundraising, candidate recruitment and development, campaign and messaging services, and, most notably, targeting Republican incumbents for defeat (Herrnson 1988; Kolodny 1998). In July of 1981, Coelho boasted to his Democratic colleagues, "For the first time, the Democratic Congressional Campaign Committee is taking an active role in urging strong Democrats to take on Republican incumbents and run for open seats."[26]

More to the point, Coelho's campaign activities were seen as part and parcel of overall House Democratic leadership media/legislative strategy. Along with Coelho, Chris Matthews from the Speaker's office and other top leadership staff members met weekly (usually more) in "Leadership Campaign Meetings" where talk of media, public opinion, electoral, and legislative strategies were intertwined. Although a great deal of the focus of these meetings involved countering the Reagan White House on the House floor and in the mass media, electoral targeting of vulnerable Republican incumbents was frequently interspersed with these other matters. For example, Matthews arranged for Patricia Bario, an expert on local and regional media and with whom he had worked in the Carter White House, to "develo[p] media strategy" on the negative impact of Reagan budget cuts and tax policies specifically tailored for delivery "in 21 swing Democrat districts and at least 10 marginal/moderate Republican districts."[27]

These efforts became dominant legislative-electoral strategies in the 1980s and 1990s and were more routine and embedded in House structures as time went on. Indeed, with notable successes in 1982 and 1986 (and comparatively few losses in 1984 given Reagan's re-election landslide), Coelho's model was emulated by subsequent Democratic campaign chairs and the new way of doing both electoral and legislative business. As Speaker Jim Wright told me, "Tony had a broader vision" and DCCC Chairman Beryl Anthony and his successors "were students of the Coelho technique." By the same token, as Gingrich gained influence in the Republican Conference and then official position as Republican Whip in 1989, the "hardball" strategies of targeting vulnerable moderate members for electoral defeat were repeated in election after election and on both sides of the aisle. On the Republican side, in an overall plan to revamp internal leadership structures and responsibilities in the early 1990s, Republicans deemed new NRCC operations (along with close coordination between NRCC and top legislative leaders) to be the "most critical":

The NRCC, along with the Leadership, will be charged with developing an overall campaign plan for House Republicans for 1994...Democrat Target List—Target list of the most vulnerable Democrat seats, along with specific plans to "soften up" those seats beginning now. Enough seats should be targeted to lead to a Republican majority in the House...Research—Research plan to track and exploit committee votes, Floor votes and statements from vulnerable Democrats.[28]

Indeed, Republican leaders believed that to the extent that they began early and were successful in these efforts, they could attract even stronger challengers to Democratic incumbents. The House Republicans' "Management Model" for the 1990s revealed that leaders were devising a *"Communication plan to take the message to vulnerable Democrats* before they have an opponent. By exploiting the weaknesses of incumbent Democrats in their own districts, the NRCC should be able to recruit better candidates."[29]

This deeper integration of CCC-tactics and internal legislative leadership also caused the majority party to display less comity toward minority party members and, indeed, to seek to marginalize them in the legislative process rather than work with them. Once potential legislative partners, moderates were now to be considered more as targets for electoral defeat. For example, as the House Democratic leadership planned a series of "road-show" committee field hearings throughout the country to highlight the negative impacts of Reagan's budget cuts, leaders became frustrated by displays of traditional bi-partisan comity (like when consensus-oriented Democratic chairmen were passing the gavel to Republican committee members allowing them to share in "chairing" the field hearings). Notes from "Leadership Campaign Meetings" reveal that party leaders thought that "Letting Republicans chair hearings (Heckler, Schneider, and possibly Roukema)...[was] destroying DCCC targeting efforts"[30] and they worked to get committees to deny Republicans such opportunities to participate. Note, too, the description of a "Leadership Campaign Meeting" as leaders planned party "Strategy for Southerners and Gypsy Moths" with regard to an impending budget fight with the White House:

> Southerners want to support the party, but they may need their own amendment...the Whip's office and Bill Alexander, will keep the lines of communication open.—[O'Neill staffer Kirk] O'Donnell asked about our strategy for the gypsy moths. Coelho—they are being targeted and therefore we don't want to legitimize them. We don't want to separate them from the GOP. [O'Neill staffer] Ari [Weiss]—should we go to the gypsy moths instead of them coming to us?[31]

Decreasing bipartisan comity, the twin purposes of polarizing party battles and targeting moderates also had the effect of decreasing the very incentives for bipartisan cooperation as party leaders increasingly opted to isolate the other parties' moderates and target them for defeat. Note, for example, the following exchange from one of Tip O'Neill's 1981 press conferences. When asked if he and the Democratic leadership were "wooing...Northeast Republicans" to get votes against Reagan on an upcoming budget vote, O'Neill revealed that he would just as soon have northern Republicans vote with Reagan so that it would be easier to pick up those seats in 1982. Observing that the starkness of the policy change represented by Reagan's budget cuts would ultimately afford slim "cover" (he used a "sunscreen" metaphor) for Northeasterners in moderate districts, the Speaker said:

> They [Northern Republicans] know the consequences...I would hate to be any one of those 14 Northeast Republicans come election day, lying in the sun with [only] a beer and the Latta-Gramm vote. They appreciate it.[32]

O'Neill frankly confessed later that his strategy in the ninety-seventh Congress was to avoid compromise because "I was less concerned about losing the legislative battle in the spring and summer of 1981 than I was with losing at the polls in the fall of 1982" (O'Neill 1987, 344).

Forged during the Reagan years, these new strategies of polarizing the parties and picking off the moderates have become staples of contemporary congressional politics. By the first decade of the twenty-first century, Democratic and Republican targeting efforts tended to focus, first, on those districts and states where the party's presidential candidate had won but the opposition still held the seat. In his 2006 efforts, DCCC Chairman Rahm Emanuel targeted Republicans who represented districts that John Kerry had won in 2004 (Giroux 2006, 2983–2987) just as Republicans, in 2008, targeted those districts that Bush had won in 2000 and 2004 but were nevertheless represented by Democrats. As one Republican put it, they considered those districts as those "out there that are ours to get" (Harris and Fried, 2010).

Public congressional leaders use of media politics intentionally to polarize party and congressional politics, to starkly frame interparty politics as "us versus them" conflicts, and to use "wedge" issues likely to force moderate members to make difficult choices that separate their centrists voters from the party's more ideological base present unique and acute problems to partisan moderates in Congress, members who are admittedly already a vanishing breed.

CONCLUSIONS

Since the first implementation of the new public congressional leadership style in the O'Neill Speakership, moderates have been most likely to be ignored (or poorly served) by their own parties' messaging operations, least likely to participate in them, and most likely to be targeted for electoral defeat by the other party's messaging efforts. Public congressional leaders' efforts to shape the party brand, advertise national party issue positions, and integrate campaigning and legislative strategies in a "permanent party campaign" run counter to moderates' governing philosophies and their strategic efforts to de-emphasize ideology and localize issue stances. Combining the cross-pressured nature of their districts back home and the increasingly inhospitable environment in Congress, moderates are disappearing.

Thus, congressional politics may not only represent America's deepening ideological divides, but also it may propel and even distort them. To be sure, the roots of contemporary congressional polarization in the broader party system and district alignments is well established in the political science literature (see, e.g., Cooper and Brady 1981; Rohde 1991; Aldrich and Rohde 1997–1998; Stonecash and Lindstrom 1999; Stonecash and Mariani 2000; Jacobson 2000; Sinclair 2006). However, if it is true that increased "sorting" and polarization in the party system outside Congress has contributed to party leaders' becoming more active and public in recent years, members of Congress, especially high-profile elected party leaders—as consequential "actors in the public sphere" (Mayhew 2001)—produce and model party rhetoric likely to be echoed by party activists and other attentive elements of the public in ways that propel further party polarization.[33] Indeed, party messaging, it seems, is far from being evenly distributed throughout the Democratic Caucus or the Republican Conference, respectively. Both parties exhibit an overreliance on their ideological extremes to deliver message, with the Republicans exhibiting an even greater tendency than the Democrats.

Viewed this way, the interrelationship between the contemporary electoral environment and congressional party communications constitutes a complex of reverberating cause and effect. If district-based polarization and increasing intraparty unity is, in part, the result of the decline of moderates in Congress, moderates' diminishing numbers, and further marginalization in both legislative parties allows for even more extreme party leadership and strident party agendas and images. Of course, as party agendas and images become more strident and public, the price of that stridency and publicity is suffered disproportionately by moderate members caught between centrist general election voters likely to be turned off by partisanship and increasingly polarized party activists likely to be energized and mobilized by it. Furthermore, as moderates continue to lose influence in the legislative parties, the consequent greater intraparty unity and greater influence of both parties' more extreme elements causes the selection of even more extreme leaders, the creation of even sharper party distinctions, and even more strident party agendas and images. Unfortunately for moderates and, indeed, for prospects for bipartisanship and deliberation in Congress, this irresistible spiral seems a powerful long-term trend.

In 2008, Tom Davis warned his Republican colleagues that the current state of the Republican brand—"if we were a dog food, they would take us off the shelf" (Davis 2008, 2)—was to become an "albatross to our candidates." He wrote, "If we don't act boldly [to re-brand the party], the best we can do over the next six months is to allow our members to brand themselves: Chris Shays, in Connecticut; Jon Porter, in Nevada; Tom Feeney, in Florida; Mark Kirk, in Illinois; and Sam Graves, in Missouri. If held hostage to the GOP brand, nobody wins" (Davis 2008, 16, 19). Notably, the balance of Davis' examples lost in 2008. Still, by 2010 these efforts to moderate or simply loosen the brand had given way to a more extreme Tea Party–driven Republican image that would shift the party rightward and constrain Speaker Boehner's efforts at governing. Similarly, as Democrats confront their own rebranding efforts, the continued loss of Blue Dogs and New

Democrats will further push the center of gravity—and the party's message and image—to the left. The hardball tactic of targeting already vulnerable moderates is likely to continue on both sides of the aisle. At least for the time being, the system is stacked in favor of polarization and against moderates.

NOTES

1. Personal interviews were conducted under the condition of anonymity with Democratic and Republican party leadership communicators as well as congressional staff affiliated with moderate Democrats and Republicans. The archival collections cited herein include the following: the Thomas P. O'Neill Papers, Special Collections, John J. Burns Library, Boston College, Chestnut Hill, Massachusetts (TPO); the Jim Wright Collection, Mary Couts Burnett Library, Texas Christian University, Fort Worth, Texas (JCW); the Papers of Thomas S. Foley, Special Collections, Washington State University, Pullman, Washington (TSF); the Robert H. Michel Collection, Dirksen Congressional Research Center, Pekin, Illinois (RHM); James H. Quillen Papers, Archives of Appalachia, East Tennessee State University (JHQ); and the Papers of Representative Newt Gingrich, Special Collections, University of West Georgia (NLG). I am pleased to acknowledge the support of the Everett McKinley Dirksen Congressional Research Center and the Caterpillar Foundation and Loyola College in Maryland, both of which supported travel to archives and interviews with congressional staff. Thanks also to Speaker Newt Gingrich and the staff at newt.org who allowed me early access to the Gingrich papers as well as to Speaker Jim Wright and congressional staff members who were generous with their time and helped put some of the archival findings in appropriate context; unattributed quotations cited below are from these interviews.

2. On Reagan's use of media, see Kernell (1997). It was in 1981 that O'Neill's appearances on television increased significantly (Harris 1998), the leadership hired multiple press and communications staff members (including Chris Matthews in O'Neill's office), and public opinion polling became a regular feature of House Democratic leadership's legislative and electoral planning (Harris 2005a); see also Sinclair (1995).

3. Most contemporary congressional party leaders are *public congressional leaders* in one form or another: some like Tip O'Neill, Newt Gingrich, Dick Gephardt, and, it seems, Nancy Pelosi play twin roles of media and opinion strategist and high-profile media spokesperson; others, like Dennis Hastert, Tom DeLay, Tom Foley, and Steny Hoyer, who are by no means anonymous, are apt to play important roles in developing and determining messages but are savvy (or more or less content) enough to let others be the media figures who go on television articulating these carefully scripted party media messages.

4. For a more extensive examination of party efforts at conflict framing, see Harris (2010).

5. "House GOP Themes" 5/10/88, F "Strategy Group Spring 1988" Box 1063, NLG.

6. Paul Begala to "Message Staff," "Re: Our Friend, the Message Frame," May 13, 1991, Press Files Box 418, F "Press Files/1990/Democratic Strategy," TSF.

7. Vic Fingerhut to Democratic Congressional Leadership 11/15/83, "Re: Themes and Symbols for a Communication Strategy for Democratic Candidates in the Coming Year," TPO.

8. "Principal Findings of the 1985 DNC Public Opinion Survey" F "DCCC 1986" Party Leadership/Administrative Files, Box 30, TPO.
9. Newt Gingrich "Dear Republican Colleague" 3/18/82, Folder "Newt Gingrich, 1982–1985" Kirk O'Donnell Files, Box 1, TPO.
10. NG: 1984 undated memorandum, F "Staff. Pitts. House Procedures, TV Broadcasting" Staff Series. Pitts. Box 6, RHM.
11. Determining exact dates for the creation of these organizations is somewhat problematic in that both had antecedents. It was in the one hundred and first and one hundred and second Congresses, respectively, that the DMB and Theme Team received some official designation from the top party leaderships.
12. Because getting a consistent message out to these audiences requires, first, per-suading members to take the time to participate and, second, to get them "on mes-sage," leaders and leadership staff offer many services designed to entice members to participate and to "subsidize" the "on-message" speech-giving (Harris 2005b). In the past, such enticements have included recognition in the form of "thank you" letters from top leaders and speech-giving "awards," strategic and technical assis-tance to try to get wider media coverage for the speech (particularly back home), and even sometimes ready-made speeches prewritten by party leadership staff. Terry Michael to Democratic Press Assistants 7/30/82, Press Relations Box 20, Folder "Reagan 1981–86," TPO. Democratic Message Board, "One Minutes – How They Work," Cage 655, Box 418, Folder "Press Files/1990/Democratic Strategy" TSF. See Lamar Smith's "Dear Republican Colleague" letter 2/4/94 Box 124, folder 10, "Republican House Theme Team, 1979–1994," JHQ.
13. "Theme Team" F "Reform. Deliberative Democracy Task Force" Legislative Series. Special Subjects. Other Box 6, RHM.
14. "Leadership Options," 6/29/1989, Cage 655 Box 417, F "Press Files/1989/ Leadership Transition," p. 5, TSF.
15. "Theme Team" F "Reform. Deliberative Democracy Task Force" Legislative Series. Special Subjects. Other Box 6, RHM.
16. Dan Meyer, Len Swinehart Tony Roda to Bill Pitts "Re: Watchdog group/fall offensive" 9/20/91, F "Theme of the Week" Box 2684, NLG. One Democratic leadership aide from the 1980s and 1990s said of the DMB membership, "We wanted people who were good on their feet, quick on their feet and we wanted balance, diversity in terms of sex, race, ideology, and region."
17. The membership list of the Democratic Message Board in the one hundred and first Congress is from the papers of Speaker Thomas S. Foley, Cage 655 Box 418, folder "Press Files/1990/Democratic Strategy," TSF. The one hundred and third Theme Team roster is from the letterhead of the Theme Team in Lamar Smith "Dear Republican Colleague" 2/4/94, JHQ. The one hundred and fourth Theme Team roster was located in Martin Hoke letter dated March 14, 1996, F "Omnibus CR" Box 2263, NLG. The one hundred and sixth Congress's Theme Team's membership list was obtained on-line at "http:// hillsource.house.gov/ThemeTeam/members.htm" on September 18, 2000. It has since been removed from the hillsource website.
18. Date obtained from Keith Poole's "Voteview" website; https://voteview.com. Thanks to Professor Poole for making these data available; readers interested in learning more about how these scores are calculated and what they reveal should visit both the website and read Poole and Rosenthal (1997).
19. "Leadership Options," 6/29/1989, Cage 655 Box 417, F "Press Files/1989/ Leadership Transition," p. 5, TSF.

20. "Management Model for Republican Leadership" undated F "Reform. Republican Leadership Management Model" Legislative Series. Special Subjects. Other. Box 6, RHM.

21. 21. Of course, several members appeared multiple times in 2007. The most frequent *Hardball* guests were Debbie Wasserman-Schulz (D-FL) and Duncan Hunter (R-CA) both of whom appeared eight times; Hunter was running for the Republican nomination for President. Other frequent guests (four or more appearances) included Jim Moran (D-VA), Joe Sestak (D-PA), Artur Davis (D-AL), Peter King (R-NY), Christopher Shay (R-CT), and Marsha Blackburn (R-TN).

22. One Main Street-affiliated staffer who insisted that party leadership materials were, in fact, useful but only so that Main Street "members can be out there against it early."

23. "RMSP History," Republican Main Street Partnership, http://www.republicanmainstreet.org/history/htm, accessed May 21, 2008.

24. Notes on Speaker's meeting with Freshman 6/23/77 F "Freshman Caucus 1977" Party Leadership/Administrative Files, Box 5, TPO; these are direct quotations of staffer's notes and not a transcript of the meeting itself.

25. John Brademas to Tip O'Neill, 2/16/77, F "Correspondence with Colleagues, 1977" Staff Files, Eleanor Kelley Box 2, TPO.

26. Tony Coelho "Dear Democratic Colleague" 7/27/81, Folder "Democratic Congressional Campaign" Box 3–26, JCW.

27. Undated budget plan document, TPO; Mark Califano to Kirk O'Donnell "Comprehensive List of Republican Representatives and District Median Incomes" 6/11/81 and "Conservative democratic Forum Income and Election Vote" 6/22/81, Kirk O'Donnell Files Box 36, TPO.

28. "Coordination with the NRCC" F "Reform. Deliberative Democracy Task Force" Legislative Series. Special Subjects. Other Box 6, RHM.

29. "Management Model for Republican Leadership" F "Reform. Republican Leadership Management Model" Legislative Series. Special Subjects. Other Box 6, RHM; emphasis added.

30. Leadership Campaign Meeting 2/16/82, Folder "Democratic Leadership Campaign Meetings, 1982, January-May" Party Leadership/Administrative Files, Box 28, TPO.

31. Leadership Campaign Meeting 2/25/82, F "D Leadership Campaign Meeting, 1982" Party Leadership/Administrative Files Box 28–4, TPO.

32. Speaker's Daily Press Conference 6/17/81, Folder 11–1 "Press Conference Transcripts, January-June 1981" Party Leadership/Administrative Files, Box 11, TPO.

33. Recent studies suggest that sharper party distinctions in Congress heighten partisanship in the electorate (Hetherington 2001) and "prim[e] partisan evaluations of Congress" (Kimball 2005) and that the images of highly visible party leaders affect a party's electoral performance (Highton 2002; Overby 2006).

REFERENCES

Ajemian, Robert. 1981. "Tip O'Neill on the Ropes." *Time* May 18, 17.

Aldrich, John H. Aldrich, and David W. Rohde. 1997–1998. "The Transition to Republican Rule in the House: Implications for Theories of Congressional Politics" *Political Science Quarterly* 112(4): 541–567.

Cooper, Joseph, and David W. Brady. 1981. "Institutional Context and Leadership Style: The House from Cannon to Rayburn." *American Political Science Review* 75(2): 411–425.

Cox, Gary W., and Mathew D. McCubbins. 1983. *Legislative Leviathan.* Berkeley, CA: University of California Press.

Davis, Tom. 2008. Memorandum to Republican Leadership "Re: Where We Stand Today." Copy in possession of author.

Downs, Anthony. 1957. *An Economic Theory of Democracy.* New York: Harper & Row.

Gilmour, John B. 1995. *Strategic Disagreement: Stalemate in American Politics.* Pittsburgh: University of Pittsburgh Press.

Giroux, Gregory L. 2006. "Voter Discontent Fuels Democrats' Day." *CQ Weekly* November 13, 2983–2987.

Hammond, Susan Webb. 1997. *Congressional Caucuses in National Policy Making.* Baltimore: Johns Hopkins University Press.

Harris, Douglas B. 2005a. "House Majority Party Leaders' Uses of Public Opinion Information." *Congress & the Presidency* 32(2): 133–155.

———. 2005b. "Orchestrating Party Talk: A Party-based View of One Minute Speeches in the House of Representatives." *Legislative Studies Quarterly* 30(1): 127–141.

———. 2010. "Partisan Framing in Legislative Debates." In *Winning with Words: The Origins & Impact of Political Framing,* edited by Brian F. Schaffner and Patrick J. Sellers, 41–59. New York: Routledge.

———. 1998. "The Rise of the Public Speakership." *Political Science Quarterly* 113(2): 193–212.

Harris, Douglas B., and Amy Fried. 2010. "Maine's Political Warriors: Senators Snowe and Collins, Congressional Moderates in a Partisan Era." *The New England Journal of Political Science* 4(1): 95–129.

Harris, Douglas B., and Garrison Nelson. 2008. "Middlemen No More? Emergent Patterns in Congressional Leadership Selection." *P.S. Political Science and Politics* 41(January 1): 49–55.

Herrnson, Paul S. 1988. *Party Campaigning in the 1980s.* Cambridge, MA: Harvard University Press.

———. 2001. *Playing Hardball: Campaigning for the U.S. Congress.* Upper Saddle River, NJ: Pearson.

Hetherington, Marc J. 2001. "Resurgent Mass Partisanship: The Role of Elite Polarization." *American Political Science Review* 95(3): 619–631.

Highton, Benjamin. 2002. "Bill Clinton, Newt Gingrich, and the 1998 House Elections." *Public Opinion Quarterly* 66(1): 1–17.

Jacobson, Gary C. 2000. "Party Polarization in National Politics: The Electoral Connection." In *Polarized Politics: Congress and the President in a Partisan Era,* edited by Jon R. Bond and Richard Fleisher, 9–30. Washington, DC: CQ Press.

Jamieson, Kathleen Hall. 1997. "Civility in the House of Representatives." The Annenberg Public Policy Center Report #10, Philadelphia, PA.

Kernell, Samuel. 1997. *Going Public: New Strategies of Presidential Leadership.* 3rd Edition. Washington, DC: CQ Press.

Kolodny, Robin. 1999. "Moderate Success: Majority Status and the Changing Nature of Factionalism in the House Republican Party." In *New Majority or Old*

Minority? The Impact of Republicans on Congress, edited by Nicol C. Rae and Colton C. Campbell, 153–172. New York: Rowman & Littlefied.

———. 1998. *Pursuing Majorities: Congressional Campaign Committees in American Politics.* Norman, OK: University of Oklahoma Press.

Matthews, Christopher. 1988. *Hardball: How Politics is Played—Told by One Who Knows the Game.* New York: HarperPerennial.

Mayhew, David R. 2001. *America's Congress: Actions in the Public Sphere, James Madison Through Newt Gingrich.* New Haven: Yale University Press.

Menefee-Libey, David. 2000. *The Triumph of Campaign-Centered Politics.* London: Chatham House.

Neuman, W. Russell, Marion R. Just, and Ann N. Crigler. 1992. *Common Knowledge: News and the Construction of Political Meaning.* Chicago: University of Chicago Press.

O'Neill, Tip with William Novak. 1987. *Man of the House.* New York: Random House.

Overby, L. Marvin. L. 2006. "Public Opinion Regarding Congressional Leaders: Lessons from the 1996 Elections" *Journal of Legislative Studies* 12(1)(March): 54–75.

Poole, Keith T., and Howard Rosenthal. 1997. *Congress: A Political-Economic History of Roll Call Voting.* New York: Oxford University Press.

Rocca, Michael S. 2007. "Nonlegislative Debate in the U.S. House of Representatives" *American Politics Research* 35(4): 489–505.

Rohde, David W. 1991. *Parties and Leaders in the Postreform House.* Chicago: University of Chicago Press.

Sellers, Patrick J. 2000. "Manipulating the Message in the U.S. Congress." *Harvard International Journal of Press/Politics* 5(1): 21–30.

Sinclair, Barbara. 1995. *Legislators, Leaders, and Lawmaking.* Baltimore: Johns Hopkins University Press.

———. 2006. *Party Wars.* Norman, OK: University of Oklahoma Press.

Stonecash, Jeffrey, and Nicole Lindstrom. 1999. "Emerging Party Cleavages in the House of Representatives, 1962–1996." *American Politics Quarterly* 27(1): 58–88.

Stonecash, Jeffrey M., and Mack D. Mariani. 2000. "Republican Gains in the House in the 1994

Elections: Class Polarization in American Politics." *Political Science Quarterly* 115(1): 93–113.

Truman, David B. 1959. *The Congressional Party: A Case Study.* New York: Wiley and Sons.

6

Profile Politics: Examining Polarization through Congressional Member Facebook Pages

José Marichal

It is increasingly apparent that polarization is on the rise within American political institutions. Less clear is the impact that social media sites such as *Facebook* have on the political processes that affect polarization. This chapter looks at how some members of Congress use Facebook to interact with their constituents. While technology changes, the motives of members remains the same. Communication with constituents, regardless of the medium, is tempered by members' desires to remain in office and also to potentially have legislative influence. In this chapter, I argue that Facebook changes the ways in which citizens connect with each other, and, as such, changes the ways in which members connect with their constituents. Rather than encourage polarization of the political electorate, Facebook communication between constituents and members more often reinforces a *personalization* of the political process. Using Fenno's *home style* thesis, I argue that Facebook expands the ability of members to connect with constituents, in ways that often have nothing to do with politics. This typically comes at the expense of other forms of communication, those who involve listening to constituent concerns and ideas.

FACEBOOK AND POLARIZATION

Facebook has become a significant mode of communication for a vast majority of the American public. In October 2012, Facebook attained a coveted milestone, reaching one billion accounts worldwide (Gross 2012, online). The Pew Foundation reported that, in May 2012, almost two-thirds of Americans used some form of social media: almost all of them (92 percent) reported being Facebook users (Brenner 2012). Among 18–29 year olds, 86 percent reported using social media.

Despite the growing presence of Facebook in American life, its impact on political polarization is difficult to localize. A number of books have popularized the view that the Internet generally reinforces an "echo chamber," whereby information is filtered based on ideological preferences (Negroponte 1995; Manjoo 2008; Sunstein 2009; Pariser 2011). In 1995, Negroponte noted that the growing ubiquity of the Internet allowed for the formation of a *"daily me,"* of content driven by the user's personal predilections. More recently, Pariser (2011) argues that social media, such as Facebook, promotes a *filter bubble* where users can select information that reinforces their preexisting beliefs.

The prospect of an "echo chamber" effect poses an interesting dilemma for members of Congress. If Facebook is indeed an echo chamber, then public officials and/or advocacy groups could use the medium to speak directly to ardent supporters both inside and outside of their districts. Facebook can serve as a tool of advocacy for galvanizing public support around issues of concern to members. More importantly, it would be a tool that allowed members to bypass media gatekeepers and provide information directly to constituents in ways that can build support for members' projects.

Facebook's own research, however, suggests that the site is not an echo chamber. Bakshy et al. (2012) found that while Facebook users were most likely to share links from close friends, they also regularly shared links from *weak-ties* (Granovetter 1974) of more distant acquaintances. Bakshy et al. (2012) found that the information shared through weak-ties was most likely to be information users would not see otherwise. This finding is supported by other work. Goel et al. (2012) found that Facebook friends were only slightly more ideologically homogeneous than randomly assigned groups (75 percent for Facebook friends vs 63 percent for random group). Facebook networks can range from the high-school student who "friends" someone from summer camp or the brother who friends his sister who has moved five states away.

While Facebook is not an echo chamber, it is not an Athenian agora either. A 2012 Pew survey found that less than 5 percent of social media users report going to the site for political information. Because individuals do not seek political material on Facebook, the political information they see is that which comes to them. Even if individuals usually seek out information that agrees with their preexisting views (a phenomenon called *selection-bias*), they are more likely to find contradictory information on Facebook because they see political material that came to them via their social network (Garrett 2009; Brundige 2010). This "inadvertency thesis" (Brundige 2010) increases the possibility of coming across information one might not necessarily seek out.

Given this view of Facebook, members of Congress should be cautious in Facebook communications. Not only is political communication seldom discussed, but also it is seldom sought after. To be heard at all on Facebook, members must recognize they are speaking to a broad range of constituents: from the mildly engaged to the ardent. Additionally members' posts can be sent throughout Facebook via weak-ties to a broad range of users, including those with whom they are not ideologically aligned. In this case, Facebook becomes a vexing medium that can harm a member as much as help, particularly if a controversial post flows through weak-tie networks into the hands of political opponents. In this way, Facebook is more similar to traditional forms of communication with constituents (e.g., face-to-face, television, radio, and newsletters).

FACEBOOK AND VIRTUAL HOME STYLE

How do members traditionally communicate with constituents? A classic view of this question is Richard Fenno's (1978) work on Congressional member behavior. In *Home Style*, Fenno argues that members have three goals (reelection, power in Congress, and producing good policy). Members develop a "home style" to achieve the first of these objectives with the aim of achieving the latter two over time.

Fenno builds on sociologist Erving Goffman's (1959) work to argue that members build trust through three elements: a *presentation of self* through which to "connect" with constituents, credit claiming for legislative action, and position-taking on issues of concern to segments of their constituency. Members seek to present themselves as both "one of the people" (intimately connected to their community) and as effective national leaders (powerful within their political institutions). Mayhew (1974) argues that members seek to connect through *advertising* or creating a favorable image of themselves with little to no issue content attached (49).

This presentation might vary according to national conditions. For example, a low approval rating of Congress might encourage the member to distance himself/herself from the institution, an "outsider strategy." While trust gained from constituents provides members flexibility within their districts to engage in pet projects, this process takes time and effort. To build trust requires repeated visits back to the district for countless events and opportunities for members to meet with constituents. Fenno calls this the "expansionist phase," where members are trying to build a base of support. However, once that base is secure, they move beyond to attempt to gain power within the body and to have an influence on policy.

How is this *home style* process changing in the Internet era? It would appear that member use of the medium is largely driven by the architecture of the technology itself. Early work found that members of Congress used Websites for position taking and credit claiming but that sites were less geared toward "connecting" through *advertising* and that political content was mostly neutral (Messmer et al. 2000).

Pole (2006) found that members of Congress who maintained blogs were more likely to credit claim and take positions, but less likely to engage in advertising. Given the nature of blogs are to express opinion, this finding makes sense. Microblogging, on the other hand, provides different norms and expectations for appropriate communication. Golbeck et al. (2010) found that members used Twitter less to credit claim and position take and more to provide constituents information and to update location/notify members about events. Eighty two percent of over 6,000 tweets studied fell into one of these two categories.

Facebook's architecture is distinct from all other Web 2.0 tools. Because Facebook is based on socially proximate communities (friends and family) rather than communities of interest or communities of strangers, communication on that site is focused more on connection and disclosure than on information dissemination. The site's great power lies in its ability to lower the transaction costs involved in what Dunbar (1998) calls *social grooming*, or the need to periodically "check in" with friends you seek to keep.

Social media such as Facebook may change the dynamics of home style because Facebook allows for "social grooming" between friends irrespective of time or distance, cultivating trust between constituent and member may move online. While status updates on Facebook pages do not have same level of intimacy as communication within private networks, the potential exists for members to use Facebook to engage in a *virtual home style* that emphasizes more advertising or affect-based communication over different forms of interacting with constituents.

Members' ability to create a virtual home style has been greatly enhanced in the past few years. Web 1.0 tools were costly to implement, requiring a technically advanced staff member or consultant, and hence more likely to be used by well-funded candidates who could afford to pay for site maintenance (Bimber and Davis 2003; Druckman et al. 2007). Web 2.0 tools, however, allow for communication with constituents at virtually no cost beyond the time involved in posting (Williams and Gulati 2010). Indeed, recent work finds that members of Congress generally used social media (Twitter in this case) to enhance their home style in a cost effective manner (Chi and Yang 2010; Lassen and Brown 2011).

METHODS

However, how does this *virtual home style* differ from members' traditional communication with constituents? To examine the ways in which members of Congress interact with constituents via Facebook, I conducted an ethnographic content analysis of member status updates. Between September 15 and October 1, 2012, I examined over 430 status updates from the official Congressional page of 25 randomly selected members of Congress (appendix A). Of the 25 members I examined, all of them had Facebook pages that were regularly updated.[1] Twenty three of the twenty five members had posted within the 15 day window. While this might be the result of proximity to an election campaign, it signals the perceived importance of communicating with constituents through this medium.

Using a *constant comparative analysis* approach (Glaser and Straus 1967), I evaluated cases in order to reveal recurring patterns: this systematic approach allowed me to group the status updates into discrete categories based on the type of communication content in which members were engaged.[2] The original grouping yielded seven categories of members' updates: constituent event, constituent service, position-taking, self-promotion, nationalization, and personalization. A second round of analysis clarified four distinct types of member status updates: constituency service, position-taking, credit claiming, and personalization.

FINDINGS

How did members use their pages? In general, members used the site in ways that we would expect from Fenno's *Home Style* thesis. They sought to stay away from hyperpartisan attacks, instead emphasizing either their own accomplishments, alerting members to newspaper op-eds or television appearances, or displaying photographs taken either at district events or with constituents. This suggests an awareness of Facebook as consisting of both strong and weak ties, not as being an echo chamber. Each member's Facebook page revealed a great deal about the communication style members were using to shape their presentations of self to constituents.

CONSTITUENCY SERVICE

Members sought to frequently connect with constituents in a variety of ways. Some used Facebook to engage in traditional forms of constituency service by disseminating pertinent information within the district (a little over 10% of all status updates sampled). For example, Jim Costa (CA-20) used the site to let his constituents know about information relevant to those who have had their homes foreclosed erroneously:

> Over 430,000 Californians who lost their homes due to foreclosure and may be eligible for a settlement payment, will receive application forms in the coming weeks. The California Department of Justice is encouraging borrowers to return their claims as soon as possible or file online at www.nationalmortgagesettlement.com.

Judy Biggert (IL-13) used a status update to engage in direct constituency service by posting information regarding a missing college student.

> The search for missing Northwestern University student, Harsha Maddula, continues. Anyone with information is asked to call the university police at 847–491–3456.

Indeed, one member even defended the practice of constituency service in a status update: Rush Holt (NJ-12) promoted a letter he sent to the *New York Times* in defense of constituency service.

> After reading a recent op-ed, I was moved to write a letter to the New York Times in defense of representative government as inclusive of constituent services. Constituent service is my way of showing people that their government cares about them regardless of their station in life and of beating back cynicism about self-government.

Joe Donnely (IN-2) was one of the few members that used the site to "push" constituents to other Internet tools, where he could further develop positions and arguments. Much like a blogger or book author, Donnely used his status updates to link to his personal homepage where he would have a regular "Donnely Dispatch" newsletter with in-depth descriptions of his "home style."

POSITION TAKING

Members of Congress also used status updates to take positions on issues important to their districts (about 21% of the status updates sampled). There were several instances of members engaging in *position taking* that would appeal to their constituency. Jim Costa (CA-20) a member that represents the Fresno, CA, area used the site to alert people to an op-ed to advocate for farm issues of relevance to his district:

> Our dairymen and livestock producers need help. In light of the drought, we need flexibility to make sure our food isn't being used for fuel. Read my op-ed from The Hill and learn how we can provide long-term solutions for agriculture.

Some members used Facebook status updates to straddle the line between "expansionist" efforts within their districts and "nationalization." A handful of members used Facebook to advocate for or criticize national policy. Betty McCollum (MN-4) used the site to defend the Affordable Care Act, while linking its defense to its positive impact on her district:

> Today, the Department of Health & Human Services announced that the Affordable Care Act will save Americans on Medicare $5,000 from 2010 to 2022. In 2012, seniors in Minnesota saved $69.9 Million on prescription drugs, and 188,937 received free preventive care.

Like Fenno noted in *Home Style* (1978), more established members of Congress who had concluded their "expansionist" phase were more likely to move to present themselves as effective national policy leaders. James Clyburn's (SC-6) Facebook page almost exclusively focused on updates linking to upcoming and completed news-network video appearances.

As Fenno found, members who had developed trust within districts had the flexibility to branch out and engage in national issues (75 out of 434 status updates). Tom Price (GA-6), a senior member of the Republican Party leadership, has some efforts to engage in "personal connection," but used much of the site to forward policies and criticize the Obama administration. One post emphasized the attempts made by House Republicans to create jobs (in contrast to the Democrats):

> Today marks the beginning of Fiscal Year 2013. In the last two years, House Republicans have passed two budgets and over 30 bills to help encourage

job creation, while Senate Democrats have not produced a budget in over 1,000 days.

Even well-established candidates, however, did not entirely abandon using the Facebook page to build trust with their constituents. Michelle Bachman (MN-6) appears to straddle the line between "nationalizing" and "connecting." Most of her posts are critical of the Obama administration and Congressional Democrats. However, interspersed in the collection of updates are expressions of gratitude for community and photos of her doing constituency service. As an example, this post on 9–28:

> Yesterday I had the opportunity to visit with a number of Washington County residents at Keys Café & Bakery in Forest Lake. Thank you to everyone who took time out of their busy schedules to join me for coffee. I truly enjoyed meeting you and hearing your comments and concerns.

Even a member with overtly national aspirations still engages in "connection" strategies on Facebook; rather than presenting a simple report of Congressional activity or critical op-eds that would make the candidate appear too formal.

One of the key goals of a member of Congress, as Fenno observed, is to achieve policy goals. More senior members used their status updates to serve as policy advocates. Members would use the status updates to inform voters of upcoming legislation or relevant news articles pertaining to "pet" issues for the member. As an example, Edward Markey (MA-7) used the site to alert member of activity on his natural Resources Committee and to link to articles that reinforced his views on key policy areas. Markey linked to a study on the effect of the chemical Bisphenol A (BPA):

> A new study linking the toxic chemical BPA to childhood obesity demands we take action. It is time to remove this dangerous chemical from all food and beverage containers, especially those that children have contact with.
>
> Read more: http://markey.house.gov/press-release/markey-bpa-link-childhood-obesity-demands-action.

CREDIT CLAIMING

Members often used Facebook status updates to engage in what Fenno (1978) called *credit claiming*, signaling to one's district that the member is able to secure benefits for their district (approximately 28% of sampled status updates). Gwen Moore (WI-4) used status updates to announce to constituents that the district had received funding for a local health initiative.

> I am proud, once again, that Milwaukee was chosen to receive this grant funding.
>
> *Gwen Moore Announces Grant Funding for Milwaukee Health*
>
> 1.usa.gov

Similarly, John Oliver (MA-1) posted a congratulatory post to a local community organization that deals with at-risk youth for securing a grant from the US Department of Health and Human Services. The member framed his post as congratulating the organization, but if one clicks on the article, there is a mention of the member's efforts in helping to secure the grant.

> Congratulations to DIAL/SELF on their $2 million grant.
>
> DIAL/SELF has a 35-year successful history in our community for running effective and innovative programs. This funding will allow them to continue their extraordinary work on behalf of vulnerable youth here in western Massachusetts.
>
> *Congressman John Olver announces $2 million grant to help support DIAL/ SELF youth programs over next.*
>
> www.gazettenet.com

Often, members beyond their "expansionist" phase would use Facebook to "credit claim" in ways that establish a "national brand" that might be of little influence within the district but could have national benefits. Brian Bilbray (CA-5) used the page to position himself as a nonideological problem solver by highlighting an award he received from a bipartisan consensus-oriented group.

> *Congressman Brian Bilbray* shared a link.
>
> September 20
>
> I was approached by the organization "No Labels," a group dedicated to finding bipartisan solutions to Washington's most pressing issues, as one of their go-to legislators. I am honored that they recognize my work and would ask me to help fulfill their mission. I look forward to working with the group's founder, Nancy Jacobson (pictured), and the rest of their board. For more information, check out their website at www.nolabels.org.

This particular appeal is not necessarily targeted toward his district (Bilbray won his last election by a comfortable 18 percent margin in 2010), but could be seen as an effort to position himself for other office or to be a centrist leader within the chamber on forthcoming policy issues. Jack Kingston (GA-1) used a status update to notify his "broader constituency" that he supports and is actively working to provide fiscal responsibility.

> We owe our children and grandchildren better than a life indebted to China. I supported the Balanced Budget Amendment and introduced a plan to balance the budget and begin paying down the debt within five years.

PERSONAL CONNECTION

A significant majority of status updates (approximately 66 percent of the updates) during the period examined fell under the category of "personal connection."

Mayhew (1974) identified *advertising* as a key component of a member's presentation of self to constituents. More often than not, advertising would include presenting the candidate to constituents absent of issue content.

Personal connection on Facebook often included "location updates" that featured the member at a constituent event (approximately 29 percent of all updates). Seldom did these visits correspond to political issues. Betty McCollum (MN-3), for example, updated her page with the comment: "Attending the grand re-opening of the Oakdale Best Buy." Patrick Meehan (PA-7), posted on a visit to a mushroom farm within his district:

> *Visit to Joseph Silvestri & Son Mushroom Farm* (7 photos)
>
> Today I visited the Joseph Silvestri & Son Mushroom Farm located in Boothwyn. It is the only mushroom farm located in Delaware County and has been in business for over 85 years. During the visit, I learned more about Silvestri's mushroom growing and composting operations.

In essence, Facebook's page feature allows members to present "photo-ops" directly to their constituents without the need to rely on the news media. Almost all of the members I studied did some level of constituent "photo-op." However, members often went beyond traditional photo-ops by posting about events or experiences that had little to nothing to do with politics. JoAnn Emerson (MO-8) is a representative of members not only using Facebook to promote photo-ops but also to make emotional connections with constituents. Two examples are particularly instructive:

> Just home from seeing Grease! performed by the students at SEMO. It was an incredible production and after the first 30 seconds you forget this was a university production and not Broadway! The students were remarkable as was the direction, production and choreography! Congratulations to the Department of Theatre and Dance for an amazing performance!
>
> So excited to visit the Dawson's new cotton gin in Malden. Today was the first day of operation, and it is quite impressive! Very high tech evening.

This is a key difference that characterizes a "virtual home style." Members can use Facebook as a tool to personalize themselves (e.g., be "one of the people") virtually. Members still need to return to their districts to perform constituent service, but this involves direct face-to-face contact with members. Facebook pages give members and their staff complete autonomy over the member's "presentation of self." Before Facebook, they could send members a newsletter of these events, but it might seem silly for a member to send constituents an apolitical slideshow of their district visits. However, on Facebook, when Ileana Ros-Lehtinen FL-18 posts a "week in pictures" slideshow about her travels throughout the district that has almost nothing to do with politics, it seems entirely appropriate.

Members of Congress also used the site to personalize themselves in ways that might have been previously difficult (37 percent of all status updates).

Andre Carson (IN-7) included in one of his posts a photo of himself shooting baskets with the caption:

> Between visiting classrooms, meeting with school leadership, and talking to teachers, Congressman Carson takes a moment to sink a free throw in the gymnasium at Beech Grove's Central Elementary School.
> http://www.facebook.com/photo.php?fbid=486718541347261&set=a.1827 00648415720.42235.123884330964019&type=1&relevant_count=1

Certainly, Congressman Carson's staff could have set up a photo opportunity with the media, but these take up staff time and resources and might be difficult to pull off without connections to politics or policy. Members can also personalize themselves in small, less costly ways. A number of members used the site to express support for local sports teams. As an example, Rep Jack Kingston (GA-07) posted before a University of Georgia football game "Go Dawgs! Sic 'em!"

Even member profile pages sought to personalize by connecting the member to their districts or to desirable icons. Joe Gaudy (SC-4) has an illuminated night background image of the Riverwalk in Greenville, SC. This suggests an influence to "connect" with the region's voters through signaling that the member finds the district s/he represents as being worthy of showcasing on their Facebook profile.

This was by no means the only way members sought to present themselves. By contrast, JoAnn Emerson (MO-8) used her profile background to highlight the range of endorsments she has received from conservative and probusiness organizations. These included large logos of the National Right to Life Committee, the National Rifle Association, and the US Chamber of Commerce. Hers was one of the few sites where one could explicitly determine the member's political orientation from the profile background image. Tom Price (GA-6) also sought a background image that did not immediately identify the district he represents. His background image contained a row of American flags in a nondescript field.

DISCUSSION: PERSONALIZATION OR POLARIZATION?

This work suggests that members of Congress use Facebook as an extension of their home style by managing their *presentation of self* online, what I call a *virtual home style*. While members of Congress have been able to cultivate a virtual home style using Websites, blogs, or other Internet-related tools, Facebook allows for a different type of communication by emphasizing more personal, apolitical connection with constituents over aspects of members' self-presentations that involved the actual work of Congress. This suggests that the type of Internet tool used structures communication between members and constituents.

Instead of polarization, Facebook contributes to a long-standing trend of personalization of the political process. While in the United States, parties have enjoyed a resurgence of influence, the *personalization* of individual candidates remains strong. The idea that candidates need to come across as an "everyman or woman" rather than as a legislator has accelerated in the past several decades (Holtz-Bacha 2004; Van Zoonen 2005). The resulting communications between members and their constituents reflect a shift from emphasizing professional accomplishments emphasizing personal feelings and attributes.

Facebook provides us with a distinct form of communication, one in which we can simultaneously interact with intimate loved ones and distant friendly acquaintances. Managing this broad network of relationships requires moderation of how one "talks" to this vast archipelago of people. Examining how members and constituents talk about politics on Facebook requires reexamining how Facebook structures the types of "talk" that maintain relationships. Political talk is seldom that kind of communication. Eliasoph (1998) notes that politics is a subject that most Americans avoid because of its potential to be confrontational and unpleasant. Given this, members of Congress have incentive to emphasize status updates on Facebook that have little to nothing to do with politics or policy.

Facebook emphasizes talk that maintains and expands networks. This results from Facebook's *architecture* that emphasizes *disclosure and connection* (Marichal 2012). It does this in a variety of ways. The "like" button, for instance, is an example of how the medium is biased toward those disclosures that prioritizes connection through affirmation rather than other, less pleasant, forms of discourse. Indeed, this process of disclosure is central to Facebook's business model. Politics, particularly in "mixed" company, does not encourage affirmation or connection. As Goel et al. (2011) note,

> (Facebook users) are probably surrounded by a greater diversity of opinions than is sometimes claimed, (but they) generally fail to talk about politics, and that when they do, they simply do not learn much from their conversations about each other's views...the extent to which peers influence each other's political attitudes may be less than is sometimes claimed (10).

This is understandable given Facebook's primary purpose. Users who want to connect with a network of intimates and semi-intimates seek to do so through personal disclosure. A recent accomplishment ("just got accepted!"), an athletic achievement ("ran my first half-marathon!"), recent family vacation photos, or an innocuous, affect-laden observation ("beautiful day here in Los Angeles!") are more appropriate for social grooming than an expression of controversial political beliefs.

Given disclosure and connection as Facebook's *raison d'etre*, members of Congress face a difficult decision when presenting themselves on Facebook. Are they best served by maintaining formality and detachment from constituents, thereby coming of as aloof and distant? Or, do they risk a "when in Rome" strategy and share pictures of their pets with constituents?

Sennett (1974) forewarned of the dangers of removing the "formality" of politics. As politics becomes more personal, he argued, our expectations of politicians and what is possible through the political is elevated and leads to cynicism when it is betrayed. VanZoonen (1991) refers to this as a process of *intimization* where private feels and emotion become the stuff of public politics. Personal transgressions that may have never been reported in the past become the central element of political campaigns and processes (e.g., Clinton's Monica Lewinsky scandal).

Facebook is succeeding at changing social norms of interactions: what used to be private is now often made public, disclosed as a way of connecting with one's social network. Rather than sharing in private phone conversations with a friend, Facebook encourages the sharing of personal updates over an individualized quasipublic network. This network has the feel of a public sphere, and Facebook is not alone in facilitating this shift. Back in 1985, Meyrowitz noted that one of technology's main effects is to blur the line between the public and private sphere.

These are distinct, but related concepts. Personalization suggests a turn toward viewing political identity through the lens of the personal and away from the public. This means a turn away from discursive communication toward communication that is affect based. From a political perspective, this means turning away from a "politics of things" toward a "politics of feelings." Facebook's impact upon the political is to condition us toward communication that "connects" rather than a communication that discusses or deliberates. I offer that this includes how we talk about politics, even when members of Congress are communicating with their constituents.

Letting voters know that you like the same music they like goes beyond seeming like a "regular" guy or gal. There is an effort to make a direct personal connection with constituent/voters, almost as if you were trying to become "friends." Even if voters know that they are not really "friends' with their member of Congress, this type of talk shifts the evaluative focus away from accomplishments and policy positions toward affective evaluations of candidates. A political consultant who works with candidates and social media made a prescient observation about how Facebook encourages this type of communication:

> "Facebook is the thing that we do while we're at work, and we do it as a distraction from work. We don't do it as extra work," said J.P. Freire, a consultant at New Media Strategies. "Messages that work are 'Pay attention to this thing,'...or 'Give us money.' Things that don't work are 'Read this white paper.'" (Friere in Phillip 2011, Online)

The truth of this statement is reflected in the fact that not one of the over 434 status updates I examined sought to engage constituents in dialogue over policy issues. Curiously absent from member posts was any effort to glean their constituents opinion on any subject or to generate any dialogue or discussion about policy issues. When members asked for constituent action, it typically centered on reminders to register to vote.

In only one instance was a statue update even used to inform voters of an upcoming meeting. James McGovern (MA-3) used the site to inform voters of upcoming public discussion:

> Worcester-area friends: join members of the Worcester legislative delegation, leaders from Worcester's diverse ethnic, immigrant and refugee communities, and me as we discuss building a broad based coalition that supports opportunity and access for all members of the Worcester community this Friday evening

Even in this instance, voters were asked to be part of "building a broad based coalition," not a deliberation over ideas. Absent in all of the "talk" on Facebook was any mention of a "town hall" or any invitation to express dissent by the member. While expressions of dissent and conversations among issues were prevalent in discussions based on the status updates, few if any members responded or even acknowledged having seen them. This finding is in keeping with other work on the effect of Facebook on political discourse.

CONCLUSION

I argue in this work that Facebook reinforces a trend toward a personalization of politics. Personalization through Facebook results in less of a dialogue between member and constituent (Web 2.0) and more a management of a candidate's public presentation. This is not just a US-based trend. Livak et al. (2011) find that members of the Israeli Knesset (MK's) use Internet webpages to enhance their presentation of self and encouraging a personalization of Israeli politics.

Public figures face a dilemma. They can adapt to Facebook's "architecture of disclosure" (Marichal 2012) and engage in a more informal style of communication, disclosing in order to connect with their constituents—at the risk of appearing glib or flippant. Or, they can seek to engage constituents in a deliberative dialogue about core issues affecting the district and nation. Typically, members seek the former, but, I argue, that they do so at the risk of democratic legitimacy.

Personalization is related to, but distinctly different than polarization. Polarization is rooted in the idea of filtering out contrary information and basing one's beliefs unreflective on dogmatic ideology. Personalization is rooted in a failure to acknowledge the *idea* of *a public*. Public life presumes a *polis* "out there" engaged in a collective process of determining policy outcomes. This can either be through a battle between two loosely affiliated coalitions with distinct interests and little time for "talk" (a pluralist model). The second, deliberative view presumes a polity engaged in a collective search for the right political outcomes.

Fenno's classic work on Congress remains instructive. Members use Facebook in ways that would be familiar to members in the 1970s when Fenno was doing his seminal work. The difference between *virtual home style* and *home style* rests in the blending of the public and private sphere. In a virtual home style, members have tools at their disposal that can reduce their need to *listen* to constituents. Crawford (2009) differentiates between different types of listening on line. If members listen at all, she argues, they do so through "delegated listening" where public officials outsource the process to staff. True listening is "reciprocal listening," exemplified when members are face to face with constituents hearing their concerns and responding in real time.

While there are different models of Congressional representation, it is telling that not one post of a member of Congress in my sample sought out citizen feedback through Facebook; not one asked constituents for their opinion about pressing issues. It may appear naive to ask members to heed Diana Mutz (2006) advice and place themselves in venues where they "hear the other side," or to encourage a well-informed constituency that helps vet policy via exposure to cross-cutting deliberation and dialogue. There are far too many institutional pressures to behave in such a manner. Members who might be so inclined, particularly those in "safe" seats, are likely to receive few benefits from an electorate who would prefer they play the role of party loyalist.

In studying the Web pages of British members of parliament, Jackson and Lilleker (2009) found an emphasis on managing communication rather than a dialogue between citizen and representative, a phenomenon they refer to as (Web 1.5).

While this approach might make sense for members who seek to avoid uncomfortable conversations or different positions, this phenomenon runs the risk of alienating voters. As Wilson (2009) rightly points out:

> Users of social media expect, rightly or wrongly, a much more conversational and unaffected style of political communication…there is visible frustration on services like Twitter and Facebook when politicians will not engage in the dialogue that many users take to be the key function these spaces afford. (Online)

Web 2.0 is supposed to be interactive. It was to allow many-to-many forms of communication. Jenkins (2006) argues that the participatory nature of Web 2.0 would create norms and expectations of participation amongst a populous socialized to be *content creators* online. Indeed in the marketplace, consumers have a plethora of opportunities to provide feedback (Amazon.com, Angie's List, Yelp, etc.).

Facebook is not responsible for the personalization of politics. Mass media's effect on politics has been a multidecade process. However, the emphasis on affect and feeling in politics can lurch too far to the extreme. Having and expressing a public voice is a critical element of a democratic society, but finding venues where that public voice can be heard is even more critical. Members may try to address this vacuum by conducting vapid "virtual town halls" where citizen feedback is ignored. However, that may lead to even more mistrust of government. The challenge for scholars in this field is to find a middle ground between Web 1.5 (Jackson and Lilleker 2009 and a culture of continuous, but ultimately empty, feedback.

Appendix A

List of Members Selected and Coding Scheme

Congressperson	Total Posts	Constituent Events	Constituent Services	Position Taking	Credit Claiming/ Promotion	Partisan Nationalization	Personalization
Bachmann, Michele	27	3	2	10	2	16	5
Biggert, Judy	9	4	1	0	4	0	2
Bilbray, Brian	2	1	1	0	1	0	0
Carson, Andre	17	6	1	3	3	1	9
Clyburn, James	1	0	0	0	1	0	0
Costa, Jim	12	6	2	2	3	0	4
Donnelly, Joe	5	1	0	1	2	1	1
Emerson, Jo Ann	27	20	2	4	1	0	9
Gowdy, Trey	24	6	0	5	15	2	3
Grimm, Michael	12	6	1	5	6	2	2
Holt, Rush	5	2	0	2	2	2	3
Kingston, Jack	17	2	0	6	10	9	4
Markey, Edward J.	7	1	1	5	3	2	1
McCollum, Betty	30	10	0	3	6	8	8
McGovern, James	6	2	1	4	0	0	3
Meehan, Patrick	15	7	1	5	6	2	3
Moore, Gwen	19	5	3	6	5	4	16
Mulvaney, Mick	6	4	0	0	5	0	3
Nunes, Devin	4	0	0	3	4	1	0
Olver, John	9	3	4	3	1	2	5
Price, Tom	12	1	0	5	5	3	6
Rooney, Thomas	0	0	0	0	0	0	0
Ros-Lehtinen, Ileana	150	31	12	20	32	20	73
Ryan, Paul	0	0	0	0	0	0	0
Sablan, Gregorio Kilili Camacho	18	4	12	1	4	0	1
	434	125	44	93	121	75	161

Notes

1. One cannot assume that the member does his/her own updates because this task may be outsourced to a trusted staff member who potentially has guidance from the member as to what to post/not post.
2. A heartfelt thanks to my brilliant research assistant Rebecca Cardone who was of invaluable assistance in helping to code and analyze the data. I am grateful for her hard work.

References

Bimber, B. A., and R. Davis. 2003. *Campaigning Online: The Internet in US Elections.* New York: Oxford University Press.

Brundidge, J. 2010. Encountering "Difference" in the Contemporary Public Sphere: The Contribution of the Internet to the Heterogeneity of Political Discussion Networks." *Journal of Communication* 60 (4): 680–700.

Chi, F., and N. Yang. 2010. "Twitter in Congress: Outreach vs Transparency." MPRA Paper 24060. Posted July 23, 2010. http://mpra.ub.uni-muenchen.de/24060/

Crawford, K. 2009. "Following You: Disciplines of Listening in Social Media." *Continuum: Journal of Media & Cultural Studies* 23(4): 525–535.

Druckman, J. N., M. J. Kifer, and M. Parkin. 2007. "The Technological Development of Congressional Candidate Web Sites How and Why Candidates Use Web Innovations." *Social Science Computer Review* 25(4): 425–442.

Dunbar, R. 1998. *Grooming, Gossip, and the Evolution of Language.* Cambridge, MA: Harvard University Press.

Eliasoph, N. 1998. *Avoiding Politics: How Americans Produce Apathy in Everyday Life.* Cambridge: Cambridge University Press.

Fenno, R. F. 1978. *Home style.* Boston: Little Brown.

Garrett, R. K. 2009. "Echo Chambers Online?: Politically Motivated Selective Exposure among Internet News Users. *Journal of Computer-Mediated Communication* 14(2): 265–285.

Glaser B., and S. A. Straus. 1967. *The Discovery of Grounded Theory.* Chicago: Aldine Publishing.

Goel, S., D. J. Watts, and D. G. Goldstein. 2012. "The Structure of Online Diffusion Networks." *Proceedings of the 13th ACM Conference on Electronic Commerce,* Valencia, Spain, pp. 623–638. http://dl.acm.org/citation.cfm?id=2229058.

Golbeck, J., J. M. Grimes, and A. Rogers. 2010. "Twitter Use by the US Congress." *Journal of the American Society for Information Science and Technology* 61(8): 1612–1621.

Goffman, E. 1959. *The Presentation of Self in Everyday Life.* New York: Doubleday.

Granovetter, M. S. 1973. "The Strength of Weak Ties." *American Journal of Sociology* 78(6): 1360–1380.

Holtz-Bacha, C. 2004. "Political Campaigning Communication: Coordinated Convergence of Modern Media Election." *Comparing Political Communication: Theories, Cases and Challenges,* 213–230. Cambridge: Cambridge University Press.

Jackson, N. A., and D. G. Lilleker. 2009. "Building an Architecture of Participation? Political Parties and Web 2.0 in Britain." *Journal of Information Technology & Politics* 6(3–4): 232–250.

Jenkins, H. 2006. *Convergence Culture: Where Old and New Media Collide.* New York: NYU Press.

Lassen, D. S., and A. R. Brown. 2011. "Twitter: The Electoral Connection?" *Social Science Computer Review* 29(4):419–436.

Livak, L., A. Lev-On, and G. Doron. 2011. "MK Websites and the Personalization of Israeli Politics." *Israel Affairs* 17(3): 445–466.

Marichal, J. 2012. *Facebook Democracy: The Architecture of Disclosure and the Threat to Public Life*. London: Ashgate Publishing, Ltd.

Mayhew, D. R. 1974. *Congress: The Electoral Connection*, Vol. 26. New Haven, CT: Yale University Press.

Messmer, J. P., D. Carreiro, and K. A. Metivier-Carreiro. 2000. "Cyber-communication:

Congressional Use of Information Technologies." *Public Administration and Public Policy* 77: 281–298.

Meyrowitz, J. 1985. *No Sense of Place: The Impact of Electronic Media on Social Behavior*. New York: Oxford University Press.

Mutz, D. C. 2006. *Hearing the Other Side: Deliberative versus Participatory Democracy*. Cambridge: Cambridge University Press.

Negroponte, N. 1996. *Being Digital*. New York: Vintage Books.

Pariser, E. 2011. *The Filter Bubble: What the Internet Is Hiding from You*. New York: Penguin.

Pole, A. 2006. "Congressional Blogging: Advertising, Credit Claiming, and Position Taking." Presented at the 2006 American Political Science Association Annual Conference, Philadelphia, PA.

Sennett, R. 1977. *The Fall of Public Man*. New York: Alfred A. Knopf.

Smith, A., and J. Brenner. 2012. "Twitter Use 2012." Pew Internet & American Life Project. http://alexa.pewinternet.com/~/media/Files/Reports/2012/PIP_Twitter_Use_2012.pdf.

Sunstein, C. R. 2009. *Republic. com 2.0*. Princeton: Princeton University Press.

Van Zoonen, L. 2005. *Entertaining the Citizen: When Politics and Popular Culture Converge*. New York:Rowman & Littlefield Pub Incorporated.

Williams, C. B., and G. J. Gulati. 2010. "Communicating with Constituents in 140 Characters or Less: Twitter and the Diffusion of Technology Innovation in the United States Congress." Meeting of the Midwest Political Science Association, Chicago, IL.

7

NECESSARY AND DAMAGING?

PRESIDENTIAL BASE ELECTORAL STRATEGIES AND PARTISAN POLARIZATION

Lara M. Brown

There is a great risk of meeting a fool at home, but the candidate who travels cannot escape him. Benjamin Harrison, October 9, 1988 (Calhoun 2008, 132)

All presidential campaign strategies involve risk. Certain times, however, make some strategies riskier than others. For while it has long been understood that campaigns are about dividing an electorate in such a way as to construct a majority for one candidate, in periods when the electorate is already nearly equally split between the two parties, forging a majority coalition is a grueling task because both sides tend to fight harder and play dirtier.[1] In these moments, making the wrong strategic decision seems easier than making the right one. Equally taxing, times exist when, as historian Charles Calhoun has observed about the 1888 presidential contest, it is simply not possible to know—even in hindsight—whether or not a strategic decision will be determinative.[2] In the end, decisions may reveal more about politics than outcomes.

Yet despite all manner of treacherous terrain, serious candidates know that winning necessitates decisiveness on strategy early in the electoral cycle. Hesitation and delay seldom lead to success. Cognizant of their unique susceptibility to charges of ineptness, incumbent presidents facing reelection during "tough times" (e.g., a weak economy, an unpopular war, etc.) understand that this general campaign rule is an especially pertinent one for them. Customarily, candidates build their campaigns around one of two major strategies: persuasion (running toward the middle to win swing voters) or mobilization (running toward their base to turn out more partisan voters). While it is not appropriate to conceptualize these strategies as mutually exclusive, it is important to recognize that every campaign contends with resource constraints (e.g., time, money, and staff) that force the continual prioritization of these strategies.[3] Thus, if all candidates must choose and vulnerable incumbents must choose early (i.e., they cannot afford to wait for the opposition party to select its nominee), then how do incumbent presidents decide on their electoral strategy? So far as I am aware, this question has not been directly addressed.[4] Researchers interested in incumbent elections have instead focused on the impact of either the political conditions or the campaign's performance on the result. In essence, scholars have analyzed how and why incumbent presidents have won or lost reelection, but not how and why incumbents have made the decisions about their reelection campaigns that they made.[5]

This chapter looks to understand incumbent decision-making in what are known to be similarly fierce political times. It investigates the strategic rationales and the political circumstances that led Benjamin Harrison in 1892 to prioritize persuasion and Barack Obama in 2012 to prioritize mobilization. Working to situate these presidents within history, it verifies, as many have, that while both eras were highly competitive and the parties were nearly at parity in the electorate, the recent sorting of ideologues into their "correct" parties (i.e., liberals are mostly Democrats; conservatives are mostly Republicans) has made this period more polarized than the previous one.[6] This polarization, along with differing calculations about voters and turnout, has also made mobilization the preferred campaign strategy for the present moment.[7] In other words, the 2012 presidential election mirrored the 2004 election for a reason.[8] While Obama could have chosen persuasion, like President George W. Bush, it was more rational for him to prioritize mobilization. Similarly, Harrison could have chosen mobilization, but given the shape of the electorate and the state of the parties, persuasion was the preferred strategy. Although Harrison lost and Obama won, this chapter contends that each still made the appropriate decision given his specific circumstances. Hence, the elections' outcomes turned less on the incumbent's respective strategy than on the campaigns' execution and/or his political luck.[9]

More troubling, this analysis confirms that mobilization is not a normatively neutral strategy. In political systems with separated powers, mobilization not only makes postelection governing more challenging, but it also works to reinforce and magnify the partisan polarization already existing in the public sphere. Gary Jacobson aptly described this vicious cycle:

> Partisan reactions to presidents...have grown much stronger and more discordant over the past half-century or so...[it] shows up in the uglier rhetoric and more rancorous conflict that now marks the president's relations with rival politicians...it also shows up in the way ordinary Americans have come to regard their presidents. The actions and discourse of political leaders have primed citizens to react as partisans, while a more pervasively partisan electorate has increased the payoffs for (or at least reduced the costs of) partisan

intransigence in Washington. The Republicans' victory in the 2010 midterm elections provides a case in point; its aftermath also illustrates the corrosive effects of strategic polarization on governance and presidential leadership. (2012, 100)

Hence, mobilization appears to be a self-defeating electoral strategy when a president is unlikely to experience unified government.[10] In this sense, it appears irrational, despite its electoral benefits. However, deeper deliberation about the long-term consequences of polarization and the eventual resolution of the Gilded Age's contestation (i.e., a partisan convergence around progressive policies) suggest that our recent "Global Age" political battles and partisan vote swings may be fostering a new and different consensus (i.e., a partisan acceptance to revive federalism) in America. In sum, "even worse than it looks" may not be as bad as you think (Mann and Ornstein 2012).

Prior to presenting some data on the levels of electoral competition and partisan polarization in each of these historical eras, this chapter reviews the scholarly literature on incumbent elections and some related research on presidential decision-making. It then investigates the positions Presidents Harrison and Obama were in prior to their reelections, showing how their political circumstances, rather than their relationships with their parties shaped their campaign's strategies. Significantly, this chapter reveals that these presidents' strategic choices perpetuated, rather than altered each era's dominant politics, extending the trajectory that culminated (or in our time, seems likely to culminate) in major institutional change.

PRESIDENTIAL LEADERSHIP DECISIONS AND INCUMBENT ELECTIONS

Since this chapter is not concerned with whether incumbent presidents win or lose reelection, but how they play the game, scant literature is directly relevant.[11] That said, while examining a pervasive institutional issue titled, the *presidential leadership dilemma* (Azari et al. 2013), I explored a related decision-making process concerning presidential reelections in some of my prior research (Brown 2013).

For context, the *presidential leadership dilemma* is the difficulty that exists because "the constitutional structures of governance implore presidents to transcend political divisions, but the politically developed structures of selection ensure the president's involvement with one of the major parties. These structural conditions compel presidents to both unite and divide, or more precisely, to forge coalitions between elements they have sought to divide in their attempts to win office" (Azari et al. 2013, 4). Within this construct, the "third-year presidential leadership choice" is defined as the decision made by incumbents during their third year about the future "leadership course [national leader or party leader] that will help them not only win what is sure to be a fiercely competitive reelection campaign, but also place them on a governance trajectory that will help them define their presidency and frame their legacy" (Brown 2013, 62–63). This decision also includes the "strategic positioning and rhetorical commitments adopted for [their] reelection effort[s]" (Brown 2013, 63). Hence, this leadership choice (national or party) is intimately related to an incumbent's campaign decision to prioritize persuasion or mobilization. For should an incumbent president choose to be her party's leader, then she would also likely choose a mobilization strategy so as to reinforce her role as a committed partisan and principled ideological leader. It is also likely the case that an incumbent who was interested in becoming the nation's leader and rising above the partisan fray would choose persuasion so as to reassert her "fighting for all Americans" image.

Yet despite the similarity between these choices, I argued previously that an incumbent's third-year choice is mostly "structured…endogenously by each president's 'opportunism,' which…should be understood as not only a disposition, but also the accumulated biases (e.g., favored abilities and strategies), or the lessons learned from political experience" (Brown 2010, 20, 44, and 58, endnote 13). I further claimed that an incumbent's more recent experiences with her party (i.e., the difficulty surrounding her first nomination contest, the enthusiasm during her general election campaign, their relations during her first two years in office, and her perception of about the midterm election) constitute and inform her "accumulated biases" about politics (Brown 2013, 63). I have included "Table 3.1" from that work in appendix A. As that table shows, I asserted that "if a president's more recent experiences with his political party have taught him that he can count on their support then he dons the mantle of party leader; if his past experiences suggest that his party can be a fickle friend then he dons the mantle of national leader" (Brown 2013, 67). Lastly, I noted that while "other hypothetical permutations (e.g., 'easy' nomination, 'dutiful' election, 'critical' first two years, and 'pleased' midterm cycle) exist and may prove useful in future research," I only examined "the two most straightforward possibilities" (Brown 2013, 68).

What is interesting, however, about the two incumbents considered in this chapter (Benjamin Harrison and Barack Obama) is that neither enjoyed clear signals from their parties. While their individual partisan experiences will be discussed shortly, it is worth noting that a "straightforward" answer about which style of leadership they should pursue (party or national) was not available to them. Instead, both endured "hard" nominations, "enthusiastic" general elections, "supportive" first two years, and were highly "displeased" with the results of their first midterm elections. Hence, neither president was in a position to make an *endogenously* motivated choice. Their mixed experiences forced them outside to the *exogenous* events and conditions that were around them to choose their strategy. This study, therefore, tries to understand how these presidents perceived their similarly divisive eras and made their strategic decisions.

Along with this past scholarship, it is useful to review some of what political science knows about presidential reelections. Generally, as James

Campbell noted: "The evidence indicates that presidential incumbency has been an advantage for presidents seeking a second term...two-thirds of the twenty-one incumbents [from 1868–1996] seeking reelection were reelected" (2000, 103). Taking in more elections (1792–2000, while omitting 1824's multicandidate race), David Mayhew found the same winning proportion: "Incumbent candidacy makes a difference...in-office parties had kept the presidency exactly two-thirds of the time (20 out of 30 instances) when they ran incumbent candidates, and exactly half the time (11 out of 22 instances) when they did not" (2008, 213). In sum, when it comes to winning presidential elections, it helps to already be the president.

After probing more closely the election records of incumbents and reviewing other historical patterns (e.g., most win their reelections by larger popular and electoral vote margins than their first election), both Campbell and Mayhew offer some reasons for *why* they believe incumbents have possessed this electoral advantage.

- Campbell (2000, 110–124): (1) "political inertia," (2) "learning from experience," (3) "a unified party base," (4) "control of events and the agenda," and (5) "Rose Garden Strategy."
- Mayhew (2008, 214–225): (1) "incumbent capability acquired due to holding office," (2) "incumbent capability acquired in waging the preceding election campaign," (3) "voter attitudes" ("risk adverseness," "perceived start-up costs," "optimal contract," and "inertia"), (4) "innately superior talent," (5) "incumbent party fatigue," and (6) "strategic behavior."

Notably, the two lists show substantial overlap in terms of identifying the potential causes of incumbency advantage. Interestingly, neither work focuses much on why an incumbent might win or lose beyond these largely "personal trait" lists.[12] There is no mention of how the electorate may play a role except on Mayhew's list where it is delineated in terms of "voter attitudes" and "incumbent party fatigue," and/but these reasons mostly, describe a voter's assessment of the specific the incumbent. In other words, political events and structural conditions seem to matter little, whereas incumbent character, skill, and party unity seem to triumph. In the end, Campbell summarized that incumbency should be considered "an electoral opportunity, an opportunity that had on occasion been squandered but most often has been used to considerable advantage both before and during campaigns" (2000, 123–124).

This study pushes back some on that description of incumbency. It shows that the two presidents discussed in this research did not "squander" their "opportunities." Instead, it reveals that the circumstances under which these incumbents ran for reelection were such that many of the usual "advantages" that attend office-holding were either nonexistent, or worse perceived as liabilities. Hence, the notion of "change" was more the norm than "inertia," the "events and the agenda" were largely out of the control of the president, the president's party did not possess a "unified base," and/or the "Rose

Garden Strategy" was viewed as being "out of touch" with the people rather than "above" the partisan fray. In short, incumbency in these historical moments was not an opportunity, but a constraint. Furthermore, this notion of incumbency being a constraint seems truer now than even in the past because polarization appears to be driving an incumbent's job approval rating more than actual events or accomplishments (e.g., Pew Research Forum 2012).[13] In other words, in this modern polarized era, presidential challengers, particularly lesser known candidates, may have more room to maneuver than incumbents. Incumbents may not only be more defined by the governing duties associated with their office, but they may also be more politically confined. Thus, neither individual variation in political skill, nor past experiences with one's party may be as critical for understanding these two presidents' decisions as the historical circumstances they confronted as they embarked on their reelection campaigns.

Prior to delving into the particulars of the Gilded Age and the Global Age, it is helpful to recall the recent political experiences each president had had with his party and some of the specific issues he faced as he looked toward his reelection campaign.

1892: BENJAMIN HARRISON'S REELECTION PRIORITIZATION

The presidential boom for Senator Benjamin Harrison of Indiana began shortly after the 1886 midterm elections. Even though Harrison had lost his seat because of a Democratic gerrymander (which affected the state legislature's composition and its eventual vote for senator), he was seen as the one "available" candidate aligned with former nominee James G. Blaine who could keep Indiana in the Republican column (Calhoun 2010, 114). Still, winning the nomination was not easy. He was forced to not only compete against a large field of ambitious and seasoned Republicans, but also outmaneuver the party favorite, Blaine, who feigned disinterest, but desperately wanted to win. While much could be written about how Harrison bobbed and weaved his way through Blaine's false denials of interest in the nomination, cultivated the support of those delegates who preferred Blaine above all, but Harrison to the rest (e.g., John Sherman, Russell Alger, William Allison, and Walter Gresham), and eventually secured the party's nod on the eighth ballot at the Republican National Convention, for this research's purposes, it is sufficient to state, as hard as this may be to believe, that Harrison had the more difficult nomination of the two presidents discussed in this chapter.[14]

However, like Obama, Harrison's nomination struggle seemed to have made him not only a better, but also a better liked general election candidate. Furthermore, the deference he had shown to both Sherman and Blaine after he had secured the nomination brought on board more of his fellow partisans (Calhoun 2008, 120, 122, 124). Charles Calhoun noted: "[Harrison's] proven talents as an effective exponent of Republican beliefs impressed party leaders. Once the Republicans had chosen Harrison as their nominee, the vast majority stood ready to link arms and contend with the Democrats on the field that Cleveland had laid out in his December message to Congress [on lowering tariffs]" (Calhoun 2008, 124). With a savvy political boss, Senator Matthew Quay of Pennsylvania, in charge of the Republican national campaign, Harrison retired to his home in Indianapolis and "launched a full-fledged front porch campaign" (Calhoun 2008, 133). While his Democratic opponent, incumbent President Grover Cleveland made only one speech, keeping to a "Rose Garden" strategy, Harrison "gave over ninety speeches to more than 300,000 listeners...which [they made sure]...went to the Associated Press for publication in hundreds of newspapers...[so that] nearly every morning of the summer and fall, voters across the nation could read Harrison's words at their breakfast tables" (Calhoun 2008, 133). By the time of the election, Harrison and the Republicans had managed to push Cleveland toward his southern base (forcing him into to rely on a mobilization strategy), which allowed Harrison to capture the middle of the electorate. Hence, even though Cleveland had only argued for "tariff reform," the GOP linked him with what was then a fear-inducing phrase: "free trade" (Calhoun 2008, 145–146).

While the national popular vote went for Cleveland, both New York and Indiana went for Harrison, giving him the majority of electoral ballots and the presidency. Still, it was not as close as it looks: Cleveland only won the national popular vote because of the widespread suppression of the black vote in the South. Calhoun detailed: "Cleveland's overall plurality in the South stood at 563,869, while in the rest of the nation Harrison surpassed Cleveland by 473,273 votes" (Calhoun 2008, 179). Beyond this, Harrison earned nearly 88,000 more votes in New York than James G. Blaine did in 1884 and in his home state of Indiana he earned nearly 25,000 more votes than Blaine had four years earlier. The GOP also took the House majority and expanded their margin in the Senate. Harrison's popular vote minority was no indication of his party's enthusiasm for his candidacy.

Once inaugurated, Harrison aggressively pursued what he believed his electoral mandate had been: restoring protective tariffs, stabilizing the monetary system, and expanding the number of reciprocal trade agreements with the foreign countries (Calhoun 2005, 84). With House Speaker Thomas Reed largely agreeing with Harrison's priorities, the Congress passed several important pieces of legislation during its first session, including the McKinley Tariff Act and the Sherman Anti-Trust Act. Harrison was even adept in pushing forward the contentious Sherman Silver Purchase Act. After the act had been signed, the president's secretary recorded in his diary, "The President was feeling very good and all our friends were jubilant" (Calhoun 2005, 100). According to Charles Calhoun, "Congress adjourned on October 1, after one of the longest and most productive sessions in its history...newspapers and party spokesmen hailed the first session of the Fifty-first Congress for its 'unprecedented record'" (Calhoun 2005, 107). While Harrison had some difficulty with patronage appointments, he mostly enjoyed a criticism-free first few years.

Given his administration's legislative success, the midterm election results were surely shattering to Harrison. While the Republicans claimed that high tariffs helped to protect labor and their constituents on the eastern seaboard and in the industrial towns of the Midwest, populists across the country were increasingly growing frustrated with what they perceived as a rigged economy. Desiring a looser money supply and lower tariffs so that finished goods would be cheaper and their crops more saleable, the Farmer's Alliance became a force to be reckoned with. Fearful of the attraction to third parties in the rural and western parts of the Midwest, Harrison "took the unusual step of making a speaking tour through the region in early October to try to stem the losses" (Calhoun 2005, 108). His speeches appeared not to have made any difference. Republicans went from holding 179 seats in the House to only 86 seats (table 7.1). In the Senate, the GOP only lost four seats, but as Harrison himself explained even he thought the results were a "disaster" (Calhoun 2005, 108). Further, not long after the midterms, Blaine, whom Harrison had appointed Secretary of State, began making moves to challenge Harrison's presidential renomination.

Amid these mixed partisan messages, Harrison had no certainty over which leadership path he should choose. As such, the historical circumstances and structural conditions surrounding his presidency made persuasion a more attractive strategy than mobilization.

2012: BARACK OBAMA'S REELECTION PRIORITIZATION

Senator Barack Obama had a tough nomination race. When Obama entered the Democratic contest in February 2007, few thought he would be able to match the campaign efforts of the two "top tier" candidates: Senator Hillary Clinton of New York and former Democratic vice presidential nominee John Edwards. Both had national bases of support—hers from having served as First Lady and his from having run for president in 2004—and both had more experience in government than Obama (each had served more years in the Senate than Obama). Both were wrong. Obama not only managed to outraise both Clinton and Edwards in 2007, but in the Iowa caucuses, he also outmaneuvered each of them. Coming in first in the Hawkeye State, he upset media expectations and seriously stunned the Clinton campaign. While Clinton regrouped and won New Hampshire's primary, her campaign lost its sense of "inevitability" and was never again able to overtake Obama's message or momentum (Balz and Johnson 2009). Edwards dropped out on January 30, after coming in third in both South Carolina's primary and Florida's penalized contest, but Clinton stayed in the race all the way through the last election in June. Even though the Democratic National Convention was scripted to promote unity (i.e., Clinton interrupted and moved to suspend the roll call of the states and nominate Obama by acclamation) and Obama had support from some of the country's top Democrats (e.g., former Senator Tom Daschle and Senator Dick Durbin), there is no doubt about the fact that Obama had a long, "tough" road to winning the nomination.

Table 7.1 National Electoral Comparison of 1872–1894 and 1992–2012

Year	Winning Candidate/President (Party)	Popular Vote Margin (% of two-party Vote Share) or President's Party Midterm Seat Loss/ Gain House of Representatives (% of chamber)
1872	Grant (R)	6,431,149 (55.9)
1874	Grant (R)	−96 (32.7)
1876	Hayes (R)	−8,320,950 (48.5)
1878	Hayes (R)	−4 (1.4)
1880	Garfield (R)	9,070 (50.1)
1882	Arthur (R)	−34 (10.5)
1884	Cleveland (D)	57,579 (50.3)
1886	Cleveland (D)	−15 (4.6)
1888	Harrison (R)	−94,530 (49.6)
1890	Harrison (R)	−93 (28.0)
1892	Cleveland (D)	363,099 (51.7)
1894	Cleveland (D)	−125 (35.0)
1992	Clinton (D)	84,014,356 (53.5)
1994	Clinton (D)	−52 (12.0)
1996	Clinton (D)	86,598,880 (54.7)
1998	Clinton (D)	+4 (0.9)
2000	Bush (R)	−543,816 (49.7)
2002	Bush (R)	+9 (2.1)
2004	Bush (R)	3,012,171 (51.2)
2006	Bush (R)	−30 (6.9)
2008	Obama (D)	9,549,105 (53.7)
2010	Obama (D)	−65 (14.9)
2012	Obama (D)	4,977,275 (52.0)

Source: Data calculated by author using state vote totals available at http://www.uselectionatlas.org and party division totals available at http://history.house.gov/Institution/Party Divisions/Party-Divisions/. Modern midterm loss numbers are slightly different from those reported by the American Presidency Project (see http://www.presidency.ucsb.edu/data/mid-term_elections.php) because the numbers on the House website are those from after each congressional election and do not factor in special elections or vacancies.

At the outset of the general election, it looked as though Senator John McCain and Obama would have something of a horserace. The polls were close (Campbell 2010). Still, most believed that Obama would win the White House because the Democrats were far more enthusiastic than the Republicans and many voters had come to dislike incumbent Republican

President George W. Bush. When the economy came crashing down in mid-September, McCain's campaign came undone (Campbell 2010). McCain suspended his campaign and then suggested that the first presidential debate be postponed until legislation addressing the financial crisis was completed (Bentley 2008). McCain's rapid response was widely ridiculed rather than respected. Obama's poll lead grew and his candidacy started to appear unsinkable. On Election Day, every battleground state broke for Obama, including Virginia and North Carolina. He even picked up one electoral vote from Nebraska. Obama earned over 66 million votes, and bested McCain by a seven percent margin. Winning Independents and voters under 65, Obama was also helped by the fact that many Republican voters appeared to have stayed home (Gans 2008). If the nomination contest had left a slightly saccharin taste in Obama's mouth, then his general election was nothing but sugary sweetness with his party.

The sugar high, at least for the Democrats, lasted through Obama's first few years in office. With Speaker Nancy Pelosi leading the House and with a relatively large majority in the Senate, the Democrats were able to pass a substantial amount of legislation and President Obama was able to rack up the highest presidential success rate *Congressional Quarterly* (*CQ*) has ever given (96.7%). But as Sarah Binder explained: "[Obama] only took an official position on issues that were really important to him—those that he knew he had a very good chance of winning. He picked his battles carefully" (Gonyea 2010). By the second year of his administration, Democrats were voicing concerns about his handling of the closing down the Guantanamo Bay facility (Finn and Kornblut 2011), his sidelining of a comprehensive immigration reform bill (Jackson 2010), and his seeming unwillingness to push for a "cap and trade"' carbon tax bill (Condon 2010). Still, most were, according to Gallup's polling (2010), either "enthusiastic" (29%) or "pleased" (53%) with the passage of the Affordable Care Act of 2010. In the main, Obama's first two years were difficult in terms of his relations with Republicans, but he was largely praised by Democrats—elected officials and the public—for pursuing a partisan agenda and offering partisan rhetoric (Milkis et al. 2012).

Despite the organization and growth of the Tea Party in 2009, neither the President nor the Democrats seemed to realize how their legislative "success" had energized the GOP. When the votes were counted on Election Day, Republicans won a net gain of 63 seats in the House, which not only brought them the chamber's majority, but also was a larger net gain than any out-party had experienced since 1938 (+71).[15] Republicans also picked up six Senate seats and 11 governorships across the country. Afterward, Obama was quoted as saying that his party took a "shellacking." He further noted that Democrats had seemed to have "lost track" of their connection to the people, but he still stood by what they had accomplished with health care: "This was the right thing to do" (*NBC News* 2010).

Taken together, Obama's partisan experiences were mixed in a way similar to Harrison (tough nomination, enthusiastic general election, successful first few years, and a devastating midterm election). Interesting, however, Obama did not tack to the middle, initiate a persuasion campaign, or attempt to rise above the partisan fray. Instead he chose mobilization—the strategy consistent with his circumstances. Unlike Harrison, Obama won, but as will be discussed, this outcome also seems to be more consistent with his time.

THE GILDED AGE AND THE GLOBAL AGE

In addition to their similarly erratic relationships with their political parties, Harrison and Obama faced electorates that were not only almost equally divided between the parties, but also restless in their beliefs about which party deserved the opportunity to govern. Though public opinion was only anecdotally collected in Gilded Age, historians tend to characterize the era as one involving substantial turmoil (Weibe 1967; Painter 1989; McGerr 2003). Theodore Roosevelt later summarized the period's "great unrest" as stemming from "a fierce discontent with evil, of a determination to punish the authors of evil, whether in industry or politics" (1906). Over the last 20 years, the only time a majority of Americans have said they were "satisfied with the way things were going" was in the late 1990s. The average, dating back to 1979, has been 38% (Gallup 2013b).

Looking more closely on the 20 years prior to 1892, the nation endured a major congressional scandal (Credit Mobilier in 1872–1873); a tied presidential election with a partisan decided result (Rutherford Hayes in 1876); a patronage motivated presidential assassination (James Garfield in 1881); three majority party switches in the House (Democrats won in 1874; Republicans won in 1880; and Democrats won in 1882) and two in the Senate (Democrats won in 1878; and Republicans won in 1880); and two presidential elections (1880 and 1884) where the winners were separated from the losers in the two decisive states (New York and Indiana) by a small number of votes (Calhoun 2010, 3–9).[16] Beyond this, the popular vote for president alternated between Republicans and Democrats, and neither party seemed able to reelect their presidential incumbents. Furthermore, incumbent Chester Arthur, who had risen to the presidency after Garfield died, was unexpectedly denied the Republican nomination in 1884 (Calhoun 2010, 80–87).

Reflecting on the 20 years prior to 2012, it becomes evident that it has been a comparably tumultuous time. The country witnessed a third-party presidential candidate secure close to one-fifth of the national popular vote (Ross Perot in 1992); a partisan budget battle that culminated in two federal government shutdowns (in 1995–1996); a partisan investigation that led to only the second presidential impeachment in the nation's history (in 1998–1999); a nearly tied presidential election with a partisan adjudicated outcome (George W. Bush in 2000); the first major terrorist attack on American soil (in 2001) that resulted in two wars (Afghanistan and Iraq), in which one quickly became a partisan cause (Iraq in 2003); three majority party switches in the House (Republicans won in 1994; Democrats won in 2006; and Republicans won in 2010); and four majority party switches in Senate

(Republicans won in 1994; Republican Jim Jeffords defected from his party and forced a power-sharing agreement in 2001; Republicans won in 2002; and Democrats won in 2006). While there was more stability in the presidency (incumbents Bill Clinton and George W. Bush were each reelected), neither party seemed able to hold the office for a third term (both Vice President Al Gore and Senator John McCain lost).

Aside from the raucous partisan politics, both periods experienced major economic transformations. The Industrial Revolution kicked into high gear (railroads, electricity, interchangeable parts, assembly line production, etc.) after the invention of Bessemer steel in the 1860s and continued its expansion at a break-neck pace up until World War I. Likewise, the Information Age galloped ahead once the Internet was commercialized in the early 1990s and few believe that this technological revolution will slow down any time soon. In both of these periods, wealth increased significantly, as entrepreneurial capitalists set to work selling the new technologies to the American people and making a fortune in the process (Steele 2004, 205–263, 405–419). From railroads and electricity to web-based computing and smart phones, rapid changes in transportation and communication led to exponential increases in productivity. High levels of risky speculation, coupled with panics and busts—in 1873 and 1893, and in 2001 and 2008—contributed to the economic unpredictability of these times. Yet despite these political and economic similarities, these historical periods appear different in at least one important respect: partisan polarization.

While survey data have enabled researchers to track the growing polarization over the last 20 years (see, for instance, Pew Research Forum2012; Gallup 2013a), it is more challenging to uncover the partisan trends in the late nineteenth century. Figures 7.1 and 7.2, however, offer some sense of the distinct partisan differences between the eras. Since there were fewer states in the nation during the Gilded Age than there are now, these charts present a modified measure of the level of polarization developed by Galston and Nivola (2006, 13–14). Instead of reporting the *number* of states (including the District of Columbia) where the winning candidate's vote share was more than either 5 percentage points above or below his national average, they report the *percentage* of states (including the District of Columbia) where the winning candidate's vote share was more than either 5 percentage points above or below his national average. In addition, in order to reveal how much each party is responsible for this total level of polarization, I included the percentage of polarized states won by the Democrats and the percentage of polarized states won by the Republicans on the same figures.

Figure 7.1 shows that overall the level of polarization in the earlier period did not exceed 53 percent of the states, whereas figure 7.2 reveals that only once (1992) in the modern period was the level of polarization *below* 55 percent of states. Both periods also show an election where it appears as though the parties were very far apart from each other (1872 and 1992), but that is something of an artifact of those contests being relative landslides (Grant earned nearly 56% of the two-party vote and Clinton earned about 53.5% of

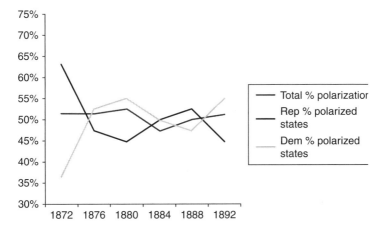

Figure 7.1 Percent of Polarized States, 1872–1892.

Source: Data calculated by author using state by state vote totals available at http://www. uselectionatlas.org (accessed April 5, 2013). Polarized states are those where the winning/ losing margin exceeds ±5 percent of the national two-party vote share for the winning candidate.

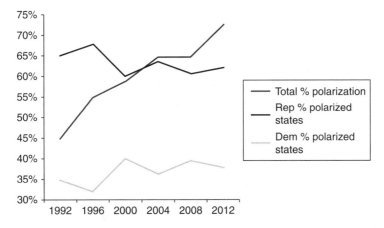

Figure 7.2 Percent of Polarized States, 1992–2012.

Source: Data calculated by author using state by state vote totals available at http://www. uselectionatlas.org (accessed April 5, 2013). Polarized states are those where the winning/ losing margin exceeds ±5 percent of the national two-party vote share for the winning candidate.

the two-party vote) and many of the competitive states siding heavily with the winning candidate. In sum, the level of polarization is more meaningful when the aggregate popular vote share is nearly split (e.g., 1880, 1884, 1888, and 2000 and 2004). Nevertheless, in the early period, Democrats and the Republicans appear to alternate responsibility for the level of polarization, though the Democrats seem more responsible for it in more elections than the Republicans. In the modern era, Republicans appear more responsible for the high levels of polarization than the Democrats. However, over the course of the period, the Republican percentage of polarized states declined (about 6%), whereas the Democratic percentage increased (about 6%). Taken together, these trends suggest three things: (1) that polarization may be driven more by the "solid" nature of the South, than by a specific party; (2) the swing toward the winning party in the competitive states often results in that party's base states becoming polarized; and (3) in the modern period, northern states (Democratic states, like New York) seem to be growing less competitive, whereas southern states (Republican states, like South Carolina) seem to be growing more competitive. For instance, in 1996, Clinton earned approximately 11% more than his national two-party vote share in New York and about 8% less than his national two-party vote share in South Carolina. In 2012, Obama's percentage in New York was about 12% and about 7% in South Carolina. While this last trend may be somewhat counterintuitive given all of the evidence showing that the recent polarization arises from the Republican Party, it is not surprising when one considers both the patterns of migration from the Rust Belt to the Sun Belt and those of immigration from foreign countries to the South. In sum, it makes sense that the region that is contracting would also be growing more homogenous and polarized, while the region that is expanding would be growing more heterogeneous or "purple." Still, this last trend appears in its infancy and it could easily reverse in the next few election cycles.

Table 7.2 offers a different, albeit more familiar perspective on polarization. It shows Poole and Rosenthal's DW-NOMINATE scores for both the House and the Senate for each historical era, going back to the Congress elected in 1878 and concluding with the Congress elected in 2010. Again, these data reveal that the parties appear to be more polarized in the modern period, even though the different chambers of Congress appear to be differently polarized. During the Gilded Age, the Democrats were the more polarized party (further from the "0" point) and the Senate was the more polarized chamber (larger difference of means). The opposite appears true today. Figure 7.3 compares the difference of party mean scores calculated by Poole and Rosenthal for the two periods. Looking at this last figure, it is clear that the overall polarization in Congress has not only grown in the modern period, but also that the trend line is substantially different from the one from the earlier period.

While the partisan story behind the modern numbers has been traced by several scholars to the realignment of the electorate since the Civil Right Movement of the 1960s, few have remarked on what these changes have meant for presidential candidates.[17] In simple terms, the two incumbents faced electorates that were nearly evenly divided between the parties, but as the data suggest, the position of these states and their representatives along an ideological spectrum were different. As figure 7.1 shows, in 1884, both parties had an equal percentage of polarized states and the total level of polarization in the country was below 50 percent. Table 7.2 reveals that the

Table 7.2 Party Means by Chamber (DW-NOMINATE), 1878–1892 and 1996–2010

Year	House			Senate		
	Democratic	Republican	Difference	Democratic	Republican	Difference
1878	−0.39	0.38	0.77	−0.60	0.23	0.83
1880	−0.40	0.37	0.77	−0.60	0.23	0.83
1882	−0.35	0.36	0.71	−0.60	0.22	0.82
1884	−0.38	0.36	0.74	−0.60	0.21	0.81
1886	−0.39	0.37	0.76	−0.59	0.21	0.80
1888	−0.41	0.39	0.80	−0.58	0.22	0.80
1890	−0.37	0.40	0.77	−0.56	0.24	0.80
1892	−0.39	0.42	0.81	−0.53	0.24	0.77
1996	−0.37	0.49	0.86	−0.37	0.38	0.75
1998	−0.37	0.51	0.88	−0.36	0.37	0.73
2000	−0.37	0.54	0.91	−0.36	0.38	0.74
2002	−0.37	0.57	0.94	−0.35	0.37	0.72
2004	−0.38	0.60	0.98	−0.37	0.40	0.77
2006	−0.36	0.63	0.99	−0.35	0.42	0.77
2008	−0.34	0.66	1.00	−0.36	0.43	0.79
2010	−0.39	0.68	1.07	−0.36	0.49	0.85

Source: Data compiled by author using the Republican and Democratic Party means on the first DW-NOMINATE dimension, available at the http://voteview.com/Political_Polarization.asp.

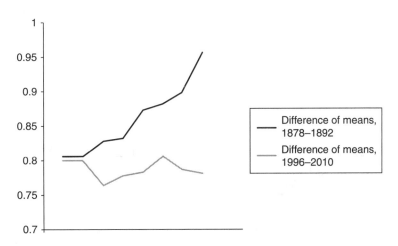

Figure 7.3 Difference of Means (DW-NOMINATE) in Congress, 1878–1892 and 1996–2010.

Source: Data compiled by author using the Republican and Democratic Party means on the first DW-NOMINATE dimension available at the http://voteview.com/Political_Polarization.asp.

mean Democratic position in the Senate that year was about 0.8 points away from the mean Republican position in Senate. On the other hand, those entries for the modern period show that in 2004, fully 65 percent of the states were polarized and the Republican states were responsible for far more of the polarization (about 64%) than the Democratic states (36%). In addition, the mean Republican position in the House was about 1 point away from the mean Democratic position in the House. Hence, when Harrison began considering his reelection campaign strategy (1891), these structural circumstances had not only largely persisted for the previous seven years, but they also suggested that persuasion may be possible. In other words, competitive states were plentiful and elected officials articulated partisan platforms that were not terribly far apart. When Obama began considering his reelection campaign strategy (2011), the polarization had grown worse in the House and had remained at a high level in the 2008 election. In other words, with few competitive states overall and more partisan solidarity in the Democratic states and among congressional Republicans, there was little room to launch a persuasion strategy. Thus, "circling the wagons" and "cheer-leading" one's party to victory (mobilization) makes the most sense given the present circumstances.

Figure 7.4 presents another facet of these electorates that the incumbents likely considered: voter turnout. The percent of the voting age population who turned out and voted in these presidential elections, as is widely known, was much greater during the Gilded Age than the Global Age. This fact made both incumbent presidents' decisions all the more rational.

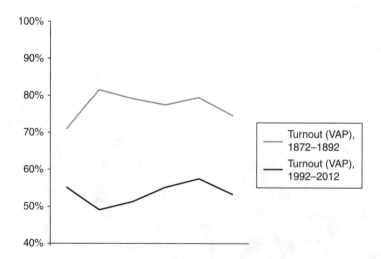

Figure 7.4 Turnout Levels (VAP) in Presidential Elections, 1872–1892 and 1992–2012.

Source: Data compiled by author using the "Voting Turnout in Presidential Elections" for those elections through 2008 available at http://www.presidency.ucsb.edu/data/turnout.php and for 2012, consulting Michael McDonald's "2012 General Election Turnout Rates" available at http://elections.gmu.edu/Turnout_2012G.html.

Harrison likely chose persuasion because the parties were already turning out impressively large numbers of their eligible voters. If he pursued mobilization, how many more voters could he realistically expect to bring to the polls? Not many. Hence, there was more room for him to expand his coalition by "converting" those who had voted than in turning out those who had not voted. The reverse calculation was true for Obama. With fewer "swing" voters and more citizens voting in line with their party identification in the modern period (Mayer 2012), the room to grow one's coalition exists in the lower turnout figures. Daron Shaw's analysis of the increase in turnout since 1996 seems to confirm this: "The increased number of voters is driven by the more effective mobilization of a growing eligible electorate" (2012, 9).

Beyond these data, there exists an interesting difference between these time periods in the sources through which partisanship was activated and reinforced. During the Gilded Age, the political parties fostered and maintained mass participation and voter engagement. Machine politics meant that the bosses were involved in the daily lives of people. Further, no opportunity was ever passed up to recruit another partisan (Riordan 1963). Today, while the parties still work hard to encourage citizen involvement, much of the partisan zeal is fueled by the increasingly diversified media. While the media, like parties, possess a pervasive interest in growing the size of their audience, they use a different method to attract people. Although the parties may try to blur distinctions (Downs 1957), the media tend to hype controversy and promote conflict to lure viewers to "tune in" (Mann and Ornstein 2012, 60–67). Unfortunately, this "out-sourcing" to the media seems to be fostering not only "increasingly negative [opinions] towards the other party and its candidates" (Shaw 2012, 12), but also smaller, more ideologically rigid parties and in nonelection years particularly, large numbers of self-identifying independents who are disenchanted with the parties (Gallup 2012).

Although there are many other distinctions between these historical eras that could be discussed in detail (e.g., the factional compositions of the parties, the turnout methods of the bosses versus today's parties, and the roles the candidates play in the campaigns, etc.), the critical take away from this structural comparative is that incumbents in the Gilded Age perceived benefits in pursuing a persuasion strategy that today's presidents do not. Thus, despite being similarly competitive, the periods promoted different political and electoral calculations. Still, the Gilded Age's "paradoxical blend of stability and disarray" offers an intriguing possibility regarding today's politics. Charles Calhoun summarized it well:

> In the last three decades of the nineteenth century, the political struggles of the Gilded Age had laid the groundwork for this transformation and the emergence of the modern American polity. In the great debates over civil rights and economic policy...the underlying question concerned what role the national government should play in the society...nationally oriented Republicans...

envisioned an expansive role for the federal government in managing the economy to further the nation's development. Unlike Cleveland Democrats, still imbued with the small-government notions of Jefferson and Jackson, these Republicans had come to accept was more than a negative force, that it could do something to stimulate the country's growth and thereby improve the lot of the people...And in pressing the argument for government action, they not only charted a course for their own time; they also set the stage for the great contest in the Progressive Era over the duty and function of government in a modern society. (2010, 182–183)

Thus, the fighting, gridlock, and pendulum swings during the Gilded Age eventually forged a new political consensus. While not realized until the Progressive Era, the sentiment in favor of an energetic, strong, and professionalized national (no longer merely federal) government grew amid the partisan wrestling. Cycle after cycle of persuasion strategies brought the parties closer together on the reform issues. Eventually, the Democrats were able to capture the middle (i.e., the key development was President Woodrow Wilson's reelection in 1916) and become the party responsible for the vast changes in the role of government and the regulation of the economy in the last century (Milkis 2009).

Given this history, the question remains: are these last 20 years of similarly unstable politics already working toward the generation of a new consensus? If this is the case, then it certainly seems possible that "even worse than it looks" may not be as "bad as you think."

IMPLICATIONS AND CONCLUSIONS

While not much explored in this chapter, there are signs that the new consensus forming may involve a rejection of Washington and a restoration and reinvention of the federalism that was overtaken by the progressive impulse (Kamarck 2007; Mele 2013). For the last two decades, "limited government" movements and candidates have caught on with the public in ways that those on the progressive end of the spectrum have not. Aside from Ross Perot's deficit cutting plea in 1992 and the Tea Party's returning constitutional principles message in 2009, Speaker Newt Gingrich's 1994 "Contract with America" and Representative Ron Paul's libertarian-leaning presidential platform both generated more enthusiasm than either of the progressive platforms offered by consumer advocate Ralph Nader or Representative Dennis Kucinich. Further, even the more recent Occupy Wall Street Movement, which sought to place the "99% before the 1%" disintegrated before they could realize any political gains. Beyond this, the movement toward states' rights does not seem to be an exclusively conservative (Brownstein 2013).

More explicitly, the longer view suggests that the Gilded Age's battle eventually forged a progressive consensus about the need to empower and professionalize Washington (e.g., Pendleton Act, Hatch Act, Federal Reserve Board, Federal Trade Commission, etc.) and eviscerate the corrupt state and local party bosses (e.g., Australian ballot and seventeenth Amendment). Hence, it seems possible that the current period's fierceness may be giving way to a new consensus that is pushing for more citizen involvement at more local and state levels (Brookings 2012; Mele 2013). In short, it seems possible that the next "post-partisan" consensus can be summed up in an old slogan: "think globally, act locally." This time, however, it may not only include things like locally grown produce and farmers' markets, but it may also well come to mean city activism and state-specific legislation. While it may sometime before this takes shape (polarization is likely to be here for a while longer, especially after the divisive 2012 presidential election), the mirror image parallels between Global Age politics and those of the Gilded Age are striking and should be explored further.

Returning to the issue of presidential campaigns and today's polarization, this chapter situated Harrison and Obama within history and showed the ways in which their political circumstances likely affected the nature of their reelection campaigns. Considering the electorate, it suggested why Harrison chose to prioritize persuasion, whereas Obama chose mobilization. It also asserted that the longer-term consequences of polarization may not be as normatively problematic as they appear at first blush. Thus, like the Gilded Age's contestation, the people and our government may be working to foster a new consensus—one that reinvigorates federalism—about the role of government in America.

APPENDIX A

REPLICATION OF TABLE 3.1 FROM "PLAYING FOR HISTORY: THE REELECTION LEADERSHIP CHOICES OF PRESIDENTS WILLIAM J. CLINTON AND GEORGE W. BUSH"

Table 3.1– Framework of a President's Past Partisan Experiences on their Leadership Choice

| | Leadership Choice | |
	Party Leader	National Leader
Partisan		
Experience		
Nomination Contest		
Easy	X	
Hard		X
Presidential Election		
Enthusiastic	X	
Dutiful		X
First Two Years in Office		
Supportive	X	
Critical		X
Midterm Election		
Pleased	X	
Displeased		X

Source: Brown, Lara. 2013. "Playing for History: The Reelection Leadership Choices of Presidents William J. Clinton and George W. Bush." In *The Presidential Leadership Dilemma: Between the Constitution and a Political Party*, edited by Julia R. Azari, Lara M. Brown, and Zim Nwokora. (Albany, NY: State University of New York Press, p.). Reprinted with permission from SUNY Press.

NOTES

1. While negative advertisements are only one indicator of electoral competitiveness, they have the advantage over some other electoral data (i.e., popular votes) of capturing the overall tone of the campaign. For instance, the Wesleyan Media

Project's authors noted that, along with "unprecedented volumes of advertising" in 2012, the advertising "was also extremely negative, especially at the presidential level, and frequently evoked the emotion of anger" (Fowler and Ridout 2013).

2. Charles Calhoun aptly described 1888: "Leaders of both major parties knew that neither could regard itself as the favorite to win the presidency. Republicans and Democrats alike recognized that they confronted an arduous struggle and that winning would require the effective management of the party machinery as well as the mounting of a persuasive campaign of education...the outcome was extremely close, and in a campaign filled with dramatic incidents, no one could discount the impact of sheer luck (2008, 125)." Benjamin Harrison earned about 14,000 more votes than Grover Cleveland out of about 1.4 million votes in New York. Had approximately 7,500 of those swung to Cleveland, he would have not only won the national popular vote majority, but also the Electoral College and reelection (Campbell 2000, 172–173).

3. While it is true that all campaigns must do both (persuasion and mobilization), the simplest way to conceptualize this choice is through the voter contact process. Over the course of a campaign, all contacted voters are placed on a five-point scale with 1 being a strong supporter, and 5 being a strong opponent. Campaigns typically do not target either 1s (definitely with) or 5s (definitely against). Instead, in the real world of limited resources (time and money), campaign must decide whether they do outreach to the 2s (leaning toward) to ensure they vote or the 3s (neither for nor against) to bring them into the campaign. Most campaigns do not bother to try to dissuade the 4s (leaning against) from turning out, but this also can be an effective strategy.

4. As I will discuss shortly, I have previously sought to answer a related question with which incumbent presidents must contend (leadership choice in the third year in office), but in the case of Harrison and Obama, my previous theory is not easily applicable.

5. While vast research exists on what makes a winning or losing presidential campaign and whether campaigns even matter (for a review of this literature, see Shaw 2006, Chapter 2), few scholars have sought to relate this literature to that which exists on the nature of presidential leadership and the importance of political time (see, for instance, Neustadt 1960; Hargrove 1966; Barber 1977; Skowronek 1993; Greenstein 2000). For an exception, see Brown 2010.

6. While this chapter follows Galston and Nivola (2006) and uses presidential vote returns as a measure of "polarization," Abrams and Fiorina criticized this approach: "far from minimizing the effects of different candidates, reliance on presidential voting returns maximizes the effects of different candidates" (2012, 203).

7. I am grateful to James E. Campbell for this insight on the "diminishing returns" reality of a mobilization strategy during the generally high-turnout elections during the Gilded Age.

8. As political scientists, Larry Sabato, Kyle Kondik, and Geoffrey Skelley at the University of Virginia explained: "What election was 2012 most like?...No election is exactly like another, but there are similarities...2012 most resembled 2004, when an incumbent president had a mixed record that had polarized Americans, but won with a superior organization, favorable demographics and effective early attacks on an opponent from Massachusetts" (*Crystal Ball*, 2012).

9. See note 2.

10. In only about six of the past 32 years (1993–1995, 2003–2007, and 2009–2011) has the president party's held the majority in both chambers of Congress. George W. Bush also enjoyed unified government for approximately the first five months of his presidency, but then Vermont Senator Jim Jeffords switched parties, which produced an even split in the partisan control of that chamber.

11. While vast research exists on what makes a winning or losing presidential campaign and whether campaigns even matter (for a review of this literature, see Shaw 2006, Chapter 2), few scholars have sought to relate this literature to that which exists on the nature of presidential leadership and the importance of political time (see, for instance, Neustadt 1960; Hargrove 1966; Barber 1977; Skowronek 1993; Greenstein 2000). For an exception, see Brown (2010).

12. Campbell, however, spent much of his book focusing on the economy's impact on presidential elections, which in his description of the structural campaign mediates an incumbent's advantage (2008, 128–142).

13. Even though more incumbents win reelection in the modern period than in the previous era (see table 7.1), this seems more related to the institutional accretion and purposive insulation (e.g., gerrymandering, party rules, and campaign finance benefit incumbents) that has occurred over time. In other words, our political system generally appears much less responsive to shifts in voter sentiment than it was 120 years ago.

14. For a complete description of Harrison's nomination challenge, see Calhoun (2008, 73–124).

15. For comparison data on a presidential party's midterm losses in Congress, see http://www.presidency.ucsb.edu/data/mid-term_elections.php (accessed April 7, 2013).

16. In 1880, James Garfield won New York by 21,003 (about 1.1 million ballots were cast) and Indiana by 6,612 votes (about 500,000 ballots were cast). Together, these states were worth 50 electoral votes and had they swung the other way, Winfield Hancock would have won the presidency. In 1884, the election was even closer. For although Grover Cleveland won both Indiana and New York for the Democrats that year, if he had lost New York's 36 electoral votes, he would have lost the presidency to James Blaine. Further, Cleveland's margin of victory in the Empire State was 1,149 votes out of the approximately 1.2 million ballots cast.

17. For an exception, see Jacobson (2012).

REFERENCES

Abrams, Samuel J., and Morris Fiorina. 2012. "'The Big Sort' That Wasn't: A Skeptical Reexamination." *PS: Political Science and Politics* 45 (April2): 203–209.

Azari, Julia R., Lara M. Brown, and Zim G. Nwokora, eds. 2013. *The Presidential Leadership Dilemma: Between the Constitution and a Political Party*. Albany, NY: State University of New York Press.

Balz, Dan, and Hayes Johnson. 2009. *The Battle for America 2008: The Story of an Extraordinary Election*. New York: Viking.

Bentley, John. 2008. "McCain Suspends Campaign." *CBS News* September 24. http://www.cbsnews.com/8301-502443_162-4475541-502443.html.

Brown, Lara M. 2010. *Jockeying for the American Presidency: The Political Opportunism of Aspirants*. Amherst, NY: Cambria Press.

Brookings Institution (A Project Managed by Bruce Katz and Mark Mauro). 2012. "Remaking Federalism | Renewing the Economy: Resetting Federal Policy to Recharge the Economy, Stabilize the Budget, and Unleash State and Metropolitan Innovation." Brookings Institution. http://www.brookings.edu/research/papers/2012/11/13-federalism-budget-economy (accessed April 13, 2013).

Brownstein, Ron. 2013. "How Washington Ruined Governors." On NationalJournal. com, released April 12. http://www.nationaljournal.com/magazine/how-washington-ruined-governors-20130411 (accessed April 13, 2013).

Calhoun, Charles W. 2005. *Benjamin Harrison.* New York: Times Books.

———. 2010. *From Bloody Shirt to Full Lunch Pail: The Transformation of Politics and Governance in the Gilded Age.* New York: Hill and Wang.

———. 2008. *Minority Victory: Gilded Age Politics and the First Front Porch Campaign of 1888.* Lawrence, KS: Kansas University Press.

Campbell, James E. 2000. *The American Campaign: U.S. Presidential Campaigns and the National Vote.* College Station, TX: Texas A&M University Press.

———. 2010. "The Exceptional Election of 2008: Performance, Values, and Crisis." *Presidential Studies Quarterly* 40, (2): 225–246.

Condon, Stephanie. 2010. "White House: 'Cap and Trade' is Out." *CBS News Online* March 31. http://www.cbsnews.com/8301–503544_162–20001508–503544. html (accessed April 8, 2013).

Down, Anthony. 1957. *An Economic Theory of Democracy.* New York: Harper and Row.

Finn, Peter, and Anne E. Kornblut. 2011. "Guantanamo Bay: Why Obama Hasn't Fulfilled His Promise to Close the Facility." *Washington Post* April 23. http://www.washingtonpost.com/world/guantanamo-bay-how-the-white-house-lost-the-fight-to-close-it/2011/04/14/AFtxR5XE_story.html (accessed on April 7, 2013).

Fowler, Erika Franklin, and Travis N. Ridout. 2013. "Negative, Angry, and Ubiquitous: Political Advertising in 2012." *The Forum* 10(4): 51–61. http://www.degruyter.com/view/j/for.2012.10.issue-4/forum-2013–0004/forum-2013–0004.xml?format=INT (accessed April 7, 2013).

Galston, William, and Pietro Nivola. 2006. "Delineating the Problem." In *Characteristics and Causes of America's Polarized Politics*, edited by Pietro Nivola and David Brady. Washington, DC: Brookings.

Gallup (Lydia Saad). 2010. "By Slim Margin, Americans Support Healthcare Bill's Passage." Released March 23. http://www.gallup.com/poll/126929/slim-margin-americans-support-healthcare-bill-passage.aspx (accessed April 20, 2013).

———(Jeffrey Jones). 2012. "Record-high 40% of Americans Identify as Independents in '11.'" Released January 9. http://www.gallup.com/poll/151943/Record-High-Americans-Identify-Independents.aspx (accessed April 20, 2013).

———(Jeffrey Jones). 2013a. "Obama's Fourth Year in Office Ties as Most Polarized Ever." Released January 24. http://www.gallup.com/poll/160097/obama-fourth-year-office-ties-polarized-ever.aspx (accessed April 20, 2013).

———(Jeffrey Jones). 2013b. "U.S. Satisfaction Improved in 2012, but Still Below Average." Released January 10. http://www.gallup.com/poll/159803/satisfaction-improved-2012-below-average.aspx (accessed April 10, 2013).

Gans, Curtis. 2008. "Much-hyped Turnout Record Fails to Materialize Convenience Voting Fails to Boost Balloting." Official Release by the Center for the

Study of the American Electorate (CSAE) on November 6. http://www.american. edu/spa/cdem/upload/csae2008gpprfull.pdf (accessed April 20, 2013).

Gonyea, Don. 2010. "CQ: Obama's Winning Streak On Hill Unprecedented." *NPR Online* January 11. http://www.npr.org/templates/story/story. php?storyId=122436116 (accessed April 10, 2013).

Jackson, David. 2010. "Obama Still Committed to 'Comprehensive Immigration Reform.'" *USA Today* September 17. http://content.usatoday.com/communi-ties/theoval/post/2010/09/obama-still-committed-to-comprehensive-immi-gration-reform/1#.UXVE88p42Sp (accessed July 10, 2012).

Jacobson, Gary. 2007. *A Divider, Not a Uniter: George W. Bush and the American People*. New York: Pearson Education.

———. 2012. "Presidents, Partisans, and Polarized Politics." in *Can We Talk?: The Rise of Rude, Nasty, Stubborn Politics*, edited by Daniel Shea and Morris Fiorina. New York: Pearson.

Kamarck, Elaine. 2007. *The End of Government...As We Know It: Making Public Policy Work*. Colorado: Lynne Rienner Publishers.

Mann, Thomas, and Norman J. Ornstein. 2012. *It's Even Worse Than It Looks: How the American Constitutional System Collided With the New Politics of Extremism*. New York: Basic Books.

Mayer, William G. 2012. "The Disappearing—but Still Important—Swing Voter." *The Forum* 10(3). ISSN (Online) 1540-8884.

Mayhew, R. David. 2008. "Incumbency Advantage in U.S. Presidential Elections: The Historical Record, *Political Science Quarterly* 123: 2 (201–228).

McGerr, Michael. 2003. *A Fierce Discontent: The Rise and Fall of the Progressive Movement in America*. New York: Oxford University Press.

Mele, Nicco. 2013. *The End of Big: How the Internet Makes David the New Goliath*. New York: St. Martin's Press.

Milkis, Sidney M. 2009. *Theodore Roosevelt, the Progressive Party, and the Transformation of American Democracy*. Lawrence, KS: University Press of Kansas.

Milkis, Sidney M., Jesse Rhodes, and Emily Charnock. 2012. "What Happened to Post-Partisanship? Barack Obama and the New American Party System." *Perspectives on Politics* 10(1) (March):57–76.

NBC News.com. 2010. "After 'Shellacking,' Obama Laments Disconnect with Voters." Released on November 3. http://www.nbcnews.com/id/39987154/ ns/politics-decision_2010/t/after-shellacking-obama-laments-disconnect-vot-ers/#.UXVH_Mp42Sp (accessed April 10, 2013).

Painter, Nell Irvin. 1989. *Standing at Armageddon: The United States, 1877–1919*. New York: W.W. Norton & Company.

Pew Research Forum. 2012. "Partisan Polarization Surges in Bush, Obama Years." Released June 4. http://www.people-press.org/2012/06/04/partisan-polariza-tion-surges-in-bush-obama-years/ (accessed April 15, 2013).

Roosevelt, Theodore. 1906. "The Man with the Muck-Rake." Address given April 14. http://voicesofdemocracy.umd.edu/theodore-roosevelt-the-man-with-the-muck-rake-speech-text/ (accessed April 10, 2013).

Shaw, Daron. 2006. *The Race to 270: The Electoral College and the Campaign Strategies of 2000 and 2004*. Chicago, IL: The University of Chicago Press.

———.2012. "If Everyone Votes Their Party, Why Do Presidential Election Outcomes Vary So

Much?" *The Forum* 10(3). ISSN (Online) 1540-8884, DOI: 10.1515/1540-8884.1519, October 2012.

Steele, John Gordon. 2004. *An Empire of Wealth: The Epic History of American Economic Power*. New York: Harper Perennial.

Weibe, Robert. H. 1967. *The Search For Order, 1877–1920*. New York: Hill and Wang.

8

A POLARIZING COURT?

ANALYZING JUDICIAL DECISIONS IN A RED/BLUE AMERICA

Kevin J. McMahon

As the year 2000 neared conclusion, the Supreme Court of the United States announced its decision in *Bush v. Gore*, putting an end to one of the most contested presidential elections in American history. Liberal critics of the ruling, which effectively declared that Republican George W. Bush would be the nation's next president, denounced the Court for undertaking nothing short of a "constitutional coup."[1] Conservatives hailed the decision for providing clarity to an election left uncertain by Florida's vote counting process and by the closeness of the vote there. Liberals pointed to the fact that the five most conservative justices joined forces to declare the more conservative of the presidential candidates the victor. Conservatives responded by noting that Republican presidents had appointed two of the four justices in dissent. Nearly everyone agreed that the decision was a prime example of the increasing polarization defining the nation's politics.

Twelve years later, with *Bush v. Gore* and the more recent *Citizens United* likely in mind, legal commentators from both ends of the ideological spectrum speculated on how the high Court might rule on the constitutionality of the linchpin of Affordable Care Act of 2010, the individual mandate. While some certainly thought otherwise, many, especially after listening to the oral arguments of the case, predicted that a conservative majority of the justices would deliver a deathblow to the law, rendering null and void the most significant piece of legislation passed by a Democratic Congress and signed by a Democratic president since the 1960s. However, of course, those predictions turned out to be wrong. In what apparently was a very difficult decision for him, Chief Justice John Roberts joined his four most liberal colleagues in reaching a ruling that upset conservatives across the land.[2] In an era defined by political polarization, the Court—filled with five Republican-appointed conservative justices and four Democratic-appoint liberal justices appointed—had failed to fulfill its expected role as the denier of this historic Democratic legislative accomplishment. There would not be another *Bush v. Gore*. But was the *National Federation of Independent Business v. Sebelius* ruling as unprecedented as many commentators suggested? In this chapter, I argue that, in fact, it represents a continuation rather than a departure from the Supreme Court's place—with obvious exceptions— in American politics since the Rehnquist Court was put into place. I further argue that the while the Court's moderating decision-making—viewed from the perspective of the principles of the larger Republican regime—has frustrated conservatives, it has lessened the level of political polarization, and in doing so, seemingly aided the GOP's electoral chances.[3] To make this case, I consider the doc-trinal product of a hypothetical Rehnquist Court before concluding with a discussion of the role of the actual decisions of the Rehnquist and Roberts Courts had on political polarization in the United States. Along the way, I offer a critique of the dominant method in political science for interpreting judicial decisions, namely, the attitudinal model. I begin, however, with a discussion of the concept of a judicial "mistake"; that is, a Supreme Court justice who failed to live up his or her ideological promise. This concept sheds light on the Court's role in the polarization of American politics since "successful" justices are likely to further divide an already ideologically split Court, which may also affect politics outside the Court.[4] I suggest that a more political—and realistic— understanding of presidential motivations with regard to the selection of Supreme Court nominees allows for a differ-ent and keener assessment of the "success" of a Supreme Court justice.

THE PURSUIT OF AN IDEOLOGICAL COURT AND THE DIFFICULTY DEFINING "SUCCESS"

Six weeks before Chief Justice William H. Rehnquist died in early September 2005, the George W. Bush White House received something of a surprise from the Supreme Court: a resignation letter signed by Associate Justice Sandra Day O'Connor. While the White House had expected such a let-ter, most there thought it would come from the ailing chief justice, not the Court's first female member. Either way, the resignation gave President Bush his first opportunity to shape the Court. During the process, the president became almost obsessed with avoiding the mistake his father had made 15 years earlier, when the elder Bush selected the stealthy David Hackett Souter. Despite his apparent conservative credentials, Souter quickly became a mod-erate justice with liberal leanings. Conservatives, who had trusted the presi-dent despite concerns about Souter, were frustrated and angry. In fact, legal journalist Jan Crawford Greenburg notes that some conservatives consider the Souter nomination "one of the biggest presidential mistakes in the twen-tieth century."[5] President George W. Bush apparently agreed.

With news of O'Connor's retirement, Republicans in the Senate also reflected on the work of the Rehnquist Court, and in doing so, eagerly high-lighted what they viewed as clear inadequacies in constitutional doctrine.

Like the president, they wanted to make sure the next nominee would not follow in the footsteps of past Republican-appointed justices who had failed to toe the conservative line. In other words, they wanted justices who fit the mold of Rehnquist, Scalia, and Thomas not of O'Connor or Justice Anthony Kennedy, and certainly not Souter. To the Senate's most conservative Republican members, these latter justices had been clear failures, pretenders to the declared counterrevolution against the decisions of the Warren and Burger Courts.[6]

Conservative critics of the Court are not the only ones who have pointed to judicial "failures." In political science literature, owing to the dominance of the attitudinal model, scholars consistently evaluate presidential efforts to transform the Court on purely ideological—and potentially political polarizing—grounds. However, overemphasizing ideology can be problematic for understanding the work of the Rehnquist Court. After all, the Republican presidents (i.e., Ronald Reagan and George H. W. Bush) responsible for selecting O'Connor, Kennedy, and Souter were not motivated by purely ideological factors when they made these choices. Nonideological motivations, such achieving electoral gain and avoiding conflictual confirmations, informed their decisions as well. Indeed, as political scientist and leading attitudinalist Jeffery Segal shows, at the time of their appointments, these three nominees were widely considered more moderate than Reagan's and Bush's other choices; nominees who were typically defined as "movement" conservatives. For these three, the perceived ideological scores—ranging from 0 (most conservative) to 1 (most liberal)—were O'Connor (0.415), Kennedy (0.365), and Souter (0.325). In contrast, the scores for the other Reagan and Bush nominees were Rehnquist (0.045), Antonin Scalia (0.000), Robert H. Bork (0.095), Douglas Ginsburg (0.000), and Clarence Thomas (0.160).[7]

Nevertheless, attitudinal scholars reach conclusions about the "success" or "failure" of a justice by suggesting that presidents seek to appoint individuals to the Supreme Court based solely on a candidate's perceived ideology. For example, as Segal and Harold Spaeth write in *The Attitudinal Model Revisited*, "a rational President will wish to nominate someone with views as close to his as possible."[8] Despite acknowledging that certain factors beyond the appointing president's control influence the ultimate selection, Segal and Spaeth nevertheless evaluate presidential success in reshaping the Court in ideological terms. Therefore, to them, compared to Ronald Reagan, "the more moderate Richard Nixon had a much greater impact in pulling the Court to the right." In fact, "Reagan, perhaps the most conservative President of the twentieth century, oversaw a Court that had only a marginally lower average score [meaning more conservative] than Ford and Carter, despite four appointees."[9]

Political scientists George L. Watson and John A. Stookey took the idea of grading justices—and by implication presidents— to another level. In their 1995 book, *Shaping America: The Politics of Supreme Court Appointments*, they provide nine justices with hypothetical reports cards—with the appointing president serving as teacher—complete with grades and comments.

While some might suggest that Justice Scalia deserves the proverbial "doesn't play well with others" comment, Watson and Stookey have Teacher Reagan remark on Pupil Scalia in the following terms: "Nino has brought to the Court exactly the philosophy and leadership that was expected of him. On occasion, his libertarian bent will show through, as it did in one case in which he joined the liberals. Such instances are sufficiently rare to warrant a *strong A*."[10]

To be fair, *Shaping America* is a textbook designed for use in the class-room, and therefore, the authors deserve a degree of latitude to make their point to their audience. Nevertheless, the argument Watson and Stookey advance is problematic. As they write, "Presidents are, for the most part, results oriented. This means that they want justices on the Court who will vote to decide cases consistent with the president's policy preferences."[11] While there is certainly much truth in this statement, the starkness of attitudinal evaluations of presidential performance on judicial appointments often masks the subtlety of real-world political life and fails to take into account the potential political consequences of an ideologically and politically polarizing "successful" Supreme Court. In other words, a rational president—especially one up for reelection—may be much better served by choosing a nominee for reasons other than ideology.

To account for these nonideological motivations, I assess presidential success from an alternative perspective, considering the potential political consequences of judicial decisions. I do so by examining the ramifications of a hypothetical "successful" Rehnquist Court—from a social conservative standpoint—on the cohesiveness of the Republican coalition. While I do not disagree that the Rehnquist Court failed to achieve the results most desired by social conservatives, I suggest that its conservative shortcomings likely diminished the possibility of a division within the GOP's coalition; divisions some Republican strategists thought would further polarize American politics, and more importantly from their perspective, deeply wound their party on Election Day. I further suggest that a more complete understanding of presidential motivations with regard to Supreme Court appointments forces a reconsideration of the notion of a "failed" justice. In other words, presidents should not be judged on the extent of their success in altering the ideological makeup of the Court if some or all their appointments were motivated by other concerns. After all, as noted above, presidents often do not think solely about ideology when selecting a nominee for the high Court. Instead, politics is usually an equal—if not a superior—concern. Therefore, scholars should avoid grading them on just one portion of the exam. In other words, the attitudinalists err in viewing presidents in the same terms as their unconstrained justices on the nation's highest bench, where they assert that ideology trumps all else. Leaving aside the question of whether justices freely act on their policy preferences, presidents—limited by political constraints—often do not. This conclusion is widely supported by scholars writing in the appointment literature; scholars who have pointed to an array of motivations that shape presidential selection, including the partisan makeup of the Senate, geographic representation on the Court, and appeals to interest groups (particularly those with a strong voice in the president's political party).[12] Assessments of presidential success in changing the Court's constitution need to account for the complexity of the political regimes to which the president and the corresponding high bench belongs; regimes that are certainly not only committed to advancing a particular ideology but also attentive to the ramifications of an unbending pursuit of those ideals. Here, I draw on the insights of both the regime politics literature[13] and the segment of the appointment literature that understands Supreme Court nominations as representative of the political order of the time.[14]

In making this case, I consider the appointments of O'Connor, Kennedy, and Souter via a discussion of Supreme Court decisions on abortion, affirmative action, and school prayer. It is important to note that I am not arguing that Presidents Reagan and Bush intentionally sought to limit the conservatism of the Court and succeeded with these nominees. They may have done so, but this is not my argument. Rather, I am suggesting that to score electoral points and to ease confirmation concerns—goals linked to the expansion and maintenance of the Republican coalition—they appointed individuals who were perceived as less ideologically pure than their other high Court nominees. In other words, Presidents Reagan and Bush may still have hoped these choices would have delivered consistently conservative doctrine, but they were willing to risk greater ideological certainty to ease confirmation and enhance their electoral chances. Significantly, these justices often joined majority opinions on politically salient issues that spoke with a moderate tone, leaving their conservative brethren frustrated in dissent. After the Reagan and the elder Bush nominees, I explore why President George W. Bush was determined to pursue a different course, and why conservatives—fearing another "failed" justice—nevertheless denounced his selection of Harriet Miers and blocked her bid for a seat on the Supreme Court.

THE TROUBLE WITH GRADES: WHEN FAILURE MAY MEAN SUCCESS

To both illustrate the drawbacks of ideological-exclusive grading and to evaluate the role of the Rehnquist Court in the polarization of American politics, let us assume hypothetically that all six appointments Presidents Reagan and George H. W. Bush made to the Supreme Court—including Rehnquist's elevation to the center chair—were successful ideological choices that offered no surprises once they settled into their chambers. Let us further assume, given the Republican Party's interest in judicially focused social concerns during this period, that Presidents Reagan and Bush appointed these individuals with the firm expectation that they would advance a conservative viewpoint on three issues at the heart of the GOP's social agenda: abortion, affirmative action, and school prayer. Finally, let us assume that each of the Reagan and Bush justices fulfilled the expectations of their appointing president by seeking to advance the position of that president or the Republican Party's platform—often the two were significantly similar—on these issues.[15] In simple terms, each would earn an A from his or her appointing president, maybe even an A+. As a result, instead of the Rehnquist Court's moderate conservative middle wing of O'Connor, Kennedy, and Souter, it would have been filled with justices who shared the constitutional outlook of Rehnquist, Scalia, and Clarence Thomas.[16] Therefore, after Thomas won approval from the Senate in 1991, the Court would have had the following makeup (in order of appointment): Byron White, Harry Blackmun, John Paul Stevens, Scalia I (replacing O'Connor), William Rehnquist, Scalia II (his actual appointment), Scalia III (replacing Kennedy), Thomas I (replacing Souter), and Thomas II (his actual appointment). In essence, the use of a hypothetical Court here is simply a means to consider the state of American politics if the Court fully endorsed Presidents Reagan's and Bush's—and/or their party's—policy goals on these issues. On abortion and school prayer, Segal and Spaeth clearly judge the Reagan/Bush effort a failure (and the Senate's conservatives of 2005 would certainly agree). As they write,

> Few Presidents had the potential opportunity to influence the Supreme Court that Ronald Wilson Reagan did. The conservative Republican reached out again and again to social conservatives, calling for the return of school prayer and the overruling of *Roe v. Wade*. Fate smiled upon the fortieth President, granting him four appointees to the high Court and hundreds of appointees to the lower federal courts. Yet the Supreme Court he left was no more conservative that the one he inherited. Moreover, despite his appointments, the twentieth century ended with school prayer unconstitutional and *Roe v. Wade* the law of the land.[17]

By examining beyond Segal and Spaeth's ideological-focused landscape, however, we might arrive at a different conclusion. In the following sections, I pursue this idea by considering the political consequences of a hypothetical "successful" Rehnquist Court on these three issues and then reevaluate the Reagan/Bush effort in electoral and coalitional terms rather than ideological ones. Specifically, I consider how a hypothetical Court would have decided the abortion case of *Planned Parenthood v. Casey* (1992); the affirmative action case of *Grutter v. Bollinger* (2003); and the two school prayer cases of *Lee v. Weisman* (1992) and *Santa Fe Independent School District v. Doe* (2000). In undertaking this analysis, I also consider Republican political reaction—via an examination of a president's words and deeds (or those of a partisan successor) —after these rulings. In constructing this hypothetical scenario, my point is a fairly simple one: leading Republicans reacted to Rehnquist Court decisions on social issues—particularly abortion— as though they viewed complete success on the development of conservative doctrine as potentially divisive to their party's coalition. This reaction suggests that by issuing less than conservative decisions in these political salient cases, the Rehnquist Court played a moderating role within Republican Party politics specifically and within American politics generally.

Abortion

Beginning at the 1980 convention, Republicans clearly articulated a strong prolife position on abortion; one that not only called for the end of *Roe v. Wade*, but also advocated—via a constitutional amendment—the "restoration" of the fundamental "right to life for unborn children." In 1984, convention delegates approved language that took this prolife stance even further, supporting "legislation to make clear that the Fourteenth Amendment's protections apply to unborn children." In 1988, the platform's language was virtually unchanged from four years earlier. Both platforms also added: "We applaud President Reagan's fine record of judicial appointments, and we reaffirm our support for the appointment of judges at all levels of the judiciary who respect traditional family values and the sanctity of innocent human life."[18] Throughout his presidency, Ronald Reagan repeatedly expressed his commitment to a prolife agenda, often in terms consistent with his party's strident platform. For example, in a debate with Democratic challenger Walter Mondale in 1984, he noted: "I believe that until and unless someone can establish that the unborn child is not a living human being, then that child is already protected by the Constitution, which guarantees life, liberty, and the pursuit of happiness (sic) to all of us."[19] Despite this belief, Reagan nevertheless supported a constitutional amendment banning abortions in all cases expect where the life of the mother was at stake. While also prolife in outlook, George H. W. Bush accepted more exceptions than his predecessor: "My position on the issue of abortion is clear. I support a constitutional amendment that would reverse the Supreme Court's decision in Roe v. Wade. I also support a human life amendment with an exception for rape, incest, or where the life of the mother is threatened."[20]

Given both the platform and the presidents' language, a hypothetical Rehnquist Court would have had little difficulty casting aside *Roe* in its 1992 *Casey* decision. With Justices White, Blackmun, and Stevens as the only holdovers from the pre-Reagan years, the Court would have seemingly flipped the vote in *Roe,* with seven justices in the majority (the four Reagan and two Bush justices joining with the *Roe*-dissenting White), and only Blackmun, *Roe's* author, and Stevens in dissent. In addition, if the actual dissents in *Casey* serve as any guide, the conservative majority would have not only overturned *Roe,* but also eviscerated its underlining principle of the right to privacy. As Justice Scalia wrote, "the issue in this case [is] not whether the power of a woman to abort her unborn child is a 'liberty' in the absolute sense...[but] whether it is a liberty protected by the Constitution of the United States. I am sure it is not."[21] Yet, as these words suggest, not even a Rehnquist Court filled with Scalia, Thomas, and their constitutional clones would have endorsed President Reagan and the Republican platform's suggestion that the word "life" in the due process clause demanded an interpretation that constitutionally forbade states from legalizing abortion without a compelling interest.[22]

Of course, the actual Rehnquist Court did not reach such a ruling, choosing instead to endorse some portions of the Pennsylvania's antiabortion law while still maintaining the principle that women had a right to choose to terminate an unwanted pregnancy. Moreover, the Court majority seemed to suggest that the politics of abortion had played an essential role in its decision to let *Roe* stand. As Justice O'Connor wrote, "Overruling *Roe's* central holding would not only reach an unjustifiable result under stare decisis principles, but would seriously weaken the Court's capacity to exercise the judicial power and to function as the Supreme Court of a Nation dedicated to the rule of law...A decision to overrule *Roe's* essential holding under the existing circumstances would address error, if error there was, at the cost of both profound and unnecessary damage to the Court's legitimacy and to the Nation's commitment to the rule of law."[23]

If presidents are truly as ideologically centered as attitudinalist grading suggests, President Bush would have issued a stringing rebuke of the Court's majority opinion in *Casey*. After all, the Republican Party had led the effort to decimate the decision soon after the Court announced the ruling and his own Justice Department had urged the Court to discard *Roe* in its amicus curiae brief.[24] Whether expected or not, President Bush did not issue any such statement. Instead, he noted that he "was pleased with the Supreme Court's decision upholding most of Pennsylvania's reasonable restrictions on abortion."[25] Bush's positive spin on the decision was likely driven by the change in public opinion on abortion. In the Reagan years, the nation was almost evenly divided on the issue. For example, in Gallup polls taken in 1981 and 1985, an equal number of respondents (approximately 20 percent) held both the strong prolife view (abortion should be illegal in all circumstances) and the strong prochoice view (abortion should be legal under any circumstances). The majority thought the procedure should be legal only under certain circumstances.[26] Perhaps more importantly, President Reagan's chief strategist and pollster Richard Wirthlin believed a decision overturning *Roe* was more likely to help rather than harm the Republican coalition.[27]

By 1989, however, public opinion on the issue was trending differently. According to a Gallup poll taken that year, 27.4 percent of respondents held the prochoice view while only 17.5 percent endorsed the prolife position. Immediately after the *Casey* decision, Gallup found that this gap had grown to more than 20 percentage points (34.4–13.4 percent).[28] Moreover, on the specific question of *Roe*, an overwhelming number of Americans wanted it to stand rather than disappear. According to a late October 1992 *Los Angeles Times* poll, 57 percent of adult Americans favored the 1973 ruling (43 percent "strongly" and 14 percent "somewhat"). Only 31 percent opposed *Roe* (24 percent "strongly" and 7 percent "somewhat").[29]

Despite this divide, many Republicans were still very committed to pursuing their party's line on abortion. Thus, despite President Bush's expressed satisfaction on the *Casey* ruling, six weeks later, when the GOP convened in Houston to nominate him to head their ticket for a second time, the party's delegates once again approved a platform that proclaimed "the unborn child has a fundamental individual right to life which cannot be infringed," and endorsed "legislation to make clear that the Fourteenth Amendment's protections apply to the unborn children."[30] The platform seemingly put the president in a precarious position. However, Bush did not seem to care, noting during one question and answer session with voters: "I'm not going to necessarily be bound [by the Republican platform]. I'm the President. I'll say what I'm for and what I'm against."[31] Again, it is hard to say what President Bush truly intended with *Roe* when he appointed Souter and Thomas. What is clear, however, is that he was willing—even eager—to deemphasize his ideological opposition to legalized abortion in hopes of attracting more votes once the Court upheld *Roe* in *Casey*.

Bush's effort to moderate his position on abortion was evident in other parts of the campaign as well. While widely reported as a campaign blunder, Vice President Dan Quayle's answer to a hypothetical question about his daughter's unwanted pregnancy— "I would counsel her and talk to her and support her on whatever decision she made"— seemed to suggest that the Bush/Quayle ticket was not as prolife as conservatives had hoped.[32] Bush's near echo response to a similar question about his granddaughter and the right to choose provided more evidence for that conclusion.[33] Finally, First Lady Barbara Bush made a strategic announcement— just days after the platform committee finished writing its unwavering prolife plank— that she believed abortion was a "personal thing" and did not belong in the platform. While she refused to state her own views on the issue, news organizations like the *New York Times* reported, "her friends say she privately favors abortion rights."

Taken together, these rhetorical actions appeared to confirm that the president's campaign wanted Republican-leaning prochoice women to know that undercutting *Roe* was not at the top of Bush's second term "to do" list. In fact, as *New York Times* reporter Alessandra Stanley speculated about Mrs. Bush's statement: "Her comments about the platform could have been intended as a signal to pro-choice women that they have a sympathetic ear in the White House."[34] David Keene of the American Conservative Union certainly understood them as one component of a three-part plan: "If just Quayle had said something, you could look at it as an accident. But with three comments like that in succession, you know it's a deliberate plan."[35] To many, it sounded as though the president was singing a different tune than four years earlier. At that time, he clearly felt it was necessary to "recast himself as an ardent foe of abortion" to attract the religious conservatives,[36] especially after Televangelist Pat Robertson pushed him into third place— both behind Bob Dole—in the GOP's Iowa caucuses. But now, with only 10 percent of voters supporting the general thrust of the party's platform— that abortion should never be allowed—and a Supreme Court seemingly just one vote short of ending *Roe* once and for all, Bush emphasized his slightly more moderate position and his lack of enthusiasm for the GOP platform. Significantly, his stance— allowing the procedure in cases of "rape or incest or where the life of the mother is at stake"[37]—attracted the support 29 percent of voters.[38] Another poll added to the evidence that the Republican Party's position on abortion was potential destructive to the president's reelection chances. Taken just after the 1992 GOP convention, this Gallup poll showed that 37 percent of registered voters were less likely to vote for President Bush because of his party's platform plank on abortion. Only 16 percent said the plank would make it more likely to vote for him.[39]

In attempting to downplay the conservative tone of his party's platform, Bush was not doing anything new. Even his hard-charging predecessor had at times sought to ease tensions within the Republican Party over the abortion issue, largely in hopes of appealing to those women who usually supported the GOP but considered themselves socially moderate or liberal. Given Republican strengths among men,[40] Bush would only need to minimize the gender gap to capture the White House for Republicans once again. In turn, the Court's decision in *Casey*, which allowed the president to avoid the politics of a post-*Roe* campaign and the likelihood of a more polarized electorate, aided this strategy. If the Court had constitutionally discarded *Roe*, Bush would have needed to defend—given both his and his party's earlier efforts— an unpopular decision that would have likely put abortion at the center of the election discussion. As journalist Robin Toner explained before the decision, "The worst case scenario for Mr. Bush, in the view of many Democrats and some of his Republican friends, would involve the High Court overturning *Roe* at the height of the campaign. That coupled with the weak economy, could have a significant impact on the younger, suburban voters who are a critical swing vote in many Presidential elections." Frank Greer, an advisor to Bill Clinton, elaborated on this thinking: "I believe George Bush has packed the Court and he's going to pay a political price for it. [A ruling reversing *Roe*] will push the issue front and center."[41] Even with the actual more moderate *Casey* decision, political scientist Alan Abramowitz concludes that the abortion issue significantly undermined Bush's chances for reelection. As he writes, "The Clinton-Gore ticket suffered few defections from pro-life Democrats because most of these Democrats either didn't know the candidates' positions on abortion or didn't care about the issue. In contrast, the Bush-Quayle ticket suffered a substantial number of defections from pro-choice Republicans, although most of these Republican defectors cast their ballots for Perot rather than Clinton."[42]

Given Bush's post-*Casey* positioning, it is informative to ask which of his two appointments to the Court were more "successful"; David Souter, who sided with the Court's moderate conservatives in upholding the "essence" of *Roe*, or Clarence Thomas, who sided with Rehnquist, White, and Scalia in calling for *Roe*'s destruction. In the eyes of most social conservatives—and the attitudinalists— Souter's unexpected vote in favor of *Roe* amounted to a Bush failure. However, given the actions of Bush and his campaign team during his bid for a second term, was Souter really a failure? After all, by allowing the Bush campaign to reach out to the 61 percent of voters who did not support the president's or the Republican platform's position on abortion, the Court's decision seemingly advanced the cause of the more conservative of the two political parties. Of course, despite this assistance, Clinton defeated Bush in a three-man race.[43] Nevertheless, the point is clear.

The *Casey* decision may have been a disappointment to social conservatives, but at least to some Republican strategists it was a blessing.

Affirmative Action

In 2003, the Rehnquist Court found another way to disappoint social conservatives. This time the Court failed to deliver on conservative hopes that it constitutionally decimate affirmative action programs that treated applicants differently based on race.[44] In its *Grutter v. Bollinger*, the Court upheld the University of Michigan Law School's race-conscious admission policy. While his legal team had not pursued as conservative a position as many affirmative action's most ardent foes preferred,[45] at the time the government's attorneys made their arguments to the Court, President George W. Bush clearly articulated his belief that Michigan's programs were unconstitutional. "At their core, the Michigan policies amount to a quota system that unfairly rewards or penalizes prospective students, based solely on their race."[46] In taking this line, President Bush was continuing a campaign by conservatives in his party and his two most recent Republican predecessors who denounced the evils of a race-based selection system. For example, the 1980 GOP platform read: "Equal opportunity should not be jeopardized by bureaucratic regulations and decisions which rely on quotas, ratios, and numerical requirements to exclude some individuals in favor of others, thereby rendering such regulations and decisions inherently discriminatory."[47] Four years later, GOP thinking on affirmation action was not much different.[48] In 1988, the language remained quite similar.[49] Moreover, Bush's stance was consistent with the 2000 Republican platform, which read:

> We believe rights inhere in individuals, not in groups. We will attain our nation's goal of equal opportunity without quotas or other forms of preferential treatment. It is as simple as this: No one should be denied a job, promotion, contract, or chance at higher education because of their race or gender. Equal access, energetically offered, should guarantee every person a fair shot based on their potential and merit.[50]

However, despite his earlier position, once the sharply split Rehnquist Court issued its decision, the president altered course, releasing a statement strikingly similar to his father's response to the 1992 *Casey* ruling.[51] On the same day, the Court announced its support for the diversity principle in affirmative action programs (in an opinion written by O'Connor), President Bush "applauded" its rulings. To him, the Court deserved such praise "for recognizing the value of diversity on our Nation's campuses." He added: "Diversity is one of America's greatest strengths. Today's decisions seek a careful balance between the goal of campus diversity and the fundamental principle of equal treatment under the law."[52] Leading conservatives, however, did not applaud. Abigail Thernstrom, for example, could not find enough words to express her disappointment with the *Grutter* decision, noting that she was "in a rage," "beside myself," "in meltdown," and "totally dismayed." She also called the decision "disgusting," adding that the Court "should be ashamed of itself."[53]

This time the two Reagan/Bush justices who joined the three most liberals members of the Court—Stevens, Ruth Bader Ginsburg, and Stephen Breyer— were O'Connor and Souter. Clearly, Thernstrom—and nearly all other social conservatives— would consider O'Connor and Souter conservative failures on affirmative action. Indeed, a hypothetical Rehnquist Court—even accounting for the Clinton appointments of Ginsburg and Breyer—would have solidly found for Thernstrom's position. In such a scenario, only Stevens and the two Clinton justices would have dissented. Justice Thomas's dissent in *Grutter* provides a strong hint for what a hypothetical majority opinion striking down Michigan Law School's affirmative action program would have looked like. To Thomas,

> No one would argue that a university could set up a lower general admission standard and then impose heightened requirements only on black applicants. Similarly, a university may not maintain a high admission standard and grant exemptions to favored races. The Law School, of its own choosing, and for its own purposes, maintains an exclusionary admissions system that it knows produces racially disproportionate results. Racial discrimination is not a permissible solution to the self-inflicted wounds of this elitist admissions policy.[54]

But unlike Thomas and Thernstrom, President Bush seemingly found no need to criticize the Court for its prodiversity ruling. For one, public opinion polls supported a more cautious stance. For example, a June 2003 Gallup poll, taken just before the Court announced its decisions in *Gratz* and *Grutter*, showed a solid majority of respondents (58 percent) generally supported affirmative action programs for racial minorities. (To be sure, if the question is asked with wording indicating a lowering of standards, support has historically been substantially lower.)[55] In addition, at the time of the Court's action, the Bush White House was reportedly seeking to reach out to minority voters—particularly Hispanics—who Republican strategists believed were essential to creating a "Big Tent" GOP. Writing in January 2003, Mike Allen and Charles Lane of the *Washington Post* noted that "winning over Hispanic and moderate suburban voters is one of the White House's chief political aims." They added "some Republicans feared that the decision" to oppose the Michigan policies—even with a brief more "narrowly tailored" than some administration conservatives had argued for—"could hurt Bush, especially after the controversy over racially charged remarks by Senator Trent Lott."[56] Indeed, according to various news accounts, chief political strategists Karl Rove and White House Counsel Alberto Gonzales successfully argued for a limited attack on affirmative action based on "the need to expand the Republican base to include minorities."[57]

In this sense, Pete Wilson's advocacy of the divisive Proposition 187— which restricted illegal immigrants from using certain public services—in

1994 provided the president with a ready example of how the Hispanic community might respond to the aggressive pursuit of racially conservative policies. Through his support of Proposition 187, Wilson had become *persona non grata* in California's Hispanic community, partially contributing to the near decimation of the party in the Golden State for close to a decade. This was not a new lesson for Bush, moreover. In 1994, while Wilson was offending Hispanic voters, Bush successfully wooed these voters in his race for the governorship of Texas. As president, then, Bush's response to the Court's affirmative action decisions was similarly politically inspired, while Thomas and Thernstrom's words were motivated by ideology.[58] Given President Bush's reaction, it is again appropriate to ask which Republican-appointed justice was more of a "success": O'Connor or Thomas?

School Prayer

The issue of school prayer offers a different type of example than abortion and affirmative action. In similar manner to its platform positioning on the other two issues, the Republican Party has offered a consistent stance on school prayer for many decades. In fact, beginning in 1972, the GOP platform asserted in one way or another, a commitment to restore prayer in the classrooms of America. In 1980, the platform's language read: "We support Republican initiatives in the Congress to restore the right of individuals to participate in voluntary, non-denominational prayer in schools and other public facilities." Four years later, the statement was a bit stronger: "We have enacted legislation to guarantee equal access to school facilities by student religious groups. Mindful of our religious diversity, we reaffirm our commitment to the freedoms of religion and speech guaranteed by the Constitution of the United States and firmly support the rights of students to openly practice the same, including the right to engage in voluntary prayer in schools." In 1988, the plank took on a more combative tone:

> "Deep in our hearts, we do believe"…In defending religious freedom. Mindful of our religious diversity, we firmly support the fight of students to engage in voluntary prayer in schools. We call for full enforcement of the Republican legislation that now guarantees equal access to school facilities by student religious groups. We enacted legislation to ensure equal access to schools for student religious groups and led congressional efforts to restore voluntary school prayer.[59]

Despite this increasingly concerned language, a majority of the Rehnquist Court did not listen, disappointing social conservatives yet again. Most importantly, in 1992, the Court issued its *Lee v. Weisman* decision, constitutionally silencing prayer at a public school graduation ceremony. With the same lineup as the *Casey* ruling—decided just five days after *Lee*— Justices O'Connor, Kennedy, and Souter joined with Justices Blackmun and Stevens to thwart the city of Providence, Rhode Island from "creating a state-sponsored and state-directed religious exercise in a public school." Rising to the occasion once again, Justice Scalia provided us with a clear statement of how a hypothetical Rehnquist Court might have ruled:

> In holding that the Establishment Clause prohibits invocations and benedictions at public school graduation ceremonies, the Court—with nary a mention that it is doing so—lays waste a tradition that is as old as public school graduation ceremonies themselves, and that is a component of an even more longstanding American tradition of nonsectarian prayer to God at public celebrations generally. As its instrument of destruction, the bulldozer of its social engineering, the Court invents a boundless, and boundlessly manipulable, test of psychological coercion.

Later in his opinion, he added:

> The Court's notion that a student who simply sits in "respectful silence" during the invocation and benediction (when all others are standing) has somehow joined—or would somehow be perceived as having joined—in the prayers is nothing short of ludicrous. We indeed live in a vulgar age. But surely "our social conventions," have not coarsened to the point that anyone who does not stand on his chair and shout obscenities can reasonably be deemed to have assented to everything said in his presence.[60]

While not as outraged as Scalia, President Bush quickly voiced his displeasure with the Court's majority ruling. On this issue, he did not disagree with his party's platform.

> I am very disappointed by the Supreme Court's decision in *Lee v. Weisman*. The Court said that a simple nondenominational prayer thanking God for the liberty of America at a public school graduation ceremony violates the first amendment. America is a land of religious pluralism, and this is one of our Nation's greatest strengths. While we must remain neutral toward particular religions and protect freedom of conscience, we should not remain neutral toward religion itself. In this case, I believe that the Court has unnecessarily cast away the venerable and proper American tradition of nonsectarian prayer at public celebrations. I continue to believe that this type of prayer should be allowed in public schools.[61]

Eight years later, Justices O'Connor, Kennedy, and Souter—together with Justices Stevens, Ginsburg, and Breyer—reaffirmed their thinking in *Lee v. Weisman* by joining the majority opinion in *Santa Fe Independent School District v. Doe*. In *Santa Fe*, the Court majority ruled that a student-led prayer over a public address system before a public high-school football game was unconstitutional. In dissent, Chief Justice Rehnquist stressed: "The Court distorts existing precedent to conclude that the school district's student-message program is invalid on its face under the Establishment Clause. But even more disturbing than its holding is the tone of the Court's opinion; it bristles with hostility to all things religious in public life. Neither the holding nor the tone of the opinion is faithful to the meaning of the Establishment Clause."[62]

Like his father before him, then Governor George W. Bush was quick to announce his displeasure with the Court majority, calling the ruling "disappointing." Bush, who had jointed an *amicus curiae* brief urging the Court to uphold the prayer practice, added: "I support the constitutionally guaranteed right of all students to express their faith freely and participate in voluntary, student-led prayer."[63] In short, both President Bushes have not been above criticizing the Court's decisions in ideological terms when such criticism appeared to be politically beneficial, which was clear in the case of school prayer. After all, an early 1992 Gallup poll showed that 61 percent of respondents would be more likely to vote for a presidential candidate who favored a constitutional amendment allowing voluntary prayer in public schools. Only 23 percent said they would be less likely to do so. A 2000 Gallup poll showed that nearly 70 percent of respondents would vote for such an amendment if they could.[64]

The decisions by Presidents Reagan and Bush to select nominees perceived to be less conservative (compared to their other choices) with these three appointments had a profound impact on the ultimately shape of the Rehnquist Court's constitutional doctrine.[65] From an ideologically conservative standpoint, Justices O'Connor, Kennedy, and Souter came up short on many of the most important social issues of the day, even if they typically did push the Court's doctrine in a conservative direction. However, the ability of Republican Party to maintain its coalition was seemingly aided by the fact that it did not have to confront the political consequences of a truly conservative Supreme Court. In other words, leaving aside the motivations of a particular justice, the Rehnquist Court's failure to deliver the ideological doctrine the constructors of the conservative Republican political regime desired may have nevertheless aided the electoral pursuits of that regime. Any assessment of the "failure" or "success" of a particular justice should consider such consequences of the Court's behavior. To date, the regime politics approach appears most adept at accomplishing this task.

CONCLUSIONS: THE ROBERTS COURT AND THE POLITICS OF POLARIZATION

The summer of 2005 was an exhilarating time for conservatives in Washington. President Bush had just won reelection, and in doing so, had won 15 states with more than 59 percent of the vote. He did so, moreover, not by appealing "swing" voters but by highlighting a conservative message and turning out his conservative base in record numbers. In the Senate, Republicans controlled 55 seats, more than at any time since Reagan's first term. The Democrats appeared to be on the ropes.

After trusting previous Republicans presidents only to be disappointed once their nominees took their places on the high Court, social conservatives in particular were unwilling to give this President Bush much leeway, even though it was widely assumed that he was committed to their cause. With his first selection, they thought he had hit a homerun. Once confirmed, a Justice John Roberts would make the Court more conservative than it had been with Sandra Day O'Connor. But then Chief Justice Rehnquist died, and in the course of finding a second nominee, conservative perception of the Bush White House began to change.

The Bush White House, which had always assumed the center chair would be the first to be vacated, acted swiftly following Rehnquist's death, shifting Roberts's nomination from the associate slot to the newly vacant chief justice position. It then began to search for another nominee. During this process, President Bush let be known that he was concerned about one of the few criticisms of his selection of Roberts. In the words of none other than Justice O'Connor, Roberts was a wonderful choice except for that fact that he was "not a woman." President Bush endeavored to make up for that lack of political symbolism with his second nominee, the person who would now replace O'Connor. In turn, the White House search focused on finding a woman or a minority. After scouring a limited pool, the president settled on Harriet Miers, his White House counsel. Miers, who was overseeing the search, was not aware she was being considered for the position until the president had nearly made up his mind. While she had had a successful legal career, she did not possess the credentials of a John Roberts, or the runner-up, Samuel Alito. To the president, this lack of a track record was not important, because he knew her, knew she was "tough as nails," a "pit bull in size six shoes." In short, he knew she would not be another Souter.[66] However, conservatives did not care. They were not prepared to risk this opportunity to shift the balance of the Court on another presidential hunch, on the possibility of another Bush mistake. In turn, once word of the Miers selection hit the street, conservatives set out to block her nomination.[67] To them, she was simply too risky, too much of an unknown commodity to fill the seat of a "moderate" swing justice. In a matter of weeks, Miers withdrew her name from consideration for the Court. In her place, the president named Alito. As they had done with the selection of Roberts, conservatives rejoiced. Jeffrey Toobin neatly sums up how things had changed in the Senate in less than two decades. In 1987, "Bork couldn't be confirmed *because* he opposed *Roe v. Wade*; in 2005, a nominee couldn't be selected *unless* he or she opposed *Roe v. Wade*."[68]

True to expectations, both Roberts and Alito have been quite conservative in their decision-making since they assumed their seats on the high bench. It was with those voting records and the transcripts from the oral arguments in mind that commentators predicted that the Roberts Court would constitutionally decapitate President Obama Affordable Care Act in early summer 2012. However, of course, only one justice had to veer off his ideological course in the health-care case. Nevertheless, in doing so, rather than exacerbating political polarization in the United States, the Court once again played a mollifying role in this regard, much to the consternation of those on the right of American politics.

Throughout this chapter, I have suggested that the Rehnquist Court decisions on social issues had a largely moderating effect on the polarization of American politics. I suggest, at least with its opinion in this highly salient health-care case, the same was true for the Roberts Court. Strikingly, however, the Court has often not played such a role in American history. As Robert McCloskey has argued, throughout US history, it has been "assumed that the legislature can focus largely on the task of 'interest representation,' while passing on to the courts a substantial share of the responsibility for considering the long-term constitutional questions that continually arise."[69] In other words, McCloskey sees a rough division of labor between the courts and the Congress. In this role, however, the Supreme Court has been the typically been the most willing arm of the federal government to push the envelope of a particular political order's ideological commitments. In other words, the Court, protected from the vagaries of the ballot box, has usually been the institution prepared to advance ideological ends of the reigning party's vision for the nation, despite the potential costs. For example, during the run-up to the 1936 presidential election, it was the most conservative justices on the Court who issued the strongest ideological challenge to President Roosevelt's New Deal. Alf Landon, his Republican opponent, offered a far meeker challenge. In the 1960s, even with the passage of the historic 1964 Civil Rights Act and 1965 Voting Rights Act, the Warren Court was far more strident in its liberalism than the Democrats in Congress. At the 1968 Democratic convention, the delegates sought to defend not legislatively extend the historic decisions of that Court.[70] But today, that is not the case. As the Rehnquist Court and to a lesser extent the Roberts Court have fallen short of conservative hopes and wishes, Republicans in Congress have not abandoned their ideology but have become more committed to it. This development has certainly further polarized the Congress, and may have influenced the electorate as well. What this means for understanding the Court's role in the polarization of American politics will require further exploration.

NOTES

1. Balkin and Levinson (2001, 1049).
2. On Roberts's decision-making process, see Toobin (2012, 283–293).
3. On conservative frustrations, see, for example, Morgan (2006).
4. On the political polarization and the judiciary from another angle, see Binder (2008).
5. Greenburg (2007, 241–242, 265). On the Rehnquist court's divisions, see also Tushnet (2005).
6. See Sunstein (2005) for a discussion of these divisions.
7. Segal's updated scores are available at: http://ws.cc.stonybrook.edu/polsci/jsegal/qualtable.pdf (last accessed by author on July 25, 2012). See also Segal and Cover (1989); Segal et al. (1995); and Segal and Spaeth (2002). But notably, even the decision to choose Scalia before Bork—who were viewed as equally conservative in the Reagan White House—was motivated by the

political symbolism, a desire to appoint the first Italian American to the Court, Greenburg (2007, 43).

8. Segal and Spaeth (2002, 181). While Segal and Spaeth do admit "political real-ity may make such a choice difficult," their main concern in this regard involves whether the nominee will be confirmed. As they write, "a President who chooses an unconfirmable nominee will lose more than he will gain." Although they do retrace the confirmation fights of recent rejected nominees, Segal and Spaeth do not explain why such a failure damages the appointing president, aside from citing a 1990 conference paper that suggests "Presidents interested in maintain-ing their popularity and prestige will attempt to avoid losing the confirmation battle, if at all possible" (185). They also add: "History will undoubtedly regard the rejection of the radical-rightist Bork as the biggest legislative failure of the Reagan administration" (178).

9. Segal and Spaeth (2002, 217, 219). To be sure, writing more recently with coau-thor Lee Epstein, Jeffrey Segal does offer a more systematic view of presidential decision-making with regard to appointments. While still favoring ideology, Epstein and Segal take care to explain the importance of other factors in the selection of nominees for the Supreme Court, including partisan and electoral goals and the qualifications of a potential choice. However, when discussing the success of presidential nominations for the Court, they revert back to the ideo-logical-based "mistakes" and "failures" thinking advanced in *The Attitudinal Model Revisited*, even repeating the words quoted above (and below) about Presidents Nixon and Reagan, Epstein and Segal (2005, 132, 138–139).

10. Watson and Stookey (1995, 71; emphasis added). According to Watson and Stookey, their scores from which they derive their hypothetical grades are based on their "perception of how the appointing presidents would evaluate their appointees with respect to their performances on all nonunanimous cases during the 1990–1991, 1991–1992, and 1992–1993 terms that involved civil rights or civil liberties claims. The scores reported in the grade cards are the percentage of cases in which the justice voted in favor of the individual's claim to a right or liberty. Such a vote is conventionally considered liberal. Thus, high scores are considered liberal, such as Blackmun's 85. Low scores are considered conservative, such as Rehnquist's 4. Our first-person evaluations by the president are our own hypothetical "best guesses" about how the appointing president might evaluate the justice's performance. They do not represent actual evaluations given by the presidents" (1995, 69).

11. Watson and Stookey (1995, 58–59). For a broader discussion of presidential expectations, see Peretti (1999, 111–132).

12. See, for example, Nemacheck (2007); Silverstein (1994); Yalof (1999); Abraham (1999); Massaro (1990); and Perry (1991).

13. Examples of this literature include Dahl (1957); Shapiro (1978); Clayton and Gillman (1999); Clayton and May (1999); Gillman (2002; 2004; 2006); Gillman and Clayton (1999); Graber (1993 ; 2005); Lovell (2003); McMahon (2004; 2011); and Whittington (2005; 2007).

14. Maltese (1995); Silverstein (1994); and Yalof (1999); see also Scherer (2005).

15. On the necessity of using caution when relying on platforms for such purposes, see Pickerill and Clayton (2004).

16. Indeed, such an expectation seemingly remains important to the Republican Party since President George W. Bush has noted his desire to appoint jurists who vote like Scalia and Thomas if he is ever given the opportunity to fill a High Court vacancy.

17. Segal and Spaeth (2002, 217).
18. Republican Party platforms of 1980, 1984, and 1988
19. Debate between the president and the former Vice President Walter F. Mondale in Louisville, Kentucky, October 7, 1984.
20. "Letter to members of the Senate Appropriations Committee on Federal Funding for Abortion," October 17, 1989, *The Public Papers of George Bush.*
21. *Planned Parenthood v. Casey,* 505 U.S. 833 (1992).
22. To be sure, the platform does call for a constitutional amendment to achieve this result. Nevertheless, the 1980 platform uses the word "restore." Conceivably, a proper interpretation of the Constitution would restore the right without the need of an amendment.
23. *Planned Parenthood v. Casey,* 505 U.S. 833 (1992), 836. Justice Souter was apparently responsible for this section of the opinion; see Garrow (1994).
24. Brief for the Unites States as Amicus Curiae Supporting Respondents, April 6, 1992.
25. Bush, "Statement on the Supreme Court Decision on Abortion," June 29, 1992, *Weekly Compilation of Presidential Documents.*
26. Gallup polls taken from 5/8/1981–5/11/1981 and 1/3/1985–1/4/1985.
27. Author Interview, July 2006. See also Apple (1989).
28. Gallup polls taken from 4/12/1989–4/13/1989 and 6/29/1992–6/29/1992.
29. Poll located at Public Opinion Online, Roper Center at the University of Connecticut.
30. 1988 Republican Party platform.
31. Bush, "Question-and-Answer Session in Secaucus, New Jersey," October 22, 1992, *Weekly Compilation of Presidential Documents.*
32. "Quayle's Words about Abortion," 1992, *New York Times,* July 24. See also, Sack (1992).
33. He answered in the following manner: "I would talk her out of it, try to. But I'd do it—let me, let me rephrase it for you. If my granddaughter said I've done something terrible. I've robbed. I've stolen something, I'd stand by her. I think that's what the Vice President was saying—didn't, didn't mean he condoned the act. But he said he'd stand by his child. Of course I'd do that. My granddaughter, my son, my daughter, whoever it is. We've done that all our life as a family. Not going to change that now. And so I, I think that's what , what Dan Quayle was talking about. It got a little out of sync in the translation. But do I, would I support my child? I'd put my arm around her and say, if she were trying to make that decision, encourage her to not do that, but of course I'd stand by my child. I'd love her and help her, lift her up, wipe the tears away, and we'd get back in the game," "Excerpts from an Interview with President Bush," *New York Times,* August 12, 1992. See also Rosenthal (1992).
34. Stanley (1992).
35. Keene quoted in Apple (1992).
36. O'Connor (1996, 116).
37. Bush, "Statement on the Supreme Court Decision on Abortion," June 29, 1992, *Weekly Compilation of Presidential Documents.*
38. According to the 1992 National Election Study's exit polls (O'Connor 1996, 150).
39. Gallup poll taken from 08/17/1992–08/17/1992.

40. On the importance of the male vote in electoral politics, see, for example, Teixeira and Rogers (2000).
41. Toner (1992).
42. Abramowitz (1995, 185).
43. Bush did effectively reduce the Republican gender gap to one percent. However, his weakness among male voters, for a Republican, cost him the election.
44. In 2003, the Court also struck down Texas' same-sex sodomy law in *Lawrence v. Texas*, 539 U.S. 558.
45. See, for example, Goldstein and Milbank (2003); Novak (2003); Greenhouse (2003); and Mauro (2003).
46. George W. Bush, "Remarks on the Michigan Affirmative Action Case," January 15, 2003, *Weekly Compilation of Presidential Documents*, 71.
47. 1980 Republican Party platform.
48. The 1984 Republican Party platform read: "Just as we must guarantee opportunity, we oppose attempts to dictate results. We will resist efforts to replace equal rights with discriminatory quota systems and preferential treatment. Quotas are the most insidious form of discrimination: reverse discrimination against the innocent. We must always remember that, in a free society, different individual goals will yield different results."
49. 1988 Republican Party platform read: "'Deep in our hearts, we do believe'... In guaranteeing opportunity, not dictating the results of fair competition. We will resist efforts to replace equal rights with discriminatory quota systems and preferential treatment. Quotas are the most insidious form of reverse discrimination against the innocent."
50. 2000 Republican Party platform.
51. *Gratz v. Bollinger*, 539 U.S. 244; and *Grutter v. Bollinger*, 539 U.S. 306.
52. He continued by noting "My Administration will continue to promote policies that expand educational opportunities for Americans from all racial, ethnic, and economic backgrounds. There are innovative and proven ways for colleges and universities to reflect our diversity without using racial quotas. The Court has made clear that colleges and universities must engage in a serious, good faith consideration of workable race-neutral alternatives. I agree that we must look first to these race-neutral approaches to make campuses more welcoming for all students.

    Race is a reality in American life. Yet like the Court, I look forward to the day when America will truly be a color-blind society. My Administration will continue to work toward this important goal."
53. Thernstrom quoted in "Voices in the News," June 29, 2003, *National Public Radio*; and in Noe (2003).
54. *Grutter v. Bollinger*, 539 U.S. 306.
55. Gallup poll taken 6/12/2003–6/15/2003. On lower standards, see, for example, Gallup poll taken 06/11/2001–06/17/2001. Seventy percent supported "setting quotas for the number of racial minorities hired or accepted, but requiring them to meet the same standards as others," while only 26 percent supported "setting quotas for the number of racial minorities hired or accepted even if it means lowering the standards in order to make up for past discrimination."
56. Allen and Lane (2003b).
57. Allen and Lane (2003a). See also Goldstein and Milbank (2003).
58. The 2004 Republican Party platform was also more moderate in tone.
59. Republican Party platforms of 1980, 1984, and 1988.

60. *Lee v. Weisman,* 505 U.S. 577 (1992).
61. "Statement on the Supreme Court Decision on the Lee v. Weisman Case," June 24, 1992, *Public Papers of George Bush.*
62. *Santa Fe Independent School District v. Doe* 530 U.S. 290 (2000).
63. Bush quoted in Greenhouse (2000); see also, Judd (2000).
64. Gallup polls taken 01/06/1992–01/09/1992 and 10/25/2000–10/26/2000.
65. Moreover, Reagan's three clearly ideological choices for the Court—Rehnquist's elevation to chief, and the nominations of Scalia and Bork—took place after Reagan had already secured reelection. Significantly, the first two of these three also took place when the Republicans controlled the US Senate. George H. W. Bush's sole ideologically conservative choice for the Court—Thomas—confronted a confirmation battle that even surpassed that of Robert Bork's in intensity and hostility. However, the evidence suggests that Thomas' race—he become only the second African American nominated to the Court— helped conservative southern Democrats to support him in the end. Thus, Thomas won confirmation (barely), even though Democrats held a majority in the Senate.
66. Greenburg (2007, 264–266).
67. William Kristol of the *Weekly Standard* led off the attack mere moments after the public nomination. "I'M DISAPPOINTED, depressed and demoralized." To him, the president had failed to name someone with a "visible and distinguished constitutionalist track record" and instead selected a nominee with "no constitutionalist credentials that I know of." Kristol could not understand why Bush had "flinched from a fight on constitutional philosophy," by making a selection that "will unavoidably be judged as reflecting a combination of cronyism and capitulation," 2005. For more on the Miers appointment, see McMahon (2008).
68. Toobin (2007, 266).
69. McCloskey (1960, 17–18).
70. See McMahon (2011).

REFERENCES

Abraham, Henry J. 1999. *Justices, Presidents, and Senators: A History of the U.S. Supreme Court Appointments from Washington to Clinton.* New York: Rowman & Littlefield.

Abramowitz, Alan I. 1995. "It's Abortion Stupid: Policy Voting in the 1992 Presidential Election." *Journal of Politics* 57(1):: 176–186.

Allen, Mike, and Charles Lane. 2003a. "President to Oppose Race-based Admissions." *Washington Post* January 15.

———. 2003b. "Rice Helped Shape Bush Decision on Admissions." *Washington Post* January 17.

Apple, R. W. 1989. "Backlash at the Polls." *New York Times* November 9.

Apple, R. W., Jr. 1992. "Behind Bush's Mixed Abortion Signals." *New York Times* August 15.

Balkin, Jack M., and Sanford Levinson. 2001. "Understanding the Constitutional Revolution." *Virginia Law Review* 87(6) (October): 1045–1104.

Binder, Sarah A. 2008. "Consequence for the Courts: Polarized Politics and the Judicial Branch." In *Red and Blue Nation?: Consequences and Correction of*

America's Polarized Politics, Volume Two, edited by Pietro S. Nivola and David W. Brady. Washington, DC: Brookings Institution Press.

Bork, Robert H. 2002. "Adversary Jurisprudence." In *The Survival of Culture: Permanent Values in a Virtual Age*, edited by Hilton Kramer and Roger Kimball. Chicago: Ivan R. Dee Publisher.

Clayton, Cornell W., and Howard Gillman, eds. 1999. *Supreme Court Decision-making: New Institutionalist Approaches*. Chicago: University of Chicago Press.

Clayton, Cornell W., and David May. 1999. "A Political Regimes Approach to the Analysis of Legal Decisions." *Polity* 32 (Winter 2): 233–252.

Clayton, Cornell W., and J. Mitchell Pickerill. 2004. "Guess What Happened on the Way to Revolution? Precursors to the Supreme Court's Federalism Revolution." *Publius: The Journal of Federalism* 34(3) (Summer): 85–114.

———. 2006. "The Politics of Criminal Justice: How the New Right Regime Shaped the Rehnquist Court's Criminal Justice Jurisprudence." *The Georgetown Law Journal* 94(5): 1385–1425.

Epstein, Lee, and Jeffrey A. Segal. 2005. *Advice and Consent: The Politics of Judicial Appointments*. New York: Oxford University Press.

Garrow, David J. 1994. "Justice Souter Emerges." *New York Times Magazine* September 25.

Gillman, Howard.. 2002. "How Political Parties Can Use the Courts to Advance Their Agendas: Federal Courts in the United States, 1875–1891." *American Political Science Review* 96: 96(3):511–524.

———. 2004. "Martin Shapiro and the New Institutionalism in Judicial Behavior Studies." *Annual Review of Political Science* 7: 363–382.

———. 2006. "Party Politics and Constitutional Change: The Political Origins of Liberal Judicial Activism." In *The Supreme Court and American Political Development*, edited by Ronald Kahn and Ken I. Kersch Lawrence: University Press of Kansas.

Gillman, Howard, and Cornell Clayton, eds. 1999. *The Supreme Court in American Politics: New Institutionalist Interpretations*. Lawrence: University Press of Kansas.

Goldstein, Amy, and Dana Milbank. 2003. "Bush Joins Admissions Case Fight." *Washington Post* January 16.

Graber, Mark A. 2005. "Constructing Judicial Review." *Annual Review of Political Science* 8:425–451.

———. 1993. "The Nonmajoritarian Difficulty: Legislative Deference to the Judiciary." *Studies in American Political Development* 7(Spring 1): 35–73.

Greenburg, Jan Crawford. 2007. *Supreme Conflict: The Inside Story of the Struggle for Control of the United States Supreme Court*. New York: Penguin.

Greenhouse, Linda. 2003. "Muted Call in Race Case." *New York Times* January 17.

———. 2000. "Student Prayers Must be Private, Court Reaffirms." *New York Times* June 20.

Judd, Alan. 2000. "Justices Restrict School Prayer," *Atlanta Journal and Constitution* June 20.

Kristol, William. 2005. "Disappointed, Depressed and Demoralized: A reaction to the Harriet Miers nomination." *Weekly Standard* October 3.

Lovell, George I. 2003. *Legislative Deferrals: Statutory Ambiguity, Judicial Power, and American Democracy*. New York: Cambridge University Press.

Maltese, John Anthony. 1995. *The Selling of Supreme Court Nominees*. Baltimore, MD: Johns Hopkins University Press.

Maltz, Earl M. 2003. "Anthony Kennedy and the Jurisprudence of Respectable Conservatism." In *Rehnquist Justice: Understanding the Court Dynamic*, edited by Earl M. Maltz. Lawrence: University of Kansas Press.

Massaro, John. 1990. *Supremely Political: The Role of Ideology and Presidential Management in Unsuccessful Supreme Court Nominations*. Albany: State University of New York Press.

Mauro, Tony. 2003. "Bush's Briefs in Affirmative Action Debate Weighed." *Legal Intelligencer* January 21.

McCloskey, Robert. 1960. *The American Supreme Court*. Chicago: University of Chicago Press.

McMahon, Kevin J. 2008. "Explaining the Selection and Rejection of Harriet Miers: George W. Bush, Political Symbolism, and the Highpoint of Conservatism." *American Review of Politics* 29(Fall): 253–270.

———. 2011. *Nixon's Court: His Challenge to Judicial Liberalism and Its Political Consequences*. Chicago, IL: University of Chicago Press.

———. 2004. *Reconsidering Roosevelt on Race: How the Presidency Paved the Road to Brown*. Chicago, IL: University of Chicago Press.

Morgan, Richard E. 2006. "The Failure of the Rehnquist Court." *The Claremont Review of Books*.

Nemacheck, Christine L. 2007. *Strategic Selection: Presidential Nomination of Supreme Court Justices from Herbert Hoover to George W. Bush*. Charlottesville: University of Virginia Press.

Noe, Chuck. 2003. "Supreme Court Split on Colleges' Racial Discrimination." NewsmMax.com June 23.

Novak, Robert. 2003. "Editorial." *Chicago Sun-Times* January 23.

O'Connor, Karen. 1996. *No Neutral Ground? Abortion Politics in an Age of Absolutes*. Boulder, CO: Westview.

Peretti, Terri. 1999. *In Defense of a Political Court*. Princeton, NJ: Princeton University Press.

Perry, Barbara A. 1991. *A "Representative" Supreme Court? The Impact of Race, Religion, and Gender on Appointments*. New York: Greenwood Press.

Pickerill, J. Mitchell, and Cornell W. Clayton. 2004. "The Rehnquist Court and the Political Dynamics of Federalism." *Perspectives on Politics* 2 (2): 233–248.

Rosenthal, Andrew. 1992. "Bush, Asked in Personal Context, Takes a Softer Stand on Abortion." *New York Times* August 12.

Sack, Kevin. 1992. "Quayle Insists Abortion Remarks Don't Signal Change in His View." *New York Times* July 24.

Scherer, Nancy. 2005. *Scoring Points: Politicians, Activists, and the Lower Federal Court Appointment Process*. Stanford, CA: Stanford University Press.

Segal, Jeffrey A., and Albert D. Cover. 1989. "Ideological Values and the Votes of U.S. Supreme Court Justices." *American Political Science Review* (June)57(3): 557–565.

Segal, Jeffrey A., and Harold J. Spaeth. 2002. *The Supreme Court and the Attitudinal Model Revisited*. New York: Cambridge University Press.

Segal, Jeffrey A., Lee Epstein, Charles M. Cameron, and Harold Spaeth. 1995. "Ideological Values and the Votes of U.S. Supreme Court Justices Revisited." *Journal of Politics* 57(3): 812–823.

Shapiro, Martin M. 1978. "The Supreme Court: From Warren to Burger." In *The New American Political System*, edited by Anthony King. Washington, DC: American Enterprise Institute.

Silverstein, Mark. 1994. *Judicious Choices: The New Politics of Supreme Court Confirmations*. New York: W.W. Norton & Company.

Stanley, Alessandra. 1992. "First Lady on Abortion: Not a Platform Issue." *New York Times* August 14.

Sunstein, Cass R. 2005. *Radicals in Robes: Why Extreme Right-Wing Courts Are Wrong for America*. New York: Basic Books.

Teixeira, Ruy, and Joel Rogers. 2000. *America's Forgotten Majority: Why the White Working Class Still Matters*. New York: Basic Books.

Toobin, Jeffrey. 2007. *The Nine: Inside the Secret World of the Supreme Court*. New York: Doubleday.

———. 2012. *The Oath: The Obama White House and the Supreme Court*. New York: Doubleday.

Toner, Robin. 1992. "New Worry for Bush." *New York Times* January 22.

Tushnet, Mark. 2005. *A Court Divided: The Rehnquist Court and the Future of Constitutional Law*. New York: W.W. Norton.

Watson, George L., and John A. Stookey. 1995. *Shaping America: The Politics of Supreme Court Appointments*. New York: Longman.

Whittington, Keith. 2005. "'Interpose Your Friendly Hand': Political Supports for the Exercise of Judicial Review by the United States Supreme Court." *American Political Science Review* 99(4): 583–596.

———. 2007. *Political Foundations of Judicial Supremacy: The Presidency, the Supreme Court, and Constitutional Leadership in U.S. History*. Princeton: Princeton University Press.

Yalof, David Alistair. 1999. *Pursuit of Justices: Presidential Politics and the Selection of Supreme Court Nominees*. Chicago, IL: The University of Chicago Press.

Part II

Bridging the Partisan Divide

9

GROWING APART: "CIVILISTA" ATTEMPTS TO BRIDGE THE PARTISAN RIFT*

Frank H. Mackaman

It has always puzzled me that in Washington we have no public vocabulary to describe civility, which I believe is among the highest of public virtues...peaks of uncommon progress can be reached by paths of common courtesy."
Robert H. Michel, Republican Leader of the House, 1981–1995

From 1996 through 2004, Illinois Republican Congressman Ray LaHood, who worked for Bob Michel and then succeeded him in the House, led a small group of House colleagues in a concerted effort to promote civility in that chamber. For the first and only time in congressional history, these men and women organized a series of four "civility retreats,"[1] as they were known, to counter the trend toward discourteous behavior in the House. After almost a decade, however, they gave up, having failed at the task.[2]

Regardless of the outcome, their efforts identified scores of obstacles to civility in the House of Representatives and proposed a series of remedies. If the past is prologue, perhaps there is something to be learned from the LaHood civility initiatives.

CIVILITY IN RETREAT

By 1996, Ray LaHood's second year in Congress, the image of the House of Representatives depicted in most textbooks as a place of reasoned debate, predictable processes, and restrained partisanship had simply disappeared. For LaHood's part, he had witnessed the coarsening of politics first hand throughout the decade at Michel's side.

Minority Leader Michel's battles not only with Democrats but also with hard-edged Republicans led by Newt Gingrich warned of the decline in civility and comity that became evident to all in 1996 during the one hundred and fourth Congress.

Just a few examples. On the floor of the House, Bob Dornan (R-CA) charged President Clinton with "giving aid and comfort to the enemy" during the Vietnam War—Dornan was formally sanctioned. John Mica (R-FL) violated House decorum when he called the president "the little bugger." Wes Cooley (R-OR) offered to punch a pregnant member of the press in the nose. Jim Moran (D-VA) shoved Duke Cunningham (R-CA) after a testy debate on Bosnia, promoting a general melee and an urgent summons to the Capitol police. Democrat Maxine Waters ordered New York Republican Peter King to "shut up" during a Banking Committee hearing.

The lack of respect extended to the very highest levels of leadership in the House. The atmosphere in the House had taken a bitter turn when Gingrich first filed ethics charges against Speaker Jim Wright in 1988, an action that eventually led Wright to resign. As fate would have it, Gingrich himself then became the target of ethics charges beginning in the mid-1990s. The impact on the relationship between Gingrich, who became speaker of the House in 1995, and Minority Leader Dick Gephardt (D-MO) was predictable. The two of them went 18 months without a single private conversation. In contrast, Minority Leader Michel met at least once a week with Democratic leaders. The relationship between the leaders in the one hundred and fourth Congress was a far cry from the days when Tip O'Neill and Bob Michel famously played golf together.

THE IDEA

What did the organizers hope to achieve? The coconveners of the first civility retreat, LaHood and Congressman David Skaggs, a Democrat from Colorado, stated the purpose of their effort in letters to Speaker Gingrich and Minority Leader Gephardt in June 1996:

> The ability of the House of Representatives to deal successfully with the challenges facing the nation depends on the level of trust and the working relationships that exist among members. We believe there is a real need for a considered and concerted effort to improve the House in this respect.
>
> Without belaboring the experience of the last several years, we all seek a greater degree of civility, mutual respect and—when possible—bipartisanship. We believe this can be accomplished without having to compromise vigorous debate or legitimate disagreement. But it will take work and a certain commitment.
>
> We are writing you...to suggest that you agree to set aside a long weekend early in 1997 for the entire membership to meet together informally at an appropriate site near Washington.

It would be premature now to try to lay out any very detailed agenda. The main purpose would be to permit members to get to know each other before the difficult work of the 105th Congress begins in earnest and to establish a more constructive spirit and ethic for member-to-member relations.

We hope you agree that such a session would help create a more congenial and productive work environment, regardless of who may have the majority after the election. We recommend that you appoint a planning committee drawn equally from each party to develop a specific proposal that could be approved by the joint leadership before *sine die* adjournment of the 104th Congress.[3]

Forty-four Republicans and 42 Democrats cosigned. Skaggs said the response to the civility proposal had been "uniformly positive," adding that when he showed people the draft of the letter to the leadership, "it was like bringing a canteen to a thirsty traveler." LaHood and Skaggs were further heartened by a survey of 50 members indicating that between 60 and 70 percent either were "very likely" or "probably" would attend a retreat.

As Gingrich and Gephardt wrote in a Dear Colleague letter urging their colleagues to keep March 7–9, 1997, open: "This unique retreat is intended simply to improve the working environment in the House. By enabling members to spend quality time with each other, along with their families, we are hopeful we can establish a more collegial atmosphere, and, thereby, better working relationships."

A group of nine members began planning for Retreat I supported by the $700,00 grant from the Pew Charitable Trusts. From the beginning, the Trusts had three concerns: The retreat should be attended by at least one-third, but preferably half, of the members of the House; the participation should be truly bipartisan, with virtually equal representation from the two parties; and the members should undertake "substantive" work, that is, the retreat should not be primarily social, recreational, or even educational. The substantive work, the funders stipulated, should address issues of relationships, not policy, with a goal of developing "social trust" among the members. These three items were formally written into the grant award as "special conditions."

THE FIRST RETREAT: MARCH 7–9, 1997

The first retreat took place in Hershey, Pennsylvania. Although press accounts would peg the final tally at 200 members, the actual attendance amounted to 197 House members, 165 spouses, and 100 of their children. The bipartisan congressional leadership was well represented: the speaker, majority whip, minority leader, and minority whip attended. In addition, 45 of the 74 freshmen elected in November 1996 took part. Senior Democrats so disliked the Republican leadership, however, that they opted out, as did many older members whose children were grown.

After presentations by several speakers, including Tom Mann, Norm Ornstein, Kathleen Hall Jamieson, and David McCullough, the members and spouses divided into 12 small working groups led by trained facilitators. Each group of 30 had an equal number of Republicans and Democrats and all had received extensive briefing materials before the meeting.

Group members began their task by responding to the question, "How has the quality of discourse in the House of Representatives affected me personally?"

Taken together, the 12 groups identified more than 500 obstacles to achieving civility in the House and more than 230 solutions. Table 9.1 arrays obstacles and solutions by category.

Following the retreat, planning committee members spent countless hours parsing the data, categorizing the causes and effects of uncivil behavior in different combinations. How much of the problem stemmed from individual actions, for example? How much lay beyond the control of members—attributable to external factors? Among the findings: personal behavior and the internal culture of the House accounted for about 25 percent of the obstacles to civility. Nearly the same proportion came from media influences, public attitudes, the nature of issues, and the speed of change in society combined—all factors largely outside the direct control of members. Yet

Table 9.1 Obstacles and Solutions to Civility

Category in Order of Frequency	Obstacles	Solutions
Personal behavior	76	15
Media	58	11
Internal culture	53	57
Campaigns	49	4
Rules/procedures	47	35
Public attitudes	43	7
Planning/scheduling	26	19
Political parties	24	1
Ideology	23	0
Socializing	22	15
Leadership	18	18
Issues	14	10
Family	12	4
One-minutes	11	12
Speed of change	8	0
Terms	7	2
Orientation	6	13
Staff	4	5
Cloakroom	4	3
Travel	3	5

another analysis counted 306 of the 508 obstacles as the result of internal rules and procedures.

Much food for thought.

The talking points developed by the civilistas to describe the first retreat captured their enthusiasm:

> For any legislature to function, its members must have a level of trust in each other. And that trust can only develop when legislators have an opportunity to get acquainted, as people, across the aisle, outside the arena of partisan combat. When people know each other, they are less likely to question the other person's motives, or to let policy differences turn into personal hostility.

> Our mission for three days has been as confounding as it has been simple. We came together to bring greater civility to the House of Representatives. No legislative business. No political games. Just members and their families taking time together, to get to know one another better, to examine the environment in the House and figure out what can be done to make it better.

> The nation is well-served by healthy and vigorous debate. That's essential to a functioning democracy. There are real and significant differences between Republicans and Democrats, and we have no desire to blur those distinctions. Rather, the retreat has been about handling those disagreements constructively, and honoring our Republic with debates that are more civil, more respectful, and ultimately more productive.

> As there is no simple cure for the incivility we see too often in American society generally, there is no simple cure for the rancor and mistrust in the House. The retreat is no panacea, but it is a start. As members of Congress, we have an enormous responsibility to the nation. With some luck and good will, what has begun this weekend will help us better meet that responsibility.

Hershey I, as it came to be known, proved to be the largest gathering of House members outside of the Capitol in the nation's history. LaHood was certain that members had started to build friendships and relationships that would last far beyond their careers in Congress, the so-called social trust demanded by the Pew Charitable Trusts. He was not alone in these beliefs. Charlie Stenholm (D-TX) told the press, "There are going to be some friendships made, and I think when you do that, you're going to have a better chance of working together." According to Robert Franks (R-NJ), "This is the first time I've ever had the opportunity to get to know people as human beings rather than as political entities. People will be far more reticent to engage in verbal warfare now that we understand the human dimensions of members."

The speaker and minority leader attended all sessions during the weekend, talked to each other, and appeared open to the suggestion that the House leadership have regular joint meetings. On the floor of the House the following week, Gingrich said that the retreat had produced "measurable progress" on the complex challenge of how to debate and legislate with respect. Gephardt, too, spoke positively about the retreat, calling it "a historic event, the only time that I know that members from both sides of the aisle and their families have had a two-day period to understand how we could better work together to solve the problems we are all trying to solve."

One of the members of the planning committee had a more reserved reaction, however. New York Republican Amo Houghton told the press, "I have high secret hopes, but low public expectations. I think we can overpromise, we can overindulge ourselves because we've all had such a wonderful time." The press also called a few members who did not attend and hit upon an attitude that would confound those who planned future retreats. As an aide to Michael Oxley (R-OH), who did not attend, put it, "He's not going because the people who need to go won't. The people who are already civil will show up."

Sam Gibbons (D-FL), whose petulant behavior in a Ways and Means Committee hearing had prompted Skaggs to approach LaHood in the first place, told a reporter,

> Good luck! Most of the time these sorts of ideas are put forth by do-gooders who want to protect themselves from scrutiny. I just don't believe you can reform this place into a nice-boys' club. The way Newt has run this place, the House membership has almost become superfluous. Newt and his staff set the agenda. He's the one who's done more than anyone else to discredit the Congress. He's been quoted numerous times as saying that in order to rebuild this country, you have to first tear it down.

Next came the task of implementing at least some of the solutions proposed at the retreat. The planning group spent considerable time trying to determine what to do next. Immediately following the retreat, staff and organizers began compiling the findings and circulating drafts of action steps.[4] LaHood's files contain various lists of ideas, suggestions, and proposals for action. They dissected the ideas in every way imaginable. For example, one draft organized the suggestions according to who could take the necessary action to improve civility:

- Suggestions that could be implemented by action of the speaker, for example, move one-minutes to the end of the day, try to make the legislative schedule family friendly, and allow the use of signal lights for each floor manager to ask his or her counterpart to seek civility among members on that side of the aisle during debate.
- Suggestions that could be implemented by joint leadership action, for example, joint leadership meetings, joint meetings of the conference/caucus, and bipartisan social events.
- Suggestions that could be implemented by changes in the House rules, for example, admit spouses to the floor during late sessions and make the ethics process less subject to abuse.
- Suggestions that could be implemented by Retreat Planning Committee action, for example, distribute the opening video to all members, obtain a Special Order to explain what happened in Hershey, and hold media, staff, and committee retreats.

- Suggestions that could be implemented by administrative action, for example, commission a group photo of the entire membership and provide on-going facilitation coaching for members.
- Suggestions that could be implemented by ethics rulings (none listed).
- Suggestions that might need funding, for example, provide member name tags, publish a spouse directory, and sponsor a lecture series.
- Suggestions that might involve family participation, for example, more use of the family room and host periodic functions for families.
- Suggestions that could be implemented by individual member action, for example, participate in a DC clean-up day, wear name-tags, mingle, and improve the tone of campaigns.

For about two months, March and April 1997, momentum seemed to be with the civility initiative. On March 13, for example, members of the civility task force met to discuss the retreat and to begin laying out a list of about 40 rules changes to make the House less combative. A list of follow-up activities and actions was attached to the agenda. While some of the suggestions should have been easy to implement, LaHood noted that others are a "little like walking through a minefield. You have to do it very delicately if you want to get it done." The committee also considered a proposal from one member titled, "Hershey Accords," which listed four general rules that this member would like to see his colleagues follow in the wake of the retreat:

1. No member shall speak ill of another member on the House floor, in committee proceedings, or to the media.
2. When rumors are heard, do not assume that another member has disparaged you. Take the time to check it out and resolve the conflict amicably and privately.
3. Always make positive contributions—when you do this you bring honor to the House, your district, and your colleagues.
4. Keep you debate and legislative agenda issue-oriented. Constituents expect us to be above making personal attacks.

Ironically, *Roll Call* reported that all four accords had been broken or stretched over a single week. Even on the day the committee met, the House broke out in partisan warfare over funding for committee budgets and voted, only after acrimonious debate, to ban the practice of partial-birth abortion. The *Peoria Journal Star*, the largest paper in LaHood's district, carried a story at the end of March that summed up in a headline the civilistas' uphill battle: "Sweet lessons of Hershey already forgotten." Ironically, in mid-April, a hearing on civility before the Subcommittee on Rules and Organization of the House had to be suspended because of an outbreak of incivility on the House floor.

Momentum soon waned. No one took on the civility initiatives as a full-time responsibility, and it was too easy for members and staff to return to their normal routines. One of the consultants to the project reminded LaHood and Skaggs that neither had what he called "sanctioning power." Both could advocate for change, but they lacked the power to impose it without the approval of others. He warned that simply knowing who could effect change did not mean that change would result. "In fact, just handing over ideas to those with the power to make the change without going through certain advocacy steps first is probably the surest way to fail at making change," he said. The next decade would prove the wisdom of his analysis. The civilistas could propose change; they could not impose change.

RETREAT II: MARCH 19–21, 1999

Events conspired against the civility initiative as planners, with the tacit support of party leaders, began preparing for Retreat II. The Clinton impeachment proceedings and the 1998 election results, which resulted in substantial losses by the Republicans and the resignation of Speaker Gingrich, fostered rancor and bitterness in the House. "You would think politicians would not need lessons in listening to each other. But after a year of hectoring over President Clinton's personal conduct, they are not a bad idea," editorialized the *New York Times* on March 1 before warning that "no amount of happy talk will raise Congress's esteem."

Unfortunately, an episode in the House Committee on Veterans Affairs the week before the retreat pointed up the challenge. Committee Democrats were outraged when Chairman Bob Stump (R-AZ) refused to allow Democrats to submit a budget proposal for debate. Although other committees often experienced partisan bickering, that was rare for Veterans Affairs. Stump's action compounded Democrats' outrage over their underrepresentation on committees.

Nevertheless, an expanded committee charged with planning Retreat II identified seven objectives:

1. Help members learn about each other and understand their partnership.
2. Focus on the process, culture, and role of the House, both now and in the twenty-first century.
3. Aim to boost House productivity.
4. Give members permission to be friends and a safe place in which to do this.
5. Look into alternative techniques for debating issues.
6. Provide for team building.
7. Talk about civility in the House.

The second retreat took place again in Hershey. In total, 450 persons from the congressional community took part, a number that included spouses and children. The retreat lacked for members, however. Ninety-four

Republicans and 92 Democrats turned out, about a dozen fewer than the 197 who attended Hershey I.

The working sessions focused on (1) the members' call to public service and how the quality of discourse in the House had affected them personally and as a member of the institution; (2) understanding the institutional obstacles to civility and effectiveness in the House; and (3) identifying specific actions that could be taken to eliminate those obstacles and enhance effectiveness.

Following the event, the planning committee reached a consensus on the "action steps" much more quickly than two years before. Frustrated by the lack of success following Retreat I, the organizers thought that if they talked about "mechanisms" instead of a long list of rules changes that they might achieve what seemed to them to be the most important items. A consensus in the committee emerged around 11 action steps:

1. Create a bipartisan mechanism to address scheduling.
2. Create a bipartisan mechanism to address members' financial needs.
3. Establish a bipartisan committee on fairness and integrity in the political process and campaigning.
4. Create a bipartisan mechanism to address floor proceedings (e.g., one-minutes, open rules, and minority party substitutes).
5. Establish a bipartisan institutional fairness committee.
6. Increase communication/coordination between the parties with regular leadership meetings; consider "mini-Hershey" retreats for chairs and ranking members.
7. Create a bipartisan mechanism to address committee ratio and resource issues.
8. Improve freshman orientation, establish cross-party mentorships, and have freshmen CODELs (congressional delegations).
9. Revisit the ethics committee process; revise the rules to be clear, flexible, and supportive of families.
10. Establish bipartisan policy forums and field hearings.
11. Develop a program of bipartisan service activities/community projects.

The contrast between these 11 action steps and the 236 remedies proposed at Retreat I is striking not only in number but also in scope. The agenda for change in 1999 was markedly less ambitious than in 1997.

The postretreat evaluation gave the civilistas reason for at least some optimism. According to the 52 members who returned surveys, 81 percent said they would attend another retreat in 2001—only one said "no." Almost 70 percent had attended the first retreat, so the planners concluded that these members and families derived some value from the experience; it did leave them wondering about how to expand attendance, however. Thirty percent of the attendees brought children, and 82 percent participated in all activities. The three most cited reasons for attending the retreat were "I hoped to improve bipartisan relations," "I wanted a chance to meet colleagues and their families," and "It was a chance to discuss what improvements can be made in the House."

On the strength of members' continuing interest, albeit expressed formally by just 52 of the 186 members who attended the 1999 retreat, the civilistas proceeded to plan a third retreat in 2001, this one to follow the presidential election of 2000.

RETREAT III: MARCH 9–11, 2001
RETREAT IV: FEBRUARY 28–MARCH 2, 2003

The civility initiative seemed increasingly fragile as LaHood once again marshaled a committee to begin planning for a third retreat, this one to take place in March 2001 at the Greenbrier in West Virginia. Officials with the Pew Charitable Trust expressed disappointment with their investment. They agreed that the civilistas had tackled a large challenge, that the first two retreats had met the attendance and bipartisan balance thresholds, and that the retreats had identified changes that would improve the quality of discourse in the House.

"Despite these accomplishments, however," Pew wrote, "the retreats have failed to produce much evidence of lasting change." Whatever increases in civility that had occurred had then "quickly disappeared in the face of the partisan tensions resulting in part from the Clinton scandal and ensuring impeachment." As a result, "none of the recommended institutional changes have been instituted." The Trust official also concluded that there was no evidence that the second retreat had increased civility "in any systematic or lasting way." Furthermore, news coverage of the event, while often positive, "had undertones suggesting that this was 'tilting at windmills' at best."

LaHood had to confess that even with more modest goals coming out of 1999, none of the proposals from the second retreat had borne fruit—even a recommendation to create a task force to examine the retreat's recommendations. Since Hershey II, the civilistas had met only briefly with Speaker Dennis Hastert or with Gephardt, and never as a bipartisan group. There was no point in avoiding the obvious.

The planning committee responded to Pew's concerns with a formal proposal seeking funding for Retreat III. "The environment that will greet the 107th Congress next January will be as difficult as ever, following what clearly will have been another very partisan, rancorous election season," the proposal began. "The opening for improved conditions that will exist will be equaled by the challenges. A new Administration is a certainty, and with it comes a certain opportunity to set a fresh tone in executive-legislative relations. There may also be changes in control of Congress." The proposal acknowledged that change is an inevitable source of anxiety and tension, all the more so with changes in political power. The civilistas realized that no matter what happened in the elections, roughly half the membership of the House would report for duty next year bitterly disappointed: that they failed to gain, or to keep, control of their chamber; that their party failed to gain, or to keep, control of the White House. All that coupled with the difficulties of the recent past promised to "aggravate the risk that political conflict and partisan rancor will stand in the way of effective governance for another two years."

The civilistas did succeed in obtaining funding for two more retreats by establishing three major criteria for measuring success going forward: substantial and roughly equal attendance by members of both parties; major changes in approach from the previous retreats; and serious, substantive programming. In sum, they said the third retreat would "aim to expand the vision of members about the great opportunities and the challenges facing the country and Congress. In the process, it will seek also to help insure that, while dealing with those opportunities and challenges, political disagreements and debate are kept within the bounds of decency and respect."

The retreat planners agreed to move away from the more introspective approach and the interpersonal orientation of the working sessions employed at the first two retreats. Instead, they told Pew they would focus on the challenges to American democracy in the new century with topical sessions on such subjects as the impact of technology on the practices of American democracy and the impact of globalization on the nation's economy and security.

The acrimony in the House continued to conspire against the civility initiative, however. Talk spread of a Democratic boycott of the third retreat. One unidentified Democrat who refused to attend explained his decision: "I need to walk the dog. That's all the excuse they deserve." For his part, Gephardt complained that the upcoming retreat would be his last. "Been there, done that, all I got was this t-shirt," he whined at a news conference in his office. "I don't want to go to West Virginia to be bipartisan. I want to be bipartisan in this building."

With fewer members than LaHood had hoped, about 125, the retreat proceeded. Attendees explored communications technology, security issues, and the biotechnology revolution in small groups, followed by a lunch at which members talked more specifically about their immediate concerns in the House.

In the weeks following Retreat III, the Bipartisan Congressional Retreat Planning Committee met to review participant evaluations of the retreat, define lessons learned, anticipate future committee activities, and decide whether or not to hold Retreat IV. Tellingly, only 22 members who attended the retreat returned evaluations; the civilistas did not have much to go on. To sustain the impact of the retreat, however, the committee did decide, somewhat tentatively, to arrange mini-retreats for committees, to sponsor a biotechnology seminar series, to consider inviting David McCullough to speak in the Capitol, and to proceed on the assumption that another retreat would occur in 2003. In hindsight, this seems like a modest agenda for action compared to Retreat I. Even so, the committee had to cancel the McCullough event for lack of participation, and none of the six committees

LaHood approached responded to the offer to host a mini-retreat just for its members.

Retreat IV took place on February 28 through March 2, 2003, again at the Greenbrier resort in West Virginia. The planning committee selected what it called "core" American values as the overarching subject for the retreat. Deciding what those core values were took time, however. They settled on the following as guidance for the guest speakers: freedom and liberty, democracy, equality of opportunity, fairness, individualism and self-reliance, and community and mutual responsibility.

LaHood saw the handwriting on the wall, however. Attendance numbers dropped, enthusiasm ebbed, even press coverage declined. The planning committee surveyed the attendees asking them to suggest follow-up activities. They only received about a half dozen suggestions, almost all of which dealt with organizing events such as bipartisan issue luncheons, committee retreats, committee dinners with families, district weekend exchange visits, and CODELs.

Bottom line: after four retreats, civility did not improve in the House. Just one example, from a *Roll Call* story headed, "Poisoned Political Water Breeds Acrimony, Contempt" authored by former Iowa congressman Jim Lightfoot:

> The air is poison. Tension grips even the most casual conversations, which have become an exercise in short, cryptic remarks, many times more grunted than spoken. Distrust is the order of the day. People keep looking over their shoulders to see if anyone has taken an unhealthy interest in them. The environment is hostile and does not lend itself to any degree of accomplishment.

According to *Congressional Quarterly*'s analysis of "party unity" votes in 2003—those that pitted a majority of one party against a majority of the other party—Congress was more polarized than it had been in the five decades that *CQ* had been tracking voting patterns.

THE END

In September 2004, LaHood and his working group canceled the bipartisan civility retreat scheduled for January 2005 but not because they had succeeded or that Congress had miraculously become a more civil place. When LaHood surveyed members to determine their interest in a fifth retreat, the demand just was not there. Only 120 members returned surveys, despite repeated efforts to solicit responses—of that number, 47 said they definitely would not attend another retreat.

What went wrong? It seems likely that four sets of factors doomed the civility initiative. First, so much of what the civilistas objected to in Congress either reflected larger issues in society or resulted from factors beyond the control of the members, never numbering more than 200, who sought change. Retreat planners could not do much about the new, hyperactive media, for example, or the proliferation of interest groups, the hardening of partisan ideologies, congressional redistricting that produced fewer competitive seats, or a style of campaigning that emphasized opposition research and constant attack. Add to those factors the narrow partisan margins in the House, which meant that both parties believed it was critical to hold down defections on key votes by framing their positions in sharp contrast to each other in anticipation of upcoming elections.

The bitterly partisan and prolonged debate over the routine appointment of a new House chaplain in 2000 seemed to epitomize the state of affairs in the House. When Speaker Dennis Hastert selected a Presbyterian, Democrats promptly accused him of anti-Catholic prejudice. Republicans responded that Democrats had turned the issue into a partisan witch-hunt. Needless to say, this sequence of events turned a customary matter into a mess. A sample of story headlines in the *Washington Post* shows how raucous the situation became: "A House Without a Prayer of Comity: Battle of Choice Over Chaplain Erodes Attempts to Restore Civility" (February 12, 2000), "Unholy Uproar on the Hill" (February 15, 2000), and "Holy War in the House: Bias Alleged After Catholic Passed Over for Chaplain" (February 19, 2000). "It's a disgrace," LaHood told a reporter from *The New York Times*, "that we have to argue about something as simple as appointing a chaplain."

Against this context, three other forces conspired against the civility initiative, factors the civilistas could not influence. First, the change in party control of the House from Democrats to Republicans following the 1994 elections proved pivotal. Democrats struggled with their newfound minority status, and Republicans had an expansive agenda to enact while dealing with a president of the opposite party. The federal government shutdowns in November and December 1995 were the culminations of this partisan bickering. Newt Gingrich got it right when he admitted in remarks to the first retreat that "we weren't very good at being in the majority, and Democrats weren't very good at being in the minority." As a Congressional Research Service report on decorum in House debate put it, "There's real anger on the Democratic side, a visceral anger at Republicans, and a sense of egregious injustice. It's hard for them to treat their former minority adversaries with respect. The 104th Congress has been terrible because of the psychological maladjustment."

The tension resulting from this role reversal was compounded by two events. The impeachment controversy in late 1998 coupled with the contested presidential election in 2000 poisoned the well beyond reclaiming.

The civilistas were handicapped by factors within the House, too. The leadership of both parties failed to support the cause. After the second retreat, Dick Gephardt told one reporter, "Hersheys come and Hersheys go. But the bottom line is, do we ever have any real change." Neither Newt Gingrich nor Denny Hastert provided much more than lip service to the effort. They failed to enact even the most simple of the institutional reforms proposed by the civilistas. Moving the one-minutes from the beginning to the end of the day, or altering committee ratios, or adopting a more family-friendly schedule—all within the power of the majority party leadership—could have made a difference.

The retreats themselves suffered from potentially fatal flaws, too. They tended not to include committee chairs, senior members, or opinion leaders in the House. The second retreat, following the impeachment controversy, for example, failed to attract most of the members directly involved in those events. Aside from Asa Hutchinson and James Rogan, the only other House manager was George Gekas, a Republican who represented Hershey in Congress. Judiciary Committee chair Henry Hyde was home in Illinois. Also absent were Bob Barr, one of the president's most vociferous critics, and Barney Frank, the committee's dogged impeachment opponent. When asked to explain his lack of attendance, Barney Frank bragged, "I have no trouble being civil when I think civility is appropriate." John Dingell, the most senior member of the House, who attended only because his wife, a coorganizer, made him, called the retreat "A prodigious waste of my time."

From the outset, LaHood believed that *only by improving relationships on a personal level* would the House become more civil. Relationships, in other words, could trump contextual, institutional, or procedural obstacles. If the problem of incivility stemmed from personal conduct, then personal relationships held the key to improving personal conduct.

How ironic, then, that the civilistas never convinced enough of their colleagues that civility served their own self-interest. LaHood and his colleagues, apparently, never answered satisfactorily this frequently posed question: "What will I get out of it?"

If the key to success sometime in the future lies with self-interest, then it may be worthwhile to suggest how working across the aisle advances a member's own agenda. The retreat planning committee actually came up with nine enticements. They are worth recounting because they suggest what might motivate members to participate in a new civility initiative:

Curiosity. Who are those people on the "other side"? What are they like? If you spend time with them, will they become friends? Or are they in fact another breed altogether?

Humility. As one leading Republican put it: "We don't have all the answers. Neither do the Democrats." The retreat is a chance to be honest about that, to stop posturing, and to see where humble dialog leads.

Partisanship. As any good partisan knows, gathering information about the other side makes good strategic sense. The more you know your opponent, the better you can advance your own causes. One reason to attend is to make sure your side learns as much as possible about the other.

Bipartisanship. Some policy issues require collaboration. What are they? How can the two sides work together? The retreat is a chance informally to begin to find out.

Image. To counteract public perceptions of House members squabbling like kids on the playground, each trying to bully the other and gain an advantage, coming to the retreat makes good sense. It conveys a public image of trying to find common ground.

Ambition. Some of the best legislation is co-sponsored by members of both parties working as partners. You can demonstrate leadership, and advance your career, by having a bipartisan strategy as well as a partisan one.

Enjoyment. The retreat could be a lot of fun.

Family. Much of the time is free for informal socializing. Your family can get to know the families of others and support each other in dealing with the lifestyle challenges that face any national leader's family life.

Community. If Congress is a community, then it must assemble as a community. Partisan retreats are simply not sufficient for genuine community-building.

Taken as a whole, success for LaHood's civility initiative came only at the margins. Yes, in many cases member-to-member relationships improved. However, the retreats failed to change the culture of the House. The proponents of civility could not infuse the institution with respect for honest differences of opinion. They lacked the capacity, the "sanctioning power," to make broad changes. They never hit upon a mechanism to ensure that their initiatives were carried through. There was no funding for it, no permanent staff, and no leadership support. They simply could not sustain the momentum. The people who were interested in keeping things the way they were, the partisan forces, overwhelmed the civilistas who could make progress only one-on-one, as individuals, but not across the Congress, as an institution.

Appendix A

Proposed Follow-up Activities for the Retreat Planning Committee, March 1997

One-minute day about the retreat

Periodic joint caucus/conference meetings

Person-to-person follow up between those attending and those who did not

Party self-policing of floor behavior

Distribution of opening retreat video to all members

Special order by planning committee to explain what happened in Hershey

Monthly coteam leader meetings

Arrange for all members to see the opening video and speeches

Wednesday sandwich night in the members' dining room for members and families

Hershey kisses in the cloakroom

Wear retreat name tags on the floor

Hold shorter retreats on a monthly or quarterly basis

Make the Speaker Pro Tempore more active in stopping bad behavior before it gets out of control

Establish a goal of having no words taken down this year

Hold another bipartisan congressional retreat next year

More foreign travel for members and family

Bipartisan freshmen orientation

More use of the family room

Combine the cloakrooms on a periodic basis

Move one-minutes to the end of the day

Retreat with the media

Write a "Hershey Accords" memorializing the agreements coming out of the retreat

Congressional staff retreat

Regular bipartisan leadership meetings

Establish a monthly lecture series around the topics of civility and the factors affecting House debate

Committee retreats

Regular bipartisan leadership meetings

Make the ethics process less subject to abuse

Work on making the schedule more family friendly

More bipartisan social events

Ongoing facilitation coaching

NOTES

* The author coined the word "civilista" to refer to the leaders of the civility initiative in the House of Representatives, 1996–2004. They did not refer to themselves in that manner.

1. See appendix A.
2. The four retreats took place on the following dates: March 7–9, 1997 (197 Members attended), March 19–21, 1999 (186 Members attended); March 9–11, 2001 (125 Members attended); and February 28–March 2, 2003 (attendance not revealed). A fifth retreat scheduled for January 2005 was cancelled because of lack of interest.
3. After leaving office, LaHood began to write a congressional memoir based on his recollections and the papers he donated to The Dirksen Congressional Center. This chapter is an adaptation of the chapter on his civility initiatives. The views expressed here are the author's own and not necessarily shared by Mr. LaHood (or anyone else, for that matter). The LaHood Collection is closed to research for a finite period.
4. The Ray LaHood Papers are closed for a period of five years after he leaves public office. Direct quotations and data are located in the DC Office, Subject Files, Civility Retreats. A fully noted copy of this chapter will be released once the access restrictions lapse.

10

Can Polarization Be "Fixed"?

California's Experiment with the Top-two Primary

Seth E. Masket

Introduction

In the summer 2010, California's voters, annoyed by legislative polarization in an increasingly dysfunctional state government, launched a statewide experiment by passing Proposition 14. This initiative instituted a top-two "jungle" primary for the state's partisan offices, beginning in 2012. The idea was that by changing the very nature of the primary—placing candidates of all parties within the same primary contest—the state could encourage the election of more moderate state legislators and discourage excessive partisanship among elected officials.

This chapter is an attempt to assess just how successful this reform has been in changing the nature of California's elected officials. To be sure, it is still quite early. At the time this is being written, those elected in the 2012 general elections have only served in Sacramento for a few months, and it is difficult to know if their behavior will be markedly different from that of the past. Nonetheless, the June 2012 elections featured the first top-two primary contest in state history, and we can glean some useful information from those results.

What those results suggest is that Proposition 14 was disruptive to some longstanding political patterns, creating greater competition in elections and reducing the electoral security of incumbents. The political parties, however, responded to this change quickly and have sought ways to control the top-two ballot and make it as close to a closed primary election as possible. The district-level results of the 2012 primary in California suggest a legislature that will not be significantly different from those that preceded it.

POLARIZATION AND ITS REMEDIES

Political observers and practitioners in California largely agree that the state is facing some sort of governing crisis. The state has faced numerous fiscal crises over the past few decades. Typically, an economic downturn leads to a decrease in state revenues, leaving lawmakers in a scramble for funds to pay the state's considerable obligations, many of which have been mandated by voters via a series of initiatives. Since running a deficit is technically illegal for the state (and most others), Democratic lawmakers often seek to raise taxes to cover the shortfall. However, the legislature's unusual two-thirds vote requirement for revenue increases often presents a barrier for the lawmakers; Democrats have held majorities for all but two years of the past four decades, but prior to 2013, they had never consistently held onto supermajorities in both chambers. Any agreement on spending cuts or revenue enhancements must, therefore, be produced via bipartisan compromise.

This has generally proven impossible, largely because of the sharply polarized nature of the California legislature. Figure 10.1 charts the mean "ideal points" (estimations of legislators' ideological preferences based on their roll call voting patterns) by party in the state Assembly since the 1940s. For a variety of reasons, California's parties have moved dramatically apart in recent decades. Even while some moderate legislative districts remain, voters in those districts must increasingly choose between a very liberal Democrat or a very conservative Republican to represent them in the state Assembly, Senate, or the US House of Representatives (Masket 2009). Although polarization is a common phenomenon across the United States, California's case

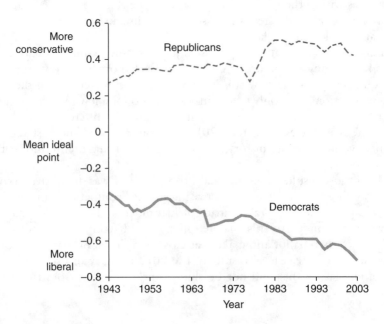

Figure 10.1   Polarization in California.

stands out. As Shor and McCarty (2011) demonstrated in their study of all 99 state legislative chambers, California's chambers are by far the most polarized in the nation, surpassing the US Congress, as well.

In such an environment, convincing even a handful of state legislators to vote against the rest of their party is virtually impossible (Kousser 2010). Republican party leaders have sometimes threatened legislators of their party, warning them that a vote to raise taxes would be their last in the legislature, and they have, on occasion, followed through with these threats, proving their credibility (Halper 2003; Halper and Vogel 2003; Cannon 2002).

Given the relative frequency of these budgetary crises in California, many political observers, reformers, and officeholders have converged on the goal of mitigating party polarization as a remedy to the state's ailments. Indeed, reducing partisanship is seen as a cure for many of the state's problems, beyond just budgetary impasses. California's reformers have pushed two specific reforms over the past few years toward this end—redistricting reform (placing a bipartisan panel of citizens, rather than the state legislature, in charge of redrawing legislative districts) and the top-two primary.

Advocates of the top-two primary proceed from the assumption that legislative partisanship is driven strongly, if not exclusively, by the rules governing who may participate in party nomination contests. California, along with over a dozen other states, has used a "semi-closed" system in its primary contests in recent years; only registered members of a party may participate in that party's primary, although unaffiliated voters may participate in a party's primary by requesting that party's ballot. In theory, primary rules that allow unaffiliated voters to participate in the contest might allow for the nomination of more moderate officeholders. Not only would there be more votes available for those advocating moderate positions, but also candidates would have more incentive to move toward the center to seek those votes.

The top-two primary is perhaps the most "open" form of primary rules. Not only can all voters participate, but also they may choose among all candidates for office, not just those within one party. Furthermore, one possible outcome of a top-two primary is two candidates of the same party going to a runoff election. Theoretically, the more moderate of the two candidates would be well positioned to win such a contest, as she could win the support not only of some of her fellow partisans, but also of independents and perhaps most of the voters of the other party.

The top-two primary won considerable support among political observers as a potential remedy to some of the countries political ailments. In a *Ventura County Star* opinion piece, for example, Thomas Elias advocated the top-two primary as an effective means to rapidly depolarize the government:

> That's the quickest way to assure putting at least some moderate centrists into the state Legislature. It's also the quickest way to give a voice to millions of voters who now essentially have no representation in state government. And it's the first step toward making state government work better, far faster and surer than a constitutional convention or any other tactic. (Elias 2009)

Jonathan Alter similarly claims that the top-two could reduce incidence of undesirable behavior among legislators. "If the concept spreads," he suggests, "the jackass quotient in state legislatures and Congress will decrease. Moderates have better manners" (Alter 2009). California's former lieutenant governor Abel Maldonado similarly reasoned,

> We have a system today where, with…a closed right primary and a closed left primary, which is Republican and Democrat, we have folks that come up there—and, frankly, they're concerned about the next election, their next position. They're concerned about party bosses. They don't worry about what's really important, and that's the state of California. We get this partisanship. (Vocke 2010)

In fact, evidence that primary rules changes can alter the partisanship of a legislature is modest, at best (Gerber and Morton 1998; Kanthak and Morton 2001; Alvarez and Sinclair 2012). A recent large-scale study of two decades of state legislative behavior and primary election rules found no consistent relationship between primary participation restrictiveness and legislative polarization at all (McGhee et al. 2010). Washington State has employed a top-two primary system for several years now, and the state's legislature remains one of the most polarized in the nation (Shor and McCarty 2011). Yet it should be noted that Louisiana has had such a system for decades and has one of the least polarized state legislatures in the country.

It is also worth noting that California's legislature was once distinct for its relative *lack* of partisanship, due in large part to the rules affecting its primary elections. From 1913 to 1959, candidates for partisan office could cross-file, meaning they could run in as many party primaries as they wished. Through this system, many (and in some years, most) incumbents won the nominations of both major parties and many minor ones, effectively winning reelection during the primary.[1] Aiding this was the fact that, up until 1952, party labels did not appear on the primary ballot, giving voters little idea of just whom they were voting for in the primary. This gave cross-filing incumbents little incentive to adhere to extreme ideological positions, and legislative partisanship collapsed during this period. While this era was notable for its bipartisan comity within the chamber, it was also notorious for its corruption—wealthy lobbyists easily bribed state legislators and assembled their own legislative coalitions, providing a structure to the chamber that the parties could not (Masket 2007; 2009; Buchanan 1963; Samish 1971).

In summary, the evidence on the manipulation of primary rules to mitigate legislative partisanship is decidedly mixed. There is certainly no guarantee that a reform like the top-two primary will have any kind of effect on polarization, and if it does, it could carry with it some significant costs. Suffice it to say that Californians' embrace of the top-two primary was based more on theory and hope than evidence.

THE PARTIES RESPOND

The switch to the top-two primary was seen as a serious threat to the state's major political parties. After all, the direct primary was established more than a century ago as a means by which parties could pick nominees—a somewhat more transparent and decisive means than the traditional approach of nomination via convention (Ware 2002). Even when the decision over nominations is opened up to a large group of voters, the choice of nominee still remains in the hands of "the party," broadly defined.

In the eyes of the law, parties have associational rights that allow them to determine who may or may not participate in their decision-making processes. This right is not absolute; the courts have held that limiting participation in primaries based on race, as was often done by Democratic organizations in the South in the early 1900s, is unconstitutional (*Smith V. Allwright* 1944). However, within broad boundaries, parties are free to determine who may vote in their primaries. As the US Supreme Court ruled in *California Democratic Party v. Jones*, when the state declares that anyone may participate in a primary (as it did under a "blanket" primary system in the late 1990s), including members of another party, it threatens to undermine the entire party system:

> [U]nder California's blanket primary system, the prospect of having a party's nominee determined by adherents of an opposing party is far from remote—indeed, it is a clear and present danger...[A] single election in which the party nominee is selected by nonparty members could be enough to destroy the party. (*California Democratic Party V. Jones* 2000)

The only way to get around this rule is to completely redefine the purpose of a primary election, and that is just what the authors of Proposition 14 did. The initiative defined the contest as a "voter-nomination primary election" rather than a party contest. In doing so, it deprived parties of their most important power, the selection of candidates for the general election ballot.

Losing the ability to choose its nominees is a serious blow to a political party,[2] and traditionally they have not suffered such ignominies gladly. In California's 2003 gubernatorial recall election, for example, party elites were active in narrowing the field of candidates through the channeling of campaign resources and in some cases outright bullying. The Republicans effectively nominated Arnold Schwarzenegger, and the Democrats (somewhat reluctantly) effectively nominated Cruz Bustamante, forcing many other high-quality candidates out of the race, even though no primary or other nomination mechanism existed in that election (Masket 2011; Mathews 2006).

In the case of the top-two election, the parties adapted by formalizing a system of endorsements. The Republicans moved first on this front (Van Oot 2011), but the Democrats soon developed a similar system of endorsements. Under the Republican by-laws, a candidate must receive at least two-thirds of the vote at either a county central committee or state central committee meeting to receive the party's endorsement.[3] Under the Democratic rules, any candidate may be considered endorsed with a 70 percent vote at a county central committee meeting, or at the state central committee meeting with a 50 percent vote for incumbents or a 60 percent vote for challengers.[4] The list of endorsees would then appear within the election handbook mailed to voters prior to the election. Notably, indications of endorsements did not appear on the sample ballot pages, but rather in a later page of the handbook.

The Effects of Reform

Political reforms have often proven disappointing for their backers, and have indeed often produced perverse results. Decades of campaign finance reform, for example, have hardly reduced the role of money in campaigns. Instead, they have largely made campaign finance a more byzantine and less transparent system, such that there are now hundreds of millions of dollars given to candidates from sources that are largely unknown, even to the recipient (Smith 1996). Open primaries were established in large part to deprive party organizations of their control over elected officials and to ensure representation of moderates, yet, as mentioned earlier, the elected officials produced by open primaries are often just as ideologically extreme as those resulting from closed primaries (McGhee et al. 2010; Kanthak and Morton 2001; Gerber and Morton 1998). The McGovern–Fraser reforms to the presidential nominating process in the early 1970s were designed to dethrone party insiders from their roles as kingmakers, and yet the last three decades of presidential elections have shown the insiders to have largely retained that power (Cohen et al. 2008).

Why would political reform movements have such an unimpressive track record? It is not as though they had no effects at all. Rather, they tend to induce a short-term shock that leaves parties reeling, but only for a few election cycles, or even one. Soon, they learn to adapt to the new regime.

How do they adapt? Parties are not monolithic, rigid entities. Rather, they are best thought of as loose networks of allies—ideological activists, donors, officeholders, opinion-makers, and others—who coordinate to control nominations and thus influence government (Bawn et al. 2012; Masket 2009; Schattschneider 1942; Schlesinger 1985; Heaney et al. 2012). If a new regulation makes it difficult for a network of allies to achieve its political goals, that group will generally seek new paths to exert influence. For example, campaign finance restrictions passed by voters in Colorado in 2002 prohibited parties from donating large sums of money to their preferred state legislative candidates. Wealthy liberal activists responded by coordinating (semiofficially) with Democratic party leaders to identify swing districts and devote millions of dollars to those races through the use of an intricate web of 527s. Through this system, liberal activists were able to achieve many of their policy goals outside the traditional campaign finance regime, as their work helped flip the state legislature from Republican to Democratic (Masket 2010).

Seen in this light, California's top-two primary reform might be expected to only have limited effects. To be sure, it would likely produce a short-term shock to the political environment, as it changes calculations over which incumbents are vulnerable, which seats are winnable, and how funding should best be allocated. However, in the long run, such a threat to the established parties must produce some sort of reaction from them, and party leaders will likely use endorsements to bring about the rough equivalent of party nominations. To what extent have we seen a shock to the system, and to what extent have the parties mitigated it? I turn to these questions in the next section.

THE IMPACT OF THE TOP-TWO SYSTEM ON THE 2012 PRIMARY ELECTION

Did the top-two reform shake up the status quo? We can examine this from a number of different perspectives. I first look at levels of competition in California primary elections. California primaries are not known to be especially competitive, at least when an incumbent is in the running. Party organizations, both formal and informal, tend to protect their incumbents (unless they have committed some unusually egregious sin) by providing them with levels of funding, endorsements, and expertise that either overwhelm challengers or, more typically, deter them from even entering the race in the first place (Masket 2009). Open-seat primaries are typically more subject to competition, especially since the outcomes of general elections to the California legislature are rarely in doubt.

Primary challenges to incumbents are not terribly common throughout the country (Boatright forthcoming), although there are notable differences across different levels of government. Within California, as in roughly half the states, term limits ensure that even the safest state legislative district will come open within a few election cycles. A safe congressional seat, conversely, may remain occupied by the same incumbent for decades. This difference has important effects on patterns in primary challenges. Challenging an incumbent is itself a potentially costly exercise, guaranteeing the challenger a set of enemies within her own party in an endeavor that is often doomed to fail. If an ambitious candidate seeks a legislative seat, it is usually in her interests to wait until that seat becomes open to avoid angering powerful people. If she seeks a congressional seat, however, it sometimes makes more sense to challenge the incumbent soon rather than wait the decade or two until the seat becomes open, during which time other rivals will be jockeying for position.

Figure 10.2 demonstrates this pattern in each election since 2002, charting the percentage of California's sitting Assembly members, state senators, and members of the House of Representatives who have been challenged by someone within their party in a primary. As can be seen, members of Congress have been far more likely to experience a challenge, with 20–30 percent of them typically facing a primary opponent. This number shot up in the 2012 election cycle, with fully half of congressional incumbents in California experiencing a challenge from within their party.

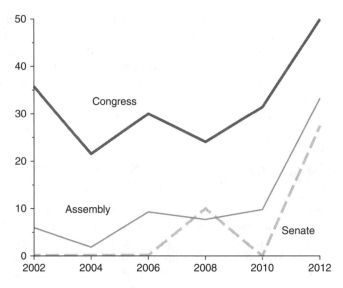

Figure 10.2 Percentage of Incumbents Challenged from Within their Party in Primaries, by Office.

Source: California Secretary of State.

The percentages of state legislators experiencing primary challenges were much lower during this time period. Less than 10 percent of Assembly members typically experienced a challenge, and in more than half of the years under study, no state senator experienced a challenge at all.[5] As with members of Congress, the rates of primary challenges increased significantly in 2012 under the top-two system, with roughly a quarter of senators and a third of Assembly members experiencing a challenge.

Figure 10.3 combines all the incumbent challenges across offices but breaks down the data by party. As can be seen, there were not extraordinary differences across party lines, either before the top-two primary or during it. However, again the same pattern emerges, with both Democratic and Republican incumbents experiencing disproportionately high levels of primary challenges from their fellow partisans under the new regime.

It should be noted that the adoption of the top-two primary for the 2012 cycle was contemporaneous with the drawing of new district lines. Redistricting, of course, may produce a heightened number of primary challenges, as incumbents' name recognition among their constituents is typically compromised and challengers thus perceive them as vulnerable. However, 2002 was also a redistricting year, and while primary challenges were more common then than they were from 2004 to 2010, they were nowhere near the levels of 2012. This additional level of incumbent insecurity can be attributed to the new top-two primary.

Electoral volatility in 2012 was not limited to primary challenges to incumbents. As McGhee and Krimm (2012a; 2012c) report, there were

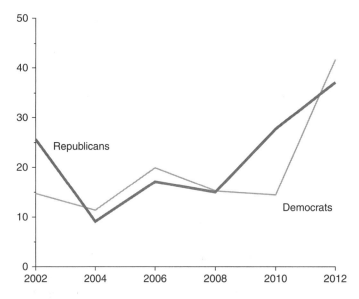

Figure 10.3 Percentages of Incumbents Challenged from Within their Party in Primaries, by Party.

Source: California Secretary of State.

disproportionately high percentages of open seat contests in 2012, indicating that an unusually high number of incumbents decided to retire rather than face reelection in such an unpredictable environment. Additionally, the 2012 primary saw atypically high numbers of districts with multiple candidates of the same party and also of districts in which one major party fielded no candidate at all. Furthermore, as McGhee and Krimm show, competition within those districts was unusually high in 2012, with smaller percentage-point differences between the first- and second-place vote-getters than was typical from 2002 to 2010.

In other areas, the differences from other elections were more muted. Rates of campaign spending in the primaries were unremarkable compared to the rates from 2002 to 2010, although spending in the general election was somewhat above average (McGhee and Krimm 2012c; 2012b). Additionally, voter turnout was similar to that of previous primary elections. About 22.5 percent of eligible voters participated in the 2012 primary election, as compared to the 24.5 percent that participated, on average, from 2002 to 2010. The 2012 rate was somewhat lower than that of other presidential primaries, although the presidential nominations of the two major parties had been functionally determined long before the June 5th election date.

DID THE PARTIES ADAPT?

As described above, the parties sought ways to adapt to this relatively chaotic electoral environment without completely losing control over their choice of nominees. They did so largely through the use of endorsements. The endorsement of incumbents was essentially automatic, and the parties also actively picked favorites in open-seat contests. To what extent did they succeed?

To a considerable degree, the parties got what they wanted. Every incumbent who sought reelection won a spot on the November ballot. Furthermore, of the 113 nonincumbent candidates for state legislature or Congress whom the parties endorsed, 101 advanced to the runoff election. As McGhee and Krimm note, "establishment" candidates tended to do very well compared to their rivals: "88 of 102 incumbents led their closest opponent by more than 10 points, as did 98 of 113 endorsed candidates who are not incumbents" (McGhee and Krimm 2012c, 3–4).

It is difficult to know the extent to which these establishment candidates succeeded *because* their party endorsed them. It is certainly possible that the parties were just being strategic, endorsing candidates who already had a good chance of winning. It is also quite possible that the party activists who dominated the county endorsement processes were impressed by candidate characteristics like charisma and coffers, much as voters might be. Preliminary analysis of the election results and of an experimental survey conducted around the same time suggest that the endorsements did, in fact, influence voters, possibly boosting vote shares for endorsed candidates by as much as ten percentage points (Kousser et al. 2013). Research on this matter is still ongoing.

Another way of determining whether the parties achieved their goals is to look at the distribution of same-party runoff elections. The possibility of a same-party runoff in a competitive district is a serious threat to the excluded major party, and some advanced coordination may be necessary to avoid such a situation. After all, in a chaotic electoral environment like that of the 2012 primary, it would certainly be possible for a large number of candidates of one major party to so split the vote as to hand the runoff spots to two candidates of the other major party. In less competitive districts, this is less of a concern for the dominant party; a runoff in a San Francisco district between two Democrats will still achieve a reasonably desirable outcome for Democratic elites regardless of what happens in November. However, the dangers of splitting the vote are very real in competitive districts, allowing for the possibility that one party could completely cede a seat to the other before fall campaigning even begins.

Figure 10.4 shows the distribution of same-party runoffs based on the Democratic voter registration in Assembly, state senate, and US House districts. The yellow bars show the frequency of all districts at various levels of Democratic party registration. Red bars illustrate instances of runoff elections featuring two Republicans, and blue bars show Democratic same-party contests. As the figure suggests, the overwhelming bulk of same-party runoffs occurred in safe districts. Republican runoffs occurred where Democratic voter registration was below 44 percent, and Democratic runoffs occurred where Democratic voter registration was above 64 percent.

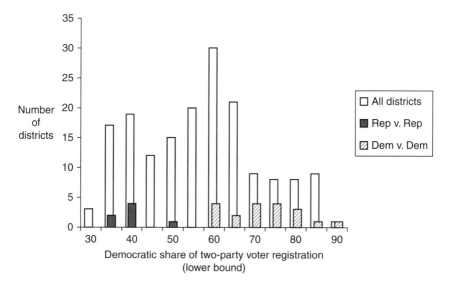

Figure 10.4   Same-party Runoffs in Assembly, Senate, and US House Elections.
Source: California Secretary of State.

There is one notable exception to this, involving the runoff contest between Republicans Bob Dutton and Rep: Gary Miller in the thirty-first congressional district, a district with a 54 percent Democratic share of the two-party voter registration. The results represent a notable failure for Democrats. Not only did the district lean slightly Democratic, but also four Democratic candidates split the primary vote, and Democrat Pete Aguilar fell short of a spot on the runoff ballot by fewer than 1,400 votes. Had any of the other three Democratic candidates withdrawn from the race, the runoff would likely have included Aguilar, who would have had a legitimate shot at winning in November. This example sends a strong message about the importance of coordinating prior to a top-two primary election. Nonetheless, it is still only one anomalous case out of the 174 state and federal districts in play this year.

DISCUSSION: THE 2012 GENERAL ELECTION AND BEYOND

In a rather ironic twist, the general election of 2012 left California considerably more governable than it had been previously by virtue of the fact that it gave Democrats two-thirds majorities (if tenuous ones) in both legislative chambers. One party now has the power to both tax and spend—a common political environment in many democracies that had nonetheless escaped California policymakers for generations. What was ironic is that this change apparently had little to do with the vaunted political reforms that went into place prior to the 2012 election cycle. The top-two primary only created one district where residents lean toward one party but were given a runoff between two members of the other party; the remaining congressional, Assembly, and state Senate districts had the same partisan outcomes that voter party identification would have led us to expect. Similarly, redistricting reform likely had only a modest effect. It may well have been responsible for some important House seat gains for Democrats, but the party would likely have achieved its two-thirds majorities in the state legislative chambers without redistricting (Kogan and McGhee 2012).

Nonetheless, the effects of these reforms could still be seen in the results of the elections. Eighteen percent of the races saw margins of victory of 10 points or less; the average for the prior decade was only seven percent. In the previous decade, the average election produced 30 new Assembly members, 10 new senators, and 3 new members of Congress in California; the 2012 general election produced 38 new Assembly members, 9 new senators, and 14 new members of Congress. Turnover and competition were simply higher in 2012 than they were previously, even if incumbents overwhelmingly retained their seats (McGhee and Krimm 2012b).

Will these increases in turnover and competition lead to changes in incumbent behavior in the coming years? It is, of course, too soon to know, yet that is the real test of the top-two primary, which was, proponents argued, a means to change the behavior of elected officials. The coming legislative session will give us some clues.

What we can see at this point, though, is a great example of the initial impacts of a party reform movement. Whether the reform depolarizes California's politicians or not, we can see that it has definitely shaken up the status quo. At least this year, elections have been more volatile than usual, and incumbents, while still overwhelmingly prevailing in elections, are not doing so with the same safety margins they used to. California's elected officials, party elites, prospective candidates, and voters are in the process of charting out the contours of a new electoral regime, and it may take several years to reach some new equilibrium.

We also see the early indications of a party system adjusting and fighting back. If California election law now says that primaries are not the way that parties determine nominees, then parties will find some other way to determine nominees. Perhaps their endorsement system will prove sufficient. Perhaps the parties will make additional demands on candidates in the future in exchange for endorsements, and if candidates come to see the party's endorsement as the key to victory, then they will legislate to the ideological extremes to keep the parties happy, just as they did up until now. Conversely, candidates may come to see party endorsements as helpful but not vital, and possibly outweighed by the prospects of winning the votes of centrists who can now more easily participate in primaries. Either way, California is truly serving as one of the nation's democratic laboratories, providing a high-leverage case about the power of institutions to affect partisanship.

NOTES

1. In 1946, for example, Earl Warren was the gubernatorial nominee of both the Republican and Democratic parties.
2. Arguably, a party that cannot determine its nominees is not a party at all (Schattschneider 1942).
3. http://cagop.org/pdf/Standing_Rules_and_Bylaws_03–20–2011.pdf, sections 3.02.03 and 3.02.04.
4. http://www.cadem.org/admin/miscdocs/files/CDP-BY-LAWS.pdf, Article VIII Section 2.
5. California senators are elected to staggered four-year terms. In a given election cycle, 20 of the state's 40 senate districts are typically subject to an election campaign.

REFERENCES

Alter, Jonathan. 2009. "The Jackass-Reduction Plan." *Newsweek* September 18.

Alvarez, R. Michael, and Betsy Sinclair. 2012. "Electoral Institutions and Legislative Behavior: The Effects of Primary Processes." *Political Research Quarterly* 65(3): 544–557

Bawn, Kathleen, Marty Cohen, David Karol, Seth Masket, Hans Noel, and John Zaller. 2012. "A Theory of Political Parties: Groups, Policy Demands and Nominations in American Politics." *Perspectives on Politics* 10(3): 571–597.

Boatright, Robert. 2013. *Getting Primaried: The Changing Politics of Congressional Primary Challenges.* Ann Arbor: University of Michigan Press.

Buchanan, William. 1963. *Legislative Partisanship: The Deviant Case of California.* Berkeley: University of California Press.

California Democratic Party V. Jones. 2000. 530 U.S. 567 530 U.S. 567, U.S. Supreme Court.

Cannon, Carl M. 2002. "California Divided." *California Journal* (January): 8–14.

Cohen, Marty, David Karol, Hans Noel, and John Zaller. 2008. *The Party Decides : Presidential Nominations before and after Reform.* Chicago: University of Chicago Press.

Elias, Thomas D. 2009. "Open Primary Should Be Top 2010 Voter Priority." *Ventury County Star* December 18.

Gerber, Elisabeth R., and Rebecca B. Morton. 1998. "Primary Election Systems and Representation." *Journal of Law, Economics & Organization* 14(2): 304–324.

Halper, Evan. 2003. "Careers at Stake, Brulte Tells Gop." *Los Angeles Times* June 5, 1.

Halper, Evan, and Nancy Vogel. 2003. "Lawmakers See Slim Chance of Meeting Budget Deadline." *Los Angeles Times* June 11, 1.

Heaney, Michael, Seth Masket, Joanne Miller, and Dara Strolovitch. 2012. "Polarized Networks: The Organizational Affiliations of National Party Convention Delegates." *American Behavioral Scientist* 56(12):1654–1676.

Kanthak, Kristin, and Rebecca Morton. 2001. "The Effects of Primary Systems on Congressional Elections." In *Congressional Primaries and the Politics of Representation*, edited by Peter Galderisis and Mike Lyons. Lanham, MD: Rowman and Littlefield.

Kogan, Vladimir, and Eric McGhee. 2012. "Redistricting California: An Evaluation of the Citizens Commission Final Plans." *California Journal of Politics and Policy* 4(1):1–22.

Kousser, Thad. 2010. "Does Partisan Polarization Lead to Policy Gridlock in California?" *The California Journal of Politics and Policy* 2(2). ISSN (Online) 1944-4370.

Kousser, Thad, Scott Lucas, Seth Masket, and Eric McGhee. 2013. "Kingmakers or Cheerleaders? Party Party and the Causal Effects of Endorsements." Presented at the Annual Meeting of the Midwest Political Science Association, Chicago, IL.

Masket, Seth E. 2007. "It Takes an Outsider: Extralegislative Organization and Partisanship in the California Assembly, 1849–2006." *American Journal of Political Science* 51(3): 482–497.

———. 2009. *No Middle Ground: How Informal Party Organizations Control Nominations and Polarize Legislatures.* Ann Arbor: University of Michigan Press.

———. 2011. "The Circus That Wasn't: The Republican Party's Quest for Order in the 2003 California Gubernatorial Recall." *State Politics and Policy Quarterly* 11(2): 124–148.

———. 2010. "The New Style: How Colorado's Democratic Party Survived and Thrived Amidst Reform." Presented at the the Annual State Politics and Policy Conference, Springfield, Illinois.

Mathews, Joe. 2006. *The People's Machine : Arnold Schwarzenegger and the Rise of Blockbuster Democracy.* New York: Public Affairs.

McGhee, Eric, and Daniel Krimm. 2012a. *California's New Electoral Reforms: How Did They Work?* San Francisco: Public Policy Institute of California.

———. 2012b. "California's New Electoral Reforms: The Fall Election." In *Just the Facts,* Public Policy Institute of California. http://www.ppic.org/main/publication_show.asp?i=1039

———. 2012c. *Test-driving California's Election Reforms.* San Francisco: Public Policy Institute of California.

McGhee, Eric, Seth Masket, Boris Shor, and Nolan McCarty. 2010. "A Primary Cause of Partisanship? Nomination Systems and Legislator Ideology." In the Annual Conference of the American Political Science Association. Washington, DC.

Samish, Arthur H. 1971. *The Secret Boss of California: The Life and High Times of Art Samish.* New York: Crown Publishers, Inc.

Schattschneider, E. E. 1942. *Party Government.* Westport, CT: Greenwood Press.

Schlesinger, Joseph A. 1985. "The New American Political Party." *The American Political Science Review* 79(December): 1152–1169.

Shor, Boris, and Nolan McCarty. 2011. "The Ideological Mapping of American Legislatures." *American Political Science Review* 105(3): 530–551.

Smith, Bradley A. 1996. "Faulty Assumptions and Undemocratic Consequences of Campaign Finance Reform." *The Yale Law Journal* 105(4): 1049–1091.

Smith V. Allwright. 1944. 321. 649, U.S. Supreme Court.

Van Oot, Torey. 2011. "Republican Chairman Pushing for New Nominating Process." *CapitolAlert* February 18. http://blogs.sacbee.com/capitolalertlatest/2011/02/crp-chair-ron-nehring.html (accessed February 18).

Vocke, Jr., William C. 2010. "Open Primaries: William Vocke Interviews Abel Maldonado, Lieutenant Governor of California." http://www.cceia.org/resources/transcripts/0282.html (accessed April 29).

Ware, Alan. 2002. *The American Direct Primary.* New York: Cambridge University Press.

11

How to Turn Democrats and Republicans into Americans

Mickey Edwards

One

Here's an interesting puzzle: We Americans are divided over a good many important political questions (no matter how much we may wish to deny it, there really is a red-state/blue-state split on a very wide range of issues), but on most of those issues, we nonetheless tend to be clustered within a fairly narrow range of opinions from "slightly-right-of-center" to "slightly-left-of-center." Political candidates and pollsters routinely seek information not only about our opinions but also about the degree of intensity with which we hold those views because in most cases while we may favor one position over another, we are hardly feverish about it. In most cases, our preferences are merely that, not reasons, to draw lines in the sand and go to battle. So why do our elected officials—chosen by us and presumably representative of our preferences—so often end up in bitter and uncompromising conflict between opposing poles? If they truly represent us, why are not they more like us?

I have defined this question as a "puzzle," not a dilemma. And that's because, as frustrating as it is, this apparent contradiction has a pretty simple answer. Our elected officials do not accurately represent us because the system we have created to elect them, and the system in which they subsequently govern, rewards them not for representing the majority of us but for acting as warriors for the most extreme minorities among us. This book's theme is about "politics to the extreme" and the forces that are driving American politics toward rival extremes are the very systems we ourselves have developed.

America's Founders had something very different in mind. In fact, they wanted something that was quite the opposite. For example, because almost every major power of the federal government was put in the hands of the people themselves (in other words, in the Congress of the United States, made up of the peoples' representatives), it was assumed that the preferences of the nation's citizens would prevail. The right to vote was originally embarrassingly limited (few blacks and no women were allowed to cast ballots) but the precedent was nonetheless set that it was in the hands of voters that power rested. Because the Constitution specifically required all US senators and representatives to be actual inhabitants of the states from which they were elected, it was therefore assumed that they would be familiar with the concerns and the economic interests of the communities they served, even if (as was originally the case with members of the Senate) their election was determined by local state legislators.

Unfortunately, the electoral system that governs American politics today produces the exact opposite result.

Two

Consider two principal reasons for this undermining of American elections. Until the beginning of the twentieth century, it was common for small and distinctly unrepresentative groups of power brokers (basically, older white men who represented the wealthy power elites of a community) to gather together in the proverbial smoke-filled rooms of the past to "choose" who would be put forth as their party's candidates for Congress (and for other major offices as well, but it is the dysfunction of the modern Congress that causes us to look at how far we have strayed from the constitutional model). That, of course, was a model with little to recommend it other, perhaps, than the ability of such insiders to gauge the relative intellectual or other merits of the various white men they would be considering for those offices—if indeed it was merit they were looking for.

The reformers of the day (members of the "Progressive" movement) rightly abhorred this "boss-centric" system and instead launched the modern political primary regime in which, presumably, all the people would be allowed to choose among all the eligible candidates and vote for the one candidate who most closely aligned with their interests. This reform was intended to restore—or introduce—democracy to what had clearly been until then a very undemocratic system. However, the laws of unintended consequences are not easily set aside and the primaries became, over time, the closed primary system of today in which relatively small and unrepresentative numbers of the most partisan, intransigent, and ideological citizens dictate election outcomes.

CONSIDER JUST TWO EXAMPLES

In the US Senate race in Delaware to select a successor to the incumbent, Joe Biden, who had been elected vice president of the United States, the prohibitive favorite, a Republican named Mike Castle, a former governor and a member of Congress, lost a party primary to a little-known outsider named Christine O'Donnell. In that primary, in a state of approximately one million people, Christine O'Donnell received only 30,000 votes. So the question becomes, "why didn't Mike Castle then run against her—and, presumably, beat her—in the general election with a larger and more representative electorate?" Because in Delaware, strangely enough, there is a law (known as a "sore loser" law) that actually prohibits a candidate's name from appearing on the general election ballot if he or she sought a party nomination and failed to achieve it. Therefore, the votes of 30,000 people who cast their ballots for O'Donnell made it impossible for the rest of the one million people of Delaware to consider whether or not they wanted Mike Castle serving in the Senate and making important decisions on their behalf about government spending, federal tax rates, and whether or not to go to war. This was hardly the "democracy" the Progressive reformers had imagined.

It was even worse in the state of Utah, where in a Republican Party convention, the votes of just 2,000 party activists in a state of three million people were sufficient to prevent incumbent Senator Robert Bennett's name from appearing on the general election ballot because Utah, as it happens, also has a sore loser law. As do 46 of the 50 states.

Thus, when members of Congress are urged to come together with their colleagues of a different political party to solve national problems, it is not the broader general electorate to which they must look for support but the relatively small numbers that actually participate in the primary selection process. It is this phenomenon that has caused political reporters to describe elected officials' fear of "being primaried" as a principal reason why it is so difficult to get Republicans and Democrats to work together to find common ground solutions to even the most urgent questions. The truth is that today our elected officials are either truly representative of the hard-liners and ideologues who dominate primaries or are so mindful of the ability of those advocates of intransigence to end their careers in the narrow electoral space of the party primary that their focus is on pleasing the few, not the many. Either way, it is the tail (the relatively small number of primary voters) that wags the dog (the public policy interests of the larger community).

THREE

This problem of unrepresentativeness is further exacerbated by laws in more than 70 percent of the states that allow whichever party controls the state legislature to redraw congressional district boundaries in ways that have the effect of both reducing representativeness and increasing polarization for the sole purpose of enhancing the power of the controlling political party.

Here I can draw on an example from my own 16-year career as a member of Congress from Oklahoma. After I was elected to Congress as the representative of a completely urban and very diverse district, the first Republican elected to Congress from Oklahoma City in nearly half a century and in a district in which registered Democrats then outnumbered Republicans by nearly three-to-one, the state legislature, which was then controlled by Democrats, redrew my district boundaries in a way that increased that party's hold on adjoining districts but left me attempting thereafter to articulate the concerns of tens of thousands of wheat farmers, cattle ranchers, and small-town merchants with whom I had very little in common. At the same time, because Oklahoma's congressional districts all thus became less diverse, the state's lone Republican district (mine) became more conservative than it had been and the adjoining Democratic districts became more liberal. There is a multiplier effect at work here: the hard-line conservatives in a more conservative district were thus more conservative and more hard-line than even the hard-liners in the old and more diverse, district I had earlier represented.

In other words, because (1) the political parties control access to the general election ballot; (2) party primaries and conventions are closed and dominated by the most ideological partisans; (3) "sore loser" laws force general election voters to choose between the candidates selected by those hardliners; and (4) the shaping of congressional districts for partisan advantage makes elected officials more and more susceptible to retaliation by nevercompromise hard-liners, the answer to "why is our Congress so dysfunctional" is "because we designed a system that makes that outcome inevitable." When we ask "why are our politics so extreme," the answer is the same: our political system rewards extreme behavior and punishes reasonableness and cooperation. If a football team gained a point every time one of its runners was thrown for a loss and was penalized a point every time its quarterback completed a pass, we would get runners being tackled by their own teammates and defensive backs standing with their hands at their sides: incentives work and we have created all the wrong incentives in our political system.

Four

Years ago it was common for candidates for local office, including those running for US House seats, to engage in what is commonly called "retail" politics, visiting voters at their front doors or in their living rooms, one on one or in small gatherings of a host's friends and neighbors. Over time, largely influenced by political consultants (who make their money from commissions on radio and television advertising) and workforce changes that meant fewer people (primarily housewives) would be home to meet candidates during the day, candidates began to put more effort into campaigning almost exclusively through the media. This has two effects: one is to reduce messages to fit the time constraints of a 30- or 60-second commercial; and the other is to greatly increase the cost of campaigns.

Raising the cost of campaigns had two effects. One was to cause candidates who had little money of their own and few wealthy friends to simply choose not to run. Recruiting good candidates for public office became harder and many good people dropped out of the pool of potential officeholders. The second effect has proven to be equally disastrous: if candidates could not function without large infusions of money, there would always be people eager to provide the money to help their favored candidates get elected.

That, of course, is a good thing within limits. It is good for citizens to be involved; supporting candidates who support the policies you believe will be good for the nation is a clear plus for a society that wants to leave decisions in the hands of the people. However, increasingly it has become possible for very wealthy people with very specific policy agendas to dominate the election system (one very egregious example came in the Republican presidential primaries of 2012, when an also-ran, Newt Gingrich, a former speaker of the House, had his semifrivolous campaign kept afloat by the infusion of millions of dollars donated by a Las Vegas casino owner). The so-called Super PACs allow the flow of large amounts of interest-driven cash into campaigns, allowing some candidates to essentially drown out the messages of competitors.

That, too, needs to be addressed.

FIVE

Before we turn to the solutions to this problem—and there are effective solutions if we adopt them—it is important to recognize that the dysfunction in Congress is not solely a result of the election process. At some point in that process, somebody actually wins and soon he or she is sworn in as a member of Congress. At which point, instead of fading from view, the extreme partisanship that dominated the election continues in a different form.

Some of the partisanship inside the Congress is cosmetic. In both the House and Senate, Republicans sit on one side of the chamber and Democrats on the other side. In the House, members who want to talk loudly, smoke, eat sandwiches, make telephone calls, read newspapers, or otherwise engage in personal activities must do so from a "cloakroom" off the House floor. However, there is not a single cloakroom where all members can congregate: Republicans have their own cloakroom and Democrats have theirs. Just as each party has its own "conference room" connected to each congressional hearing room, seating in committee meetings is dictated by which party one belongs to. Whichever party has a majority dictates what bills can be considered in committee and who will be called to provide expert testimony, almost always tailored to make an argument on behalf of the majority's position.

The committees have long been the critical chokepoints in the legislative process. If a bill is not recommended for approval at the committee level, it simply dies. How, then, does one gain a seat on a committee of particular interest? By promising in advance to stick loyally to his or her party's predetermined policy position because committee appointments are controlled not by neutral managers but by party leaders. On the committees themselves, representatives and senators are staffed by assistants who share the same partisan identity and begin with a predisposition to support the approved party line. Committees thus become not gathering places for thoughtful consideration of policy alternatives but as battlegrounds where rival armies clash over partisan agendas.

More and more, however, the committee process is being bypassed because there are other, quicker, ways to advance the party's goals. In both the House and Senate, it is becoming more common for leaders of the majority party to simply send preferred legislation directly to the floor for action without the necessity of time-consuming hearings and committee-level debate.

The incentive system described above as part of the election process is thus part of the governing system, too. If one wishes to have his or her proposals considered, or seeks a position on an important committee, those rewards flow from adherence to the party agenda; using one's own mind to act in the best interests of the country or one's constituents can lead to being marginalized and effectively removed from any influence over the making of public policy.

Six

What can be done about it?

For at least some of these problems, the answers are encouraging, largely because the public has become very aware of the partisanship that has paralyzed the federal government and is becoming increasingly determined to do something about it. A *USA Today* article in 2012 noted that citizens are fleeing from the political parties and various studies have suggested that as many as 40 percent of American voters now register as "independents."

This rebellion against the party system was set in bold relief in 2006 when voters in Washington State went to the polls and simultaneously got rid of party primaries and party control of congressional redistricting. Four years later, in 2010, voters in California took advantage of that state's "initiative petition" option to do the same thing, beating back the determined opposition of party leaders to establish a system of "open" primaries (essentially general elections with a runoff provision if no candidate gets more than 50 percent of the vote) and to place redistricting decisions in the hands of an independent, nonpartisan commission, a procedure now adopted by more than a dozen states.

In three states, Louisiana, Washington, and California, every registered voter in a constituency (statewide, congressional district, or state legislative district) can vote for any eligible candidate and every candidate, regardless of party affiliation, can run on the same ballot. In those states, every voter gets to choose among all the candidates. Because there is, at the end of the process, a runoff election, nobody can be elected to one of those offices when a majority of voters have opted for somebody else. It is a system we might call something like "democracy."

(A caveat: in some states, voters use initiative petitions to put policy decisions directly on the ballot, disregarding the cumulative cost or the possibility of voters enacting requirements that contradict each other. The Founders created a system of representative, not direct, democracy, and it is important to note that the advocates of "open primaries" are returning to voters only the control over process, not policy outcomes. However, in a democracy, it is the process—how we choose those people who will govern us and how they govern—that is ultimately determinative of the kind of nation we will live in).

Seven

While voters can take reform into their own hands in the case of primaries and redistricting (24 states allow initiative petitions and others have various provisions for referendum campaigns to allow voters to make the final decisions), reforms within Congress are more difficult to bring about.

How can we make the leadership of Congress more oriented toward solving our national problems than gaining advantage for their own parties? Speakers of the House need not even be members of Congress; committee assignments need not be made by party leaders; and committee staff members need not be chosen on the basis of party affiliation. There is no need for separate lecterns, separate cloakrooms, and separate seating. There is no need for party leaders to have control over what bills come to the House or Senate floor or the ability to restrict consideration of amendments. Yet each of those practices stems not from law but from the establishment of House and Senate rules in a process dominated by whichever party has a majority at the time the rules are adopted. Voters in their own states and congressional districts cannot change these things.

Except, of course, through the most common of American practices, the very essence in fact of political democracy. Confrontation.

Because we keep the levers of government in our own hands—every legislator must be reelected, whether it is every two years, every four, or every six—it is in their interest to return home on a regular basis to meet with constituents, usually in large public gatherings. That is where voters who want internal changes within the Congress or state legislature have an opportunity to be heard. Studies have shown that many members of Congress vote 90 percent of the time, or even more frequently, with their party leadership. They seldom vote for something proposed by a member of the opposing party and rarely cosponsor potential legislation with occupants of "the enemy camp." Those members should be met with a sizable turnout of fed-up constituents demanding that they support changes in the legislative rules to allow more open consideration of alternatives, more cooperation, nonpartisan staff, nonpartisan selection of committee members, and a return to the "regular order" of allowing legislation to be funneled through committees rather than dictated by party bosses.

Eight

The money problem is more difficult still, largely because most of the blame for this piece of the current political mess is the direct result of decisions by the US Supreme Court. It is possible, as some have suggested, that some members of the Court would welcome an opportunity to modify their previous rulings but given the reluctance to grant "standing" (the ability to be heard) except when a party is directly harmed, getting a new hearing will not be easy. The better answer may be to work with legislators and law firms to draft legislation that would pass constitutional muster by redefining who qualifies as a citizen for the purpose of making campaign contributions. My own proposal has been to eliminate any campaign funding from any source at all other individual humans—no party money, no corporate money, no labor union money, and no political action committee money. In any case, the abundance of virtually unregulated and often unreported money is a toxin in the political system that must be dealt with.

NINE

Our Founders envisioned a political system in which ultimate power would rest in the hands of the people. To a large extent, that vision has been blurred. "The People" have been replaced by small hyperpartisan, hyperideological subsets of the electorate. Representation has been replaced by the drawing of congressional district lines to suit party advantage. Those who can attract the support of the wealthy have been given massive advantage in political campaigns. The Congress itself, and most state legislatures, now act as stadiums pitting rival teams against each other instead of as Americans working together to solve our common problems.

Our political system has indeed become a war between extremes. The good news is that it is within our power to change it and become again the kind of problem-solving democracy we once were. Whether that happens will depend not on outside forces but on us. That is our challenge. It is the most important challenge of our time.

About the Authors

Scott A. Frisch is a professor and chair of political science at California State University Channel Islands. He received his PhD from Claremont Graduate University. Professor Frisch is the author of *The Politics of Pork: A Study of Congressional Appropriations Earmarks* and a coauthor with Sean Q Kelly of *Committee Assignment Politics in the U.S. House of Representatives* (Norman: University of Oklahoma Press), *Jimmy Carter and the Water Wars: Presidential Influence and the Politics of Pork* (Amherst, NY: Cambria Press), and *Cheese Factories on the Moon: Why Earmarks Are Good for American Democracy* (Boulder, CO: Paradigm Publishers).

Sean Q Kelly is a professor of political science at California State University Channel Islands. He received his PhD from the University of Colorado. Professor Kelly is a former American Political Science Association congressional fellow (1993–1994) and is a coauthor of three books with Scott Frisch, most *recently Cheese Factories on the Moon: Why Earmarks are Good for American Democracy* (Boulder, CO: Paradigm Publishers) and *Jimmy Carter and the Water Wars: Presidential Influence and the Politics of Pork* (Amherst, NY: Cambria Press). He is currently working with Scott Frisch on a book about the politics of congressional appropriations earmarks.

Lara M. Brown is an associate professor and the program director of the Political Management Program in the Graduate School of Political Management at the George Washington University. She received her PhD from the University of California, Los Angeles. She is the author of *Jockeying for the American Presidency: The Political Opportunism of Aspirants* (Amherst, NY: Cambria Press) and a coeditor and contributing author of *The Presidential Leadership Dilemma: Between the Constitution and a Political Party* (Albany, NY: SUNY Press). Prior to completing her doctorate in political science, she served in President William J. Clinton's administration at the US Department of Education in Washington, DC.

Geoffrey W. Buhl is an associate professor in the Mathematics program at California State University Channel Islands. Prior to his current position, he was a National Science Foundation Postdoctoral Fellow at Rutgers University. He received his PhD from the University of California, Santa

Cruz. He has published a number of research papers exploring mathematical structures arising from string theory in Physics.

Lawrence C. Dodd holds the Manning J. Dauer Eminent Scholar Chair in Political Science at the University of Florida. He received his PhD from the University of Minnesota in 1972. He has served as a Congressional Fellow (1974–1975), Hoover National Fellow (1984–1985), and Woodrow Wilson Center Fellow (2003–2004). His most recent book is *Thinking about Congress* (London: Routledge Press, 2012). The University of Florida selected Dodd as 2007 Teacher-Scholar of the Year, its highest faculty honor.

Matthew Dull is an associate professor of political science at the Center for Public Administration and Policy at Virginia Tech. He received his PhD from the University of Wisconsin-Madison where he won APSA's Leonard D. White Award for the best dissertation in the field of public administration. His research has appeared in *Political Research Quarterly*, the *Journal of Public Administration Research and Theory*, *Legislative Studies Quarterly*, and *Public Administration Review* among others. He is currently at work on a book-length manuscript examining results-model reform in the US federal government.

Mickey Edwards is the vice president of the Aspen Institute and serves as Director of the Aspen Institute's Rodel Fellowships in Public Leadership. Mr. Edwards was a Republican member of Congress for 16 years, serving as a member of the House Republican Leadership and as a member of the Appropriations and Budget Committees. After leaving the Congress, he taught for 11 years at Harvard University's John F. Kennedy School of Government and for five years as a lecturer at Princeton's Woodrow Wilson School of Public and International Affairs. He has served on the American Bar Association Task Force on Presidential Signing Statements and the American Society of International Law Task Force on the International Criminal Court. Edwards' latest book, *The Parties Versus the People*, was published by Yale University Press.

Douglas B. Harris is an associate professor of political science at Loyola University Maryland. He received his PhD from Johns Hopkins University. His research on Congress, political parties, and media politics include articles in *Political Science Quarterly*, *Legislative Studies Quarterly*, *American Politics Research*, *Congress & the Presidency*, *Political Research Quarterly*, *P.S.: Political Science & Politics*, *The New England Journal of Political Science*, *The Historian*, and *Presidential Studies Quarterly*. He is the coauthor of *The Austin-Boston Connection: Fifty Years of House Democratic Leadership* (Texas A&M University Press) and coeditor of *Doing Archival Research in Political Science* (Cambria Press).

Frank H. Mackaman directs the work of the Dirksen Congressional Center, Pekin, IL. He received his PhD in American history from the University of

Missouri at Columbia. He is a former director of the Gerald R. Ford Library and Museum and member of the University of Michigan faculty. Currently, he is an adjunct professor of political science at Bradley University. He edited *Understanding Congressional Leadership* (Congressional Quarterly Press) among other publications.

Thomas E. Mann is the W. Averell Harriman Chair and senior fellow in Governance Studies at the Brookings Institution. Between 1987 and 1999, he was director of governmental studies at Brookings. Before that, Mann was executive director of the American Political Science Association. He earned his BA in political science at the University of Florida and his MA and PhD at the University of Michigan. Mann is a fellow of the American Academy of Arts and Sciences and a member of the Council on Foreign Relations. He lectures frequently in the United States and abroad on American politics and public policy and is also a regular contributor to newspaper stories and television and radio programs on politics and governance. He is coauthor with Norman J. Ornstein of *The Broken Branch: How Congress is Failing American and How To Get It Back on Track* and, most recently, of *It's Even Worse Than It Looks: How the American Constitutional System Collided With the New Politics of Extremism.*

José Marichal is an associate professor of political science at California Lutheran University. He received his PhD from the University of Colorado-Boulder in 2003 and is the author of *Facebook Democracy* (Ashgate Press, 2012). He teaches courses on the Internet and Politics, public policy, race and politics, community development, and California politics. His current projects include the following: a study of the relationship between acquiring digital skills and feelings of trust/efficacy among Latinos and African Americans and an examination of how *civic hacking* affects power dynamics at the local level. In addition, he is founder of the blog ThickCulture, sponsored by *Contexts* magazine.

Seth E. Masket is an associate professor and chair of the Department of Political Science at the University of Denver. He received his PhD from UCLA in 2004. He is the author of *No Middle Ground: How Informal Party Organizations Control Nominations and Polarize Legislatures* (University of Michigan Press, 2009). He has written on state legislatures, party organizations, social networks, and campaigns and elections, and he is currently working on a book manuscript on the subject of state-level party reform movements. He is a founder of and frequent contributor to the political science blog "The Mischiefs of Faction."

Kevin J. McMahon is the John R. Reitemeyer and Charles A. Dana Research Professor of political science at Trinity College. His research examines the presidency and the political origins and consequences of Supreme Court decisions, covering a range of areas, including civil rights and liberties, constitutional law, school desegregation, political parties, and elections. His most recent book, *Nixon's Court: His Challenge to Judicial Liberalism and Its Political Consequences* (University of Chicago Press, 2011), was selected as a 2012 CHOICE Outstanding Academic Title. His book, *Reconsidering Roosevelt on Race: How the Presidency Paved the Road to Brown* (University of Chicago Press, 2004), won the American Political Science Association's Richard E. Neustadt Award for the best book published on the American presidency in 2004. He is also the coauthor/coeditor of three books on the presidency and presidential elections and author of several book chapters and journal articles.

Norman J. Ornstein is a resident scholar at the American Enterprise Institute (AEI), a Washington DC think tank. He received his PhD from the University of Michigan. Ornstein led a working group of scholars and practitioners that helped shape the law, known as McCain-Feingold that reformed the campaign financing system. His books include *The Permanent Campaign and Its Future* (AEI Press, 2000); *The Broken Branch: How Congress Is Failing America and How to Get It Back on Track, with Thomas E. Mann* (Oxford University Press, 2006); and, *It's Even Worse Than It Looks: How the American Constitutional System Collided with the New Politics of Extremism,* also with Tom Mann (Basic Books, 2012).

David C. W. Parker is an associate professor of political science at Montana State University Bozeman. He received his PhD from the University of Wisconsin-Madison. Professor Parker worked on a presidential, two Senate, and a mayoral campaign before joining the academy, and provides nonpartisan political analysis on Montana politics to local, state, national, and international media outlets including *The New York Times, USA Today,* the *Los Angeles Times, NPR,* and PBS' *Frontline.* He is the author of *The Power of Money in Congressional Campaigns, 1880–2006* (University of Oklahoma Press) and coeditor of the recently published *Doing Archival Research in Political Science* (Cambria Press). He received American Political Science Association's (APSA) 2011 Alan Rosenthal Prize with Craig Goodman for their *Legislative Studies Quarterly* article "Making a Good Impression: Resource Allocation, Home Styles, and Washington Work."

Scot Schraufnagel is an associate professor and graduate director at Northern Illinois University. He received his PhD from Florida State University in 2002. His research interests include legislative politics, political parties, and elections. His work has been published in *Representation, American Journal of Political Science,* and *Political Science Quarterly* among other leading outlets. His recently published book, *Third Party Blues: The Truth and Consequences of Two-Party Dominance* (London, UK: Routledge-Taylor Francis), has received positive reviews.

Sean M. Theriault is an associate professor of political science and university distinguished professor at the University of Texas at Austin, and researches American political institutions, primarily the US Congress. His current research examines partisan warfare in Congress. He has received numerous teaching awards, including UT Professor the Year in 2011 and the Friar Society Teaching Fellowship (the biggest undergraduate teaching award at UT) in 2009. Professor Theriault has published three books, *The Power of the People: Congressional Competition, Public Attention, and Voter Retribution* (Ohio State University Press, 2005), Party Polarization in Congress (Cambridge University Press, 2008), and *The Gingrich Senators: The Roots of Partisan Warfare in Congress* (Oxford University Press, 2013). He has also published numerous articles on subjects ranging from presidential rhetoric to congressional careers and the Louisiana Purchase to the Pendleton Act of 1883.

INDEX

Abolition of slavery, 71
Abortion, 167–71
Abramoff, Jack, 63
Advertising, Facebook, 119, 125
Affirmative action, 171–3
Affordable Care Act of 2010
　Facebook and, 122
　generally, 48
　passage of, 144
　polarization and, 161
Aguilar, Pete, 215
Alexander, Bill, 108
Alexander, Lamar, 43
Alger, Russell, 140
Alito, Samuel, 176
Allison, William, 140
Allwright, Smith v., 209
Alter, Jonathan, 208
Amendments on Senate floor, 36–9
　specific amendments offered, *38*
American Conservative Union, 169
Americans, turning Democrats and
　　　Republicans into, 219–26
　campaigns, cost of, 222–3
　dysfunctions, reasons for, 223–4
　examples, 220–1
　money problems and, 225–6
　problem solving of leaders, 225
　reasons, 220
　solutions, 224–5
　unrepresentativeness, problem of,
　　　221–2
Angle, Sharon, 28
Anthony, Beryl, 107
Anti-Trust Act, 141
Appropriations Committees,
　　　Senate and House, 3–7
　changes, 13–17
　failures, examples of, 17

House, overview, 13–17
　intra- and interparty divisions,
　　　14, 15
　new textbook Appropriations
　　　Committees
　collapse of committees, 11–13
　ideology, 7–11
　partisanship, 7–11
Senate
　intra- and interparty divisions, *16*
Armey, Dick, 9, 26, 105
Arthur, Chester, 145
Assassinations, presidential, 145
*The Attitudinal Model
　　　Revisited* (Segal and Spaeth),
　　　163, 179n9
Ayotte, Kelly, 28

Bachman, Michelle, 123
Baker, Howard, 12
Bario, Patricia, 107
Barr, Bob, 200
Barton, Joe, 104
Baucus, Max, 37, 45n15
Bauman, Bob, 97
Bayh, Evan, 23, 24
Begala, Paul, 96
Bennet, Michael, 27, 28
Bennett, Robert, 27, 221
"BEST Agenda," 95
Biden, Joe
　"fiscal cliff" and, xiii
　selection of, 220
　2011 debt-limit crisis and, 40
Biggert, Judy, 121
Bilbray, Brian, 124
Binder, Sarah, 144
Bipartisan Congressional Retreat
　　　Planning Committee, 197

Blackmun, Harry
    on abortion, 167
    Rehnquist's court and, 166
    on school prayer, 173
Blaine, James G., 140–2
Blue Dog Democrats, 103–6
Blunt, Roy, 30
Boehner, John
    "fiscal cliff" and, xiii
    television era and, 94
    television era, Congressional
        partisanship and, 110
    2011 debt-limit crisis and, 40
Bollinger, Grutter v., 171
Boll Weevil Democrats, 104
Bonilla, Henry, 12
Boozman, John, 30
Bork, Robert H., 163
Boxer, Barbara, 26
Brademas, John, 106
Brand names. *See* Party brand,
    television era
Breyer, Stephen, 172, 174
Bridgewater, Tim, 27
Brooks, Preston, 71
Brown, Scott, 25, 36, 37
Brownback, Sam, 30, 34
Buck, Ken, 27, 28
Bunning, Jim, 30
Burr, Richard, 43
Bush administration
    Iraq policy, 47
"Bush Dogs, 103
Bush, George H. W.
    on abortion, 167
    ideological court and, 163
    Landmark Laws, 86
    Presidential Support Scores, 35
    probes during time of, 53
Bush, George W., 10, 162. *See also* Bush
    administration
    on abortion, 168–70
    affirmative action and, 171–3
    appointments to Supreme
        Court, 165
    divided government and, 53, 59
    ideological court and, 165
    judicial decisions, analysis of, 161
    marginalized moderates and, 109
    persuasion as priority, 136

"Playing for History: The Reflection
    Leadership Choices of Presidents
    William J. Clinton and George
    W. Bush," 154
    Rehnquist's court and, 166
    Roberts court and, 175, 176
    on school prayer, 174, 175
    stability in presidency of, 146
    tax cuts, 79
    2000 elections, 145
    2011 debt-limit crisis and, 41
    unified government and, 156n10
    unpopularity of, 144
Bush, Laura, 169
Bush v. Gore, 161
Bustamante, Cruz, 209
Byrd, Robert, 10

Calhoun, Charles, 135, 141–2,
    151–2, 155n2
California Democratic Party v. Jones,
    209
California's experiment with the
        top-two primary, 205–18
    adaption by parties, 213–14
    budgetary crises and, 207
    electoral volatility, 212–13
    incumbents, challenges to, 211,
        212–13
    introduction, 205
    lack of partisanship, former, 208
    parties' response, 209
    reform, effects of, 210–11
    remedies, polarization and, 206–8
        nature of legislature, *206*
    same-party runoffs, distribution of,
        213, *215*
    top-two system, impact on 2012
        primary election, 211–13
    2012 general election and beyond,
        215–16
Campaigns, cost of, 222–3
Campbell, Tom, 27
Cannon, Joseph, 80
Cantor, Eric, xiii, 9, 40
Carson, Andre, 126
Carter, Jimmy, 86, 163
Casey, 167–71
Castle, Mike, 28, 220, 221
Chambliss, Saxby, 39–40

Character assassinations, 71–2
Cheney, Dick, 27
CIS. *See Congressional Information Service* (CIS)
Civil disobedience, 88
Civil rights, 76, 85
Civil Rights Act of 1964, 85
Civility, attempts to bridge partisan divide and, 187–203
  end of retreats, 198–201
  Hershey, Pennsylvania retreat (March 7–9, 1997), 189–94, 202
  Hershey, Pennsylvania retreat (March 19–21, 1999), 194
  idea of, 188–9
  obstacles to, *190*
  retreat, civility in, 187–8
  solutions to, *190*
  West Virginia retreat (February 28–March 2, 2003), 196–8
  West Virginia retreat (March 9–11, 2001), 196–8
Cleveland, Grover, 141
  Landmark Laws, 86
  votes earned, 155n2, 156n16
Clinton, Bill, 148
  on abortion, 170
  civility and, 188
  Democratic Leadership Council and, xii
  divided government and, 53
  government shutdown and, 17
  Hershey, Pennsylvania retreat (March 19–21, 1999), 194
  Lewinsky, Monica and, 128
  Obama, Barack, reelection of, 142
  "Playing for History: The Reelection Leadership Choices of Presidents William J. Clinton and George W. Bush," 154
  stability in presidency of, 146
  vote share, 148
  Whitewater investigations, 52
Clinton, Hillary, 52, 142
Club for Growth, xiii
Clyburn, James, 122
Coats, Dan, 27, 30
Coburn, Tom
  amendments on Senate floor and, 36, 38–9

  earmark ban and, 33, 34
  endorsement of, 28
  "fiscal cliff" and, xiii
  2011 debt-limit crisis and, 40
Cochran, Thad, 3, 10
Coelho, Tony, 107
Collins, Susan, 36
Congressional Government, 50
Congressional Information Service (CIS), 53–4
Congressional Research Service, 49
Conrad, Kent, 40
Constitutional Model, 51
Constrained conflict, 76
Continuing Resolutions bills, 19
"Contract with America," 152
Cook, Charlie, 25, 28
Cooley, Wes, 188
Coolidge, Calvin, 86
Coons, Chris, 28
Cordray, Richard, 36
Cornyn, John, 26, 42, 43
Corwin, Edwin, 50
Costa, Jim, 121, 122
Crapo, Mike, 37, 40
Credit claiming, Facebook and, 123–4
Crist, Charlie, 26
Cunningham, Duke, 188

Daschle, Tom, 12, 142
Davis, Tom, 104–5, 110
DCCC. *See* Democratic Congressional Campaign Committee (DCCC)
Decorum, breaches of U.S. Congress (1891–2012). *See* Incivility *below, this group*
DeLay, Tom, 9, 105
DeMint, Jim
  amendments on Senate floor and, 38, 39
  antiestablishment behavior, 43
  earmark ban and, 33
  as party polarizer, 32–3
  Presidential Support Scores and, 36
  Sunday morning talk show appearances, 42
  Tea Party movement and, 25–8
  2010 elections, 28
    campaign contributions, *29,* 30, 44n12

Democratic Caucus, 15
Democratic Congressional Campaign
    Committee (DCCC), 97, 106–9
Democratic Leadership Council, xii
Democratic Message Board (DMB), 98
Democratic National Convention, 142
Department of Justice, 63–4
Depolarized congresses, incivility in,
    75–8
Devore, Chuck, 26–7
DeWine, Mike, 36
Dingell, John, 200
Distributive politics, new textbook
    Appropriations Committees,
    11–13
Diversity, 171
Divided government, 52–4
    mean number and intensity of
        investigations, *57–8*
    publicity, high, *60–1*
    Whitewater investigations, 52
Divided We Govern (Mayhew), 53,
    59–60
DMB. *See* Democratic Message
    Board (DMB)
*Doe, Santa Fe Independent School
    District v.,* 173
Dole, Bob, 169
Donnely, Joe, 122
Dornan, Bob, 188
Downs, Anthony, 93
Durbin, Dick, 10, 40, 42, 142
Dutton, Bob, 215
DW-NOMINATE, 99–100, *100,*
    148, *149*

Earmarks, 11–13
    ban, 33–4
Economy, crash of 2008, 144
Edwards, John, 142
Eisenhower, Dwight D., 86
Election comparisons of 1872–1894
    and 1991–2012, *143*
    states, polarized, 146, *147*
Electioneering amendments, 37–8
Electoral strategies. *See* Presidential
    base electoral strategies, partisan
    polarization and
Elias, Thomas, 207
Emanuel, Rahm, 109

Emerson, JoAnn, 125, 126
Ensign, John, 37, 38
Executive Branch, overseeing, 49–52

Facebook pages, examining polarization
    through pages of Congressional
    member, 117–33
    advertising, 119, 125
    architecture of Facebook, 127
    constant comparative analysis
        approach, 120
    constituency service, 121–2
    credit claiming, 123–4
    findings, 121
    home style thesis, 117
    list of members selected, 131
    "location updates," 125
    methods, 120–1
    personal connection, 124–6
    personalization vs polarization,
        126–9
    polarization, Facebook and generally,
        117–19
    position taking, 122–3
    presentation of self, 119, 126
    social grooming, 120
    virtual home style, Facebook and,
        119–20, 126
Failure, when meaning success, 165
"Families First" agenda, 95
Fannie Mae, 63
Farmer's Alliance, 142
Feeney, Tom, 110
Feinstein, Diane, 39
Fenno, Richard, 5–6, 117, 119
    Home Style, 119, 121–2
Fiorina, Carly, 26, 27
Fire Alarm Model, 51–2
"Fiscal cliff," xiii
Fitzpatrick, Edward, 19
Ford, Gerald, 163
Founders, 219–20, 226
Fourteenth Amendment, 167–8
Frank, Barney, 200
Franken, Al, 41
Franks, Robert, 191

"Gang of Eight," xiii
"Gang of Six," 39–40
GAO. *See* General Accounting Office

Garfield, James, 145, 156n16
Gaudy, Joe, 126
Gekas, George, 200
General Accounting Office, 62, 65
Gephardt, Richard
    civility and, 188, 189
    end of retreats and, 199
    "Families First" agenda, 95
    Hershey, Pennsylvania retreat (March
        7–9, 1997), 191
    party brand and, 96
    West Virginia retreat, 196, 197
Gibbons, Sam, 192
The Gilded Age, 137, 145–52
Gingrich, Newt
    amendments on Senate
        floor and, 38
    Appropriations Committee
        meeting, 6
    campaign costs of, 223
    civility and, 188, 189
    "Contract with America," 152
    Hershey, Pennsylvania retreat (March
        7–9, 1997), 191, 192
    Hershey, Pennsylvania retreat (March
        19–21, 1999), 194
    ideology and, 8, 9
    influence of, 15
    leadership of, 62–3
    marginalized moderates and,
        105, 107
    party brand and, 96, 97
    as party polarizer, 30
    senators serving with, 17
    shutdown of government
        (1995), 199
    television era and, 94
    Wright, Jim and, 79
Ginsburg, Douglas, 163
Ginsburg, Ruth Bader, 172, 174
Giuliani, Rudy, 27
The Global Age, 137, 145–52
Goffman, Erving, 119
Gonzales, Alberto, 59, 172
Good Government Model, 51
Gordon, Joshua, 6–7
Gore, Al, 146
Gore, Bush v., 161
Gramm, Phil, 42
Gramm, Phil as party polarizer, 30

Graves, Sam, 110
Grayson, Trey, 27
Great Society, 85
Greenbrier retreat. See West Virginia
    retreat
Greenburg, Jan Crawford, 162
Greer, Frank, 170
Gregg, Judd, 27, 30
Gresham, Walter, 140
Grutter v. Bollinger, 171
Gun purchases, xiii

Hancock, Winfield, 156n16
Hardball: How Position is Played
    (Matthews), 93, 101
Hardball with Chris Matthews (TV
    show), 101–3
    appearances by Democrats and
        Republicans, 102
Harrison, Benjamin, 145
    as incumbent, 138
    Landmark Laws, 86
    partisan experiences of, 144
    persuasion as priority, 136, 151, 153
    reelection of, 137, 140–2, 150
    votes earned, 155n2
Hastert, Dennis, 9
    "BEST Agenda," 95
    civility and, 196, 199
    marginalized moderates and, 105
Hatch, Oren, 8
Hayes, Rutherford, 145
Health-care reform, 25
Heckler, Margaret, 108
Heller, Dean, 36
Herrnson, Paul S.
    Playing Hardball: Campaigning for
        the U.S. Congress, 93
Hershey, Pennsylvania retreat
    March 7–9, 1997, 189–94
        proposed follow-up activities, 202
    March 19–21, 1999, 194
Holden, Tim, 105
Holder, Eric, 48, 65
Holt, Rush, 121
Home Style (Fenno), 119, 121–2
Home style thesis
    Facebook pages, examining
        polarization through pages of
        Congressional member, 117

Hoover, Herbert, 86
Hostettler, John, 27
Houghton, Amo, 192
House and Senate Committees, results
    of investigations by, 54–61
  by chamber, 1947–2010, 55–6
  mean number and intensity of
    investigations, 57–8
House Committee on Oversight and
    Government Reform, 47–8, 65
House Committee on Veterans
    Affairs, 194
Hurricane Katrina, aftermath, 47
Hutchinson, Asa, 200
Hyde, Henry, 200

Ideological court, pursuit of, 162–5
Ideological tilts, television era, 98–103
Immigration bill, xiii
Incivility, 71–91
  depolarized congresses, in, 75–8
  differentiation between depolarized
    and polarized spectrum of
    conflict, 78
  1891–2012, measurement
    during, 81–6
    articles on incivilities, percent
      of, 84
    landmark legislation, measuring,
      85–6
    party polarization over time, 82
    polarized and depolarized
      Congresses, measuring between,
      83–5
    three forms of incivility and
      landmark productivity, bivariate
      correlations, 86
  explanatory theory regarding, 73–5
  how and why it matters
    explanatory theory regarding,
      73–5
    separate form of conflict, seeing
      incivility as, 73
  measuring and charting, 80–6
    articles on incivilities, percent
      of, 84
    1891–2012, 81–6
    landmark legislation, measuring,
      85–6
    party polarization over time, 82

  polarized and depolarized
    Congresses, measuring between,
    83–5
  three forms of incivility and
    landmark productivity, bivariate
    correlations, 86
  measuring incivility, 1891–2012, 81
  newspaper articles gauging, 89–90n1
  partisan battles, distinction from,
    74–5
  party system polarization and
    member incivility, interplay
    between, 75–80
    constrained conflict, 76
    depolarized congresses, in, 75–8
    differentiation between
      depolarized and polarized
      spectrum of conflict, 78
    polarized congresses, incivility in,
      78–80
    silence, challenging
      norms of, 76–7
    "T" point, 75
  polarized congresses, incivility in,
    78–80
  research findings, 86–9
    articles on civilities by topic, 89
    separate form of conflict, seeing
      incivility as, 73
    testing of theory on, 80–6
Incumbents
  California, challenges to,
    211, 212–13
  elections, presidential leadership
    decisions and, 137–40
  voter attitudes, 138
Industrial Revolution, 146
Information Age, 146
Inhofe, Jim, xiii, 34
Inouye, Daniel, 3, 4, 10
Investigations
  politicization of, 61–2
  weaponization of, 61
Iraq policy, Bush administration, 47
Israel, Knesset, 129
Issa, Darrell, 48, 64

Jacobson, Gary, 136–7
Jamieson, Kathleen Hall, 189
Jeffords, Jim, 146

Johanns, Mike, 41
Johnson, Lyndon, 85, 86
Johnson, Ron, 28
Joint Select Committee on Deficit
    Reduction, 40
*Jones, California Democratic
    Party v.,* 209

Keene, David, 169
Kempthorne, Dirk, 8
Kennedy, Anthony
    ideological court and, 163, 165
    Rehnquist's court and, 166
    on school prayer, 173–5
Kennedy, Ted, 8, 25
Kerry, John, 109
King, Peter, 188
Kingston, Jack, 124, 126
Kirk, Mark, 30, 34, 110
Krimm, Daniel, 213–14
Kristol, William, 181n67
Kucinich, Dennis, 152
Kyl, Jon
    amendments on Senate floor and, 38
    retirement of, 43
    Sunday morning talk show
        appearances, 42
    2011 debt-limit crisis and, 41

LaHood, Ray
    cancellation of retreat, 198
    civility and, 187–9
    end of retreats and, 199, 200
    Hershey, Pennsylvania retreat
        (March 7–9, 1997), 191–4
    West Virginia retreat, 196–8
Lamontagne, Ovide, 27, 28
Landmark Laws, 85–6
Landon, Alf, 177
Lane, Charles, 172
Lane, Mike, 172
Leadership decisions, presidential,
    137–40
Lee, Frances, 24–5
Lee, Mike, 27, 28, 30
Lee v. Weisman, 173–4
Lewinsky, Monica, 128
Lewis, Jerry, 4, 9, 13, 17
Lightfoot, Jim, 198
Livingston, Bob, 8, 9, 15

Lizza, Ryan, xiii
Lott, Trent, 172
Lowden, Sue, 28

Madison, James, 49, 64
Main Street Republicans, 103–6
Maldonado, Abel, 208
Manchin, Joe, xiii, 42
Mann, Tom, 189
Markey, Edward, 123
Martin, Joe, 93–4
Matthews, Christopher
    Hardball: How Position is Played,
        93, 101
    Hardball with Chris Matthews (TV
        show), 101–3
Mayhew, David
    congressional oversight and, 53,
        59–60, 64
    landmark legislation and, 85
    on advertising, 119, 125
    on voter attitudes, 138
McCain, John
    amendments on Senate floor and,
        37–9
    chief adviser of, 28
    on congressional supporters, 23
    election loss, 146
    foreign policy views, 45n15
    nomination of, 12
    Sunday morning talk show
        appearances, 42–3
    Tea Party movement and, 27
    2008 elections, 143–4
McCarthy, Joe, 71–2
McCloskey, Robert, 177
McCollum, Betty, 122, 125
McConnell, Mitch
    Appropriations Committee
        meeting, 3
    earmark ban and, 34
    ideology and, 10
    leadership of, xii–xxiii
    Sunday morning talk show
        appearances, 42–3
    Tea Party movement and, 26–7
    2011 debt-limit crisis and, 41
McCormack, John, 94
McCubbins, Mat, 51
McCullough, David, 189

McGhee, Eric, 213–14
McGovern, James, 129
McHenry, Patrick, 63
McKernan, John "Jock," 106
McKinley Tariff Act, 141
McKinley, William, 86, 145
Medicare, xiii
Meehan, Patrick, 125
Meek, Kendrick, 26
Menendez, Bob, 42
Mica, John, 188
Michel, Bob, 187, 188
Microblogging, 119
Miers, Harriet, 165, 176
Miller, Gary, 215
Miller, Joe, 28
Minibus bills, 19
Mobilization, 136–7, 151, 153
Moderates, Congressional
    television era, Congressional
        partisanship in, 103–9
    marginalized moderates and
        electoral defeat, 106–9
    national party image and the
        marginalized moderates, 104–6
Mondale, Walter, 167
Moore, Gwen, 123
Moran, Jerry, 30
Moran, Jim, 188
Murkowski, Lisa, 28

Nader, Ralph, 152
National Federation of Independent
    Business v. Sebelius, 162
National party image and the
    marginalized moderates,
    104–6
National Rifle Association (NRA),
    65, 126
National Right to Life
    Committee, 126
New Deal, 85
New Democrats, 103–4
Newtown massacre, xiii
New York Times
    on Congressional oversight, 62
    on divided government, 53, 59–60
    incivility, incidents of, 81–2,
        89–90n1

9/11. See September 11, 2001
Nixon, Richard, 86, 163
No Child Left Behind, 79
NOMINATE algorithm, 20n14
Norquist, Grover, xiii, 40
Norton, Jane, 27, 28
NRA. See National Rifle Association
    (NRA)
NRCC, 106–8

Obama administration
    criticisms of, Facebook and, 122–3
    divided government and, 53
Obama, Barack, 71. See also Obama
    administration
    approval of, 25
    earmark ban and, 33
    "fiscal cliff" and, xiii
    ideology and, 10
    as incumbent, 138
    mobilization as priority, 136,
        151, 153
    nomination struggle, 140
    Presidential Support Scores, 35–6
    reelection campaign strategy, 150
    reelection of, 137
    reelection prioritization, 142–5
    reelection victory, xii
    Rice, Susan, nomination of, 90n3
    Sunday morning talk show
        appearances and, 42
    2011 debt-limit crisis and, 40
    vote share, 148
Obey, David, 4, 8, 9
Occupy Wall Street, 152
O'Connor, Sandra Day
    on abortion, 168
    affirmative action and, 171, 172
    ideological court and, 162,
        163, 165
    Rehnquist's court and, 166
    Roberts court and, 176
    on school prayer, 173–5
O'Donnell, Christine, 28, 221
O'Donnell, Kirk, 108
Office of Management and
    Budget, 19
Oliver, John, 124
Omnibus bills, 19

O'Neill, Tip
  civility and, 188
  marginalized moderates and, 106,
    108, 109
  party brand and, 95, 96, 97
  television era and, 94
Ornstein, Norm, 189
Oversight, Congressional, 47
  divided government, 52–4
    mean number and intensity of
      investigations, *57–8*
    publicity, high, *60–1*
  Executive Branch, overseeing, 49–52
  House and Senate Committees,
    results of investigations by,
    54–61
    by chamber, 1947–2010, *55–6*
    mean number and intensity of
      investigations, *57–8*
  investigations, 47–69
  politicization of, 61–2
  weaponization of, 61
Oxley, Michael, 192

Palin, Sarah, 26, 27
"Partisan bickering," 24
Partisan divide, bridging
  Americans, turning Democrats and
    Republicans into, 219–26
    campaigns, cost of, 222–3
    dysfunctions, reasons for, 223–4
    examples, 220–1
    money problems and, 225–6
    problem solving of leaders, 225
    reasons, 220
    solutions, 224–5
    unrepresentativeness, problem of,
      221–2
  attempts to bridge, civil, 187–203
    end of retreats, 198
    Hershey, Pennsylvania retreat
      (March 7–9, 1997), 189–94,
      202
    Hershey, Pennsylvania retreat
      (March 19–21, 1999), 194
    idea of, 188–9
    retreat, civility in, 187–8
    West Virginia retreat (February
      28-March 2, 2003), 196–8

  West Virginia retreat (March 9–11,
    2001), 196–8
California's experiment with the
    top-two primary, 205–18
    adaption by parties, 213–14
    introduction, 205
    parties' response, 209
    reform, effects of, 210–11
    remedies, polarization and,
      206–8
    top-two system, impact on 2012
      primary election, 211–13
    2012 general election and beyond,
      215–16
  "fixing" of polarization, 205–18
Partisan polarization, causes and
    consequences of
  abortion, 167–71
  affirmative action, 171–3
  amendments on Senate floor, 36–9
  Appropriations Committees, Senate
    and House, 3–7
  decorum, breaches of U.S. Congress
    (1891–2012). (*see* Incivility)
  Democrats, polarization scores
    for, *32*
  earmark ban, 33–4
  Facebook pages, examining
    polarization through pages of
    Congressional member, 117–33
    constituency service, 121–2
    credit claiming, 123–4
    findings, 121
    home style thesis, 117
    list of members selected, 131
    methods, 120–1
    personal connection, 124–6
    personalization vs polarization,
      126–9
    polarization, Facebook and
      generally, 117–19
    position taking, 122–3
    virtual home style, Facebook and,
      119–20, 126
  failure, when meaning success,
    165–75
    abortion, 167–71
    affirmative action, 171–3
    school prayer, 173–5

Partisan polarization, causes and
consequences of—*Continued*
financial aspects of partisanship, 3
Appropriations Committees,
changes, 13–17
textbook appropriations, 5–7
Gingrich senators, 23–46. (*see also*
Gingrich, Newt)
amendments on Senate
floor, 36–9
earmark ban, 33–4
linking to Tea Party senators,
23–30
as partisan warriors, 33–43
as party polarizers, 30–3
Presidential Support
Scores, 35–6
"Secret Santa," 41–2
Sunday morning talk show
appearances, 42–3
2011 debt-limit crisis, 39–41
ideological court, pursuit of, 162–5
incivility, 71–91
explanatory theory regarding,
73–5
how and why it matters, 73–80
measuring and charting, 80–6
measuring incivility, 1891–2012,
81–6
party system polarization and
member incivility, interplay
between, 75–80
research findings, 86–9
separate form of conflict, seeing
incivility as, 73–5
testing of theory on, 80–6
judicial decisions in a Red/Blue
America, 161–2
new textbook Appropriations
Committees
Committees, collapse of, 11–13
distributive politics, 11–13
earmarks, 11–13
ideology, 7–11
partisanship, 7–11
oversight, Congressional, 47
divided government, 52–4
Executive Branch, overseeing,
49–52

House and Senate Committees,
results of investigations by,
54–61
investigations, 47–69
weaponization of investigations, 61
polarizing court, 161–84
abortion, 167–71
affirmative action, 171–3
failure, when meaning success,
165–75
ideological court, pursuit of, 162
judicial decisions in a Red/Blue
America, 161–2
prayer in schools, 173–5
Roberts Court, 175–7
"success," defining, 162–5
prayer in schools, 173–5
presidential base electoral strategies,
partisan polarization and,
135–59
The Gilded Age, 145–52
The Global Age, 145–52
1892: Benjamin Harrison's
Reelection Prioritization, 140–2
implications and conclusions,
152–3
incumbent elections, presidential
leadership decisions and, 137–40
leadership decisions, presidential,
137–40
Obama, Barack, reelection
prioritization of 2012, 142–5
states, polarized, 146, *147*
Presidential Support Scores, 35–6
Republicans, polarization scores
for, *31*
Roberts Court, 175–7
"success," defining, 162–5
Sunday morning talk show
appearances, 42–3
Tea Party senators, 23–46. (*see also*
Tea Party)
amendments on Senate floor, 36–9
earmark ban, 33–4
linking to Gingrich senators,
25–30
as partisan warriors, 33–43
as party polarizers, 30–3
Presidential Support Scores, 35–6

"Secret Santa," 41–2
Sunday morning talk show
    appearances, 42–3
2011 debt-limit crisis, 39–41
television era, Congressional
    partisanship in, 93–115
Congressional communications,
    ideological tilts, 98–103
marginalized moderates and
    electoral defeat, 106–9
moderates, Congressional, 103–9
national party image and the
    marginalized moderates, 104–6
party brand, polarization and,
    94–103
party conflicts, framing, 95
textbook appropriations, 7–13
2011 debt-limit crisis, 39–41
Partisan warfare, generally, 24
Partisan warriors, specific, 33–43
Party brand, television era, 94–103
    framing party conflicts, 95–8
Party polarizers, specific, 30–3
Party system polarization and member
    incivility, interplay between,
    75–80
constrained conflict, 76
depolarized congresses, in, 75–8
polarized congresses, incivility in,
    78–80
silence, challenging norms of, 76–7
Paul, Rand, 27–8, 30, 39
Paul, Ron, 152
Pelosi, Nancy
    Congressional oversight and, 47
    "Six for 06," 95
    television era and, 94
    2008 elections, 144
Perot, Ross, 145
Personal connection, Facebook and,
    124–6
Personalization vs polarization,
    Facebook, 126–9
Persuasion, 136
Pew Charitable Trusts, 117, 191, 196
"Playing for History: The Reflection
    Leadership Choices of Presidents
    William J. Clinton and George
    W. Bush," 154

Playing Hardball: Campaigning
    for the U.S. Congress
    (Herrnson), 93
Polarized congresses, incivility in,
    78–80
Political party, definition, 93
Porter, Jon, 110
Portman, Rob, 30, 41
Position taking, Facebook and, 122–3
Prayer in schools, 173–5
Presentation of self, 119, 126
Presidential base electoral strategies,
    partisan polarization and,
    135–59
    1892: Benjamin Harrison's
        Reelection Prioritization,
        140–2
    The Gilded Age, 145–52
    The Global Age, 145–52
    implications and conclusions,
        152–3
    incumbent elections, presidential
        leadership decisions and,
        137–40
    leadership decisions, presidential,
        137–40
    mobilization and, 136–7, 151, 153
    Obama, Barack, reelection
        prioritization of 2012, 142–5
    persuasion and, 136, 151, 153
    "Playing for History: The Reflection
        Leadership Choices of Presidents
        William J. Clinton and George
        W. Bush," 154
    states, polarized, 146, 147
Presidential Support Scores, 35–6
Price, Tom, 122, 126
Pro Quest, 81
Problem solving of leaders, 225
Proposition 14. See California's
    experiment with the top-two
    primary
Publicity on divided government, 60–1

Quay, Matthew, 141
Quayle, Dan, 169

Raese, John, 28
Rayburn, Sam, 93, 94

Reagan, Ronald, 86
  on abortion, 167
  appointments to Supreme Court, 165
  House and Senate Committees,
      results of investigations by, 54–5
  ideological court and, 163, 165,
      181n65
  marginalized moderates and, 108
  party brand and, 97
  popularity of, 96
  Rehnquist's court and, 166
  Roberts court and, 175
  on school prayer, 175
Red/Blue America, judicial decisions,
    161–2
"Red Scare," 71–2
Reed Rules (1891), 87
Reed, Thomas, 141
Rehnquist, William
  on abortion, 167, 170
  affirmative action and, 171, 172
  center chair, elevation to, 165
  court of, 166, 177
  ideological court and, 162–4
  Roberts court and, 176
  on school prayer, 173–5
Reid, Harry, 10, 28, 38, 42
Republican National Convention
    (1892), 140
"Republican Revolution," 6
Republican Theme Team, 99, 101
Rice, Susan, 90n3
RINOs (Republicans in Name
    only), 103
Roberts, John, 161, 162, 175–7
Robertson, Pat, 169
Roe, 167–70
Rogan, James, 200
Rogers, Hal, 9
Rohde, David, 83
Roll calls, 20n14, 72
  amendments on Senate
      floor and, 39
  Hershey, Pennsylvania retreat
      (March 7–9, 1997), 193
  incivility in polarized Congresses, 78
  West Virginia retreat, 198
Roosevelt, Franklin, 85, 86
Roosevelt, Theodore, 86, 145
Ros-Lehtinen, Ileana, 125

Rossi, Dino, 28
Roukema, Marge, 108
Rove, Karl, 172
Rubio, Marco, 26, 30, 36
Rudman, Warren, 27
Rush, Richard, ix

Salazar, Ken, 27
Santa Fe Independent School
    District v. Doe, 173
Scalia, Antonin
  on abortion, 167, 170
  ideological court and, 163–4
  Rehnquist's court and, 166
  on school prayer, 174
Schneider, Claudine, 108
Schumer, Chuck, 42
Schwartz, Thomas, 51
Schwarzenegger, Arnold, 209
Sebelius, National Federation of
    Independent Business v., 162
"Secret Santa," 41–2
Selection-bias, 118
September 11, 2001, 79, 145
Sex offenders, paying for Viagra of, 37
Shaping America, 164
Shaw, Daron, 151
Shays, Chris, 110
Shelby, Richard, 36
Sherman Anti-Trust Act, 141
Sherman, John, 140
Sherman Silver Purchase Act, 141
Shutdown of government (1995), 17,
    18, 145
Silver Purchase Act, 141
"Six for 06," 95
Skaggs, David, 188–9, 192, 194
Smith v. Allwright, 209
Snowe, Olympia, 23, 24, 26, 36
Social grooming, 120
Social Security, xiii
Souder, Mark, 27
Souter, David Hackett
  affirmative action and, 172
  ideological court and, 162–3, 165
  Rehnquist's court and, 166
  on school prayer, 173, 174, 175
Specter, Arlen, 26
Stanley, Aleesandra, 169
Stenholm, Charlie, 191

Stevens, John Paul
  on abortion, 167
  affirmative action and, 172
  Rehnquist's court and, 166
  on school prayer, 173, 174
Stevens, Ted, 10, 11
Stump, Bob, 194
Stutzman, Marlin, 27
"Success," defining, 162–5
Sumner, William, 71, 72
Sunday morning talk show
    appearances, 42–3

Tariff Act, 141
"Taxpayer Protection Pledge," 40
Tea Party, 110, 152. *See also* Tea Party
    senators
  election of members, 13
Tea Party senators, 23–46
  amendments on Senate
    floor, 36–9
  earmark ban, 33–4
  linking to Gingrich senators,
    25–30
  as partisan warriors, 33–43
  as party polarizers, 30–3
  Presidential Support Scores, 35–6
  "Secret Santa," 41–2
  Sunday morning talk show
    appearances, 42–3
  2011 debt-limit crisis, 39–41
Television era, Congressional
    partisanship in, 93–115
  Congressional communications,
    ideological tilts, 98–103
  Democratic Message Board (DMB),
    98–103
  DW-NOMINATE, 99–100, *100*
  ideological tilts, 98–103
  marginalized moderates and electoral
    defeat, 106–9
  moderates, Congressional, 103–9
    marginalized moderates and
      electoral defeat, 106–9
    national party image and
      the marginalized moderates,
      104–6
    national party image and
      the marginalized moderates,
      104–6

party brand, 94–103
  framing party conflicts, 95–8
  polarization and, 94–103
  Republican Theme Team, 99, *101*
Thernstrom, Abigail, 171–3
Thomas, Clarence
  on abortion, 170
  affirmative action and, 172–3
  ideological court and, 163
  Rehnquist's court and, 166
  "Secret Santa" and, 42
Thomas, Ginni, 42
Thune, John, 38
Tillman, Pat, 63
Toner, Robin, 170
Toomey, Pat, xiii
  earmark ban and, 34
  as party polarizer, 30
  "Secret Santa" and, 42
  Tea Party movement and, 26, 28
  2011 debt-limit crisis and, 41
Top-two primary, California.
    See California's experiment with
    the top-two primary
Tower, John, 79
Turnout, elections, *150*
2011 debt-limit crisis, 39–41
  Super Committee". (*see* Joint
    Select Committee on Deficit
    Reduction)

Unrepresentativeness, 221–2
U.S. Chamber of Commerce, 126

Viagra amendment, 37
Vitter, David, 36, 38, 39

Waco standoff, 63
Walker, Bob, 97
Warner, Mark, 39
Warren, Elizabeth, 36
"Washington culture," 13
Washington Post, on incivility incidents,
    81–2, 89–90n1
Watergate, 60
Waters, Maxine, 188
Waxman, Henry, 47, 48
Weaponization of investigations, 61
Weekly Standard, 63
Weisman, Lee v., 173–4

Weiss, Ari, 108
Wesleyan Media Project, 154–5n1
West Virginia retreat
   February 28-March 2, 2003, 196–8
   March 9–11, 2001, 196–8
White, Byron, 166, 167, 170
White, Joseph, 5–6, 11
Whitewater investigations, 52
Wilson, Joe, 71
Wilson, Pete, 172–3

Wilson, Woodrow, 50, 86
Wirthlin, Richard, 168
Wright, Jim
   civility and, 188
   ethics charges against, 63
   Gingrich, Newt and, 79
   incivility during Speakership, 83
   marginalized moderates and, 107

Young, Bill, 9

Printed and bound in the United States of America